Living with the Torpedo

USS Willis

1945

A torpedo track passes under the ship, upper left to lower right.

Living with the Torpedo

Anti-Submarine Warfare, Command, and Shipboard Life in the US Navy During World War II

George P. Sotos
Captain, USN (Ret.)

Mt. Vernon, Virginia ■ Mt. Vernon Book Systems

2020

Printing 1.0

Copyright © 2020 by George P. Sotos. All Rights Reserved. No part of this book may be reproduced in any form by any means (electronic, mechanical, xerographic, photonic, quantum, or other) or held in any information storage and retrieval system without written permission from the copyright holder.

Mt. Vernon Book Systems
P.O. Box 21
Mt. Vernon, VA 22121

Visit us at: `www.sotos.navy` or `www.mtvernonbook.com`

Printing 1.0
Please email comments to: `mail@mtvernonbook.com`
Kindly include the printing number.

Printed in the United States of America

This book was produced using Macintosh computers, Scrivener, and the TeXShop front-end for the TeX and LaTeX typesetting systems. TeX is a trademark of the American Mathematical Society. TeXShop is by Richard Koch and Dirk Olmes, and includes work by Gerben Wierda.

ISBN 978-0-9818193-9-6 (softcover)

Also by the author:

Plateau of Chains

Contents

List of Figures		ix
Foreward		11
Introduction		17
1	Ensign, USNR	21
2	Fire	37
3	Load the Guns	53
4	U-Boats	69
5	PC 476	85
6	Near Miss	99
7	Aground	109
8	A Failure to Communicate	129
9	PC 451	135
10	We Lose the R-12	145
11	The Big League	153

Contents

12	Fox is at the Dip!	161
13	Aircraft Carrier Operations	171
14	Battle Stations	177
15	Attack!	185
16	Three Kills	199
17	We Lose a Carrier	211
18	We Lose the USS F. C. Davis	227
19	Guam	239
20	U.S. Subs vs. U.S. DEs	261
21	Going Home	273
22	Wilbur	287
23	Life Span	293
	Acknowledgements and Alibis	301
A	The Walter Willis Story	304
B	Photo Credits	307
C	Bibliography	309
	Index	311

List of Figures

USS Willis	ii
Sinkings by U-boats	16
Tonnage sunk by U-boats	19
German torpedo	20
Schematic of USS Nitro's main steam line	27
My sextant	30
USS Nitro (AE 2)	36
What war?	52
Wild news dispatches	58
Depth charge racks on USS Janssen (DE 396)	68
Depth charge explosion	73
PC 476	84
Loaded K-gun	98
Heavy seas aboard PC 451	108
Smoke screen	128
PC 451	134
Target practice	139
USS R-12 (SS-89)	144
Tranquility at sea	152
Aircraft on the USS Bogue flight deck	160
Making the approach for refueling	170
USS Bogue	172
Avengers from USS Bogue	176
Hedgehogs	184
Hedgehog pattern	187
USS Janssen (DE 396) picks up survivors of the U-575	198

List of Figures

Rubber from Japanese submarine I-52 207
Survivors of USS Block Island 210
Icing topside 217
More ice in the North Atlantic 218
High line during refueling 226
Survivors of the U-546 234
USS Franklin burning and listing 238
Crew for a 3"/50 gun 240
Gun 1 on USS Willis 241
Victory over the Japanese 243
Guam's harbor 246
American torpedo 247
Willis pier-side in Guam 250
Japanese prisoners of war on Guam 252
USS Sperry hulking over three DEs 260
Crossing the line ceremonies aboard the Willis 272
Wilbur 286
USS Willis after the war 292
Green Cove Springs before construction of piers 294
Green Cove Springs after construction of piers 295
About the author 313

Orthographic Notes

There is no standard spelling for the syncope of "forecastle." This book uses *foc'stle*.

Military ranks are not capitalized, unless they directly precede a personal name.

Ship names occur so frequently that they are not italicized.

Some personal names have been changed.

Foreward

In this engaging memoir of war at sea in the Second World War, Captain George Sotos manages to paint a vivid, entertaining, and occasionally harrowing portrait of the "Greatest Generation" at sea. As he tells the story of five years at sea on several US Navy warships in both the Atlantic and Pacific during the war years, his humor, sharp eye for detail, and balanced sense of human nature provide a rich tapestry of life underway for the reader.

As he says, "I was at sea on the first day of the war, and on the last day. For me, it was not a war of pervasive carnage or of grand strategic decisions. To be sure, I did see death, injury, and fury; but the chief emotions that I lived with, day and night, were suppressed suspense and apprehension." As was the case for so many naval officers at sea, the foreboding sense of an inbound torpedo followed the ships everywhere, and Captain Sotos captures this perfectly.

Beginning as a young reservist fresh out of university, he details the feelings of the "90 day wonder" reporting aboard his first ship just before Pearl Harbor – in this case a heavy ammunition carrier, USS NITRO. The portraits of his shipmates, both junior and senior, crackle with reality and personality. For anyone who has had a difficult Executive Officer harassing the wardroom or a thoughtful officer mentor teaching navigation in new ways, the memories of just beginning in the Navy come through across the generations and decades and would be fully recognizable for an Ensign from the class of 2020 walking onto a new ship. That Captain Sotos still has the small sextant and now bat-

Foreward

tered cruise box that he was presented onboard NITRO after 70 years is no surprise.

The heart of the book really begins after the author transfers from NITRO, spends a fairly brief time in two small PCs (tiny 170 foot, 55 man sub chasers) and embarks USS WILLIS, the EDSALL class destroyer escort ship he will ultimately command and spend 31 months in both the Atlantic and Pacific fleets in combat. Having been swiftly advanced to become the Exec and then Captain himself, Captain Sotos shows us the hard-earned wisdom he has acquired, both in leadership and in seamanship.

For me, the time spent on WILLIS rings very true, as it will for anyone who has served in today's surface forces as well. So much of the sailor's experience is universal:

- The long, boring voyages punctuated by fierce stints of combat operations, many for WILLIS in company with larger carriers like USS BOGUE in a hunter-killer group.

- Back-and-forth interplay between the junior officers, the CO and XO, and the senior enlisted which keep the ships operating in the best way.

- Longing for a conflict and a cruise to be over, but regretting the knowledge that the end will break up a warm camaraderie at sea.

Some of the best and most poignant writing in the book comes toward the end, as Captain Sotos is appointed commander of a three ship group and ordered to take them out of the Pacific and back to the southeast coast of the USA to be laid up at the end of the war. On the way he says goodbye to the ship's dog, Wilbur, who had gone through the entire war onboard and never set a paw ashore. Wilbur is taken home by a departing sailor, and the Captain and crew gather on the deck to hug him goodbye.

"It was with genuine feelings of sadness that I said goodbye to Wilbur. We all hugged him there at the quarterdeck, then watched as he walked hesitantly ashore at the end of something he had never experienced in his entire life: a leash." Metaphor for a crew having spent so long at sea together, I suspect.

At the end of this five-year adventure with Captain Sotos, the reader has come to like him and his calm, matter-of-fact sea stories that capture life at sea in the war. He was the only officer to spend the entire life of the ship – 31 months – onboard WILLIS. He says, "In less than five years I had jumped from college student to being a task unit commander with responsibilities, challenges, excited, and professional growth opportunities seen by few guys my age." Indeed.

It is of course no surprise that Captain Sotos went on to have a total of six commands at sea and retire as a full Captain. But I am sure he looks back on his time in destroyer escort WILLIS with the greatest of affection. In that sense in particular, this love of a sailor for the ship that forms him or her, *Living With the Torpedo* is a small classic.

– James Stavridis, PhD
  Admiral, USN (Ret.)

Admiral Stavridis' 37-year career in the Navy included six commands – the favorite being his first destroyer command, USS BARRY (DDG-52). He afterwards became Dean of The Fletcher School of Law and Diplomacy at Tufts University.

To Georgette

The amazing ability of young Americans to learn the unwelcome and unsought-for profession of fighting U-boats, their fortitude in meeting the wartime perils of the deep and of the air, their skill in operating ships and planes, surprised their friends and confounded their foes.

– Rear Admiral Samuel Eliot Morison[1]

---

[1] Morison, page 248.

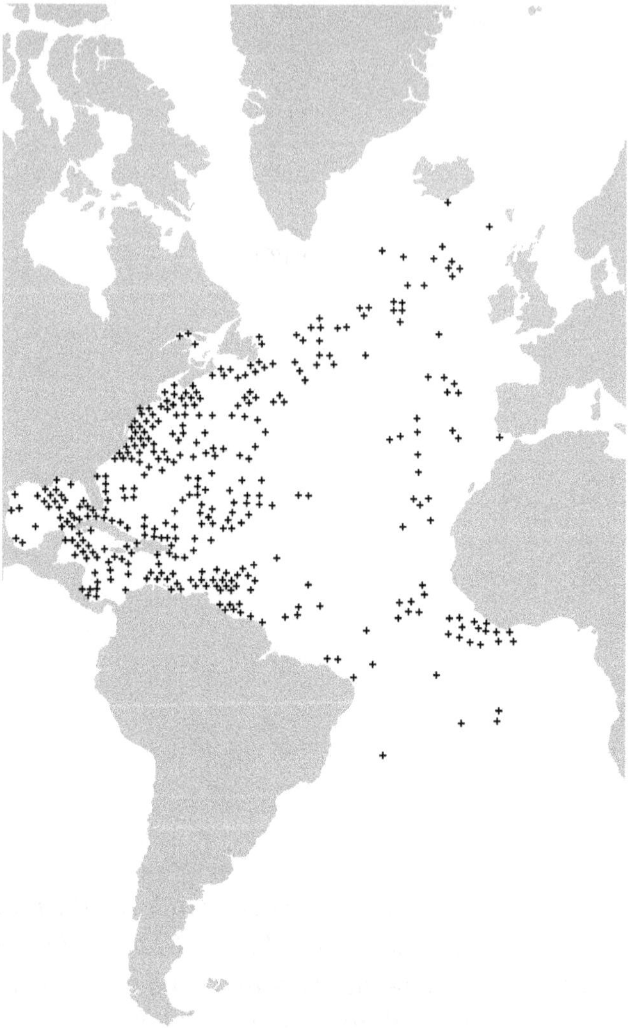

Figure 16: **Sinkings by U-boats.** At each + a German U-boat sank a merchant ship between December 1941 and July 1942, inclusive. Most attacks were close to the east coast of the United States or in the Caribbean area. In the Gulf of Mexico and the Caribbean, U-boats sank more than 160 merchant ships during the second quarter of 1942, including 69 in June alone. So many oil tankers were sunk that the United States had to start rationing fuel at home. During that same June, the US Navy sank two U-boats, and the British, one. Data from Morison.

Introduction

World War II ended more than 70 years ago, but I still dream about it.

I was at sea on the first day of the war, and on the last day. For me, it was not a war of pervasive carnage or of grand strategic decisions. To be sure, I did see death, injury, and fury, but the chief emotions that I lived with, day and night, were suppressed suspense and apprehension.

Throughout the war, my home and work-place was a floating piece of metal. Every moment of every day that we were at sea, I knew we were a potential target for a U-boat torpedo. The fact that my first sea-going home was an ammunition ship, and that any resulting explosion would be audible 100 miles away, did not ease the tension.

In the many years since then, I've felt those emotions again in my sleep, about once a month as I re-live standing an underway watch on the bridge of our destroyer escort. The dreams vary. Sometimes it's the mid-watch on a dark night. Other times it's a routine watch in the morning or afternoon. In all of them I hear clearly, again and again, the familiar, reassuring ping... ping... ping... sounds of our sonar gear searching for U-boats. With nerves on edge, I await the WHOOSH echo that will signify a contact. When I do hear an echo, the suppressed apprehension that a torpedo might be heading towards us gives way to a flush of fear and aggression combined in an almost automatic response to kill before being killed.

Sometimes the dream will end after the explosions of our

Introduction

first depth charge attack, and I will wake up in a small sweat. In others, we don't even get a contact. The pinging just goes reassuringly on and on with no disturbance to my sleep. In all of them, we never make any mistakes. Everyone does his job perfectly, and I find that very comforting.

• • •

Before December 7, 1941, readiness for war was the furthest thing from my mind. But Japan's success in attacking Pearl Harbor was by no means the most glaring example of the Navy's unreadiness. The complete lack of any defense against U-boats along the Atlantic coast in 1942 "was as much a national disaster as if saboteurs had destroyed half a dozen of our biggest war plants."[2]

In the first four months of 1942, U-boats sank 82 merchant ships off the U.S. east coast, plus another 55 around Bermuda.[3] Americans standing on beaches in Florida, or North Carolina, or New York, or just about anywhere, could look with their naked eye out over the water and see American ships on fire and sinking. Cities all along the coast ordered blackouts at night because the glow from their lights would silhouette any ship sailing between shore and a U-boat, telling the U-boat commander exactly where to aim his torpedoes.

On the other side of the Atlantic Ocean, Great Britain was dying. Only aid from the United States kept it alive, but that aid was carried by sea, and the U-boats were sending enormous amounts of it to the bottom. The U-boats were Winston Churchill's single greatest fear. "The only thing that ever really frightened me during the war was the U-boat peril... the U-boat attack was our worst evil. It would have been wise for the Germans to stake all upon it."[4]

President Franklin Roosevelt had started some preparations for war before Pearl Harbor, but, in retrospect, not enough. Thus,

---
[2] Morrison-I, page 127.
[3] Morison, page 7. Pages 35-36 and 49 also provide data for this section.
[4] Hickam, page vii. (Also Churchill vol. II p529 and vol. IV p107.)

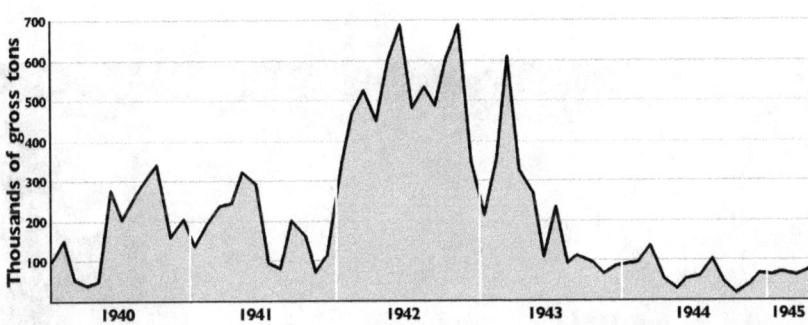

Figure 19: **Tonnage sunk by U-boats.** The British fought the U-boats starting in 1939, but it was in 1942, after the United States entered the war, that the U-boats had their field day. The graph shows, monthly, how many tons of merchant cargo that U-boats sank. It does not show combat ships sunk. Data from Churchill.

in 1942, the first full year of the war, the Navy's highest construction priority was for two small types of anti-submarine ships: patrol craft ("PC boats") and wooden-hulled subchasers. Mass production of destroyer escorts started in February 1943, and by December 260 had entered service. I served on east coast PC boats from February 1942 to November 1943, then on a destroyer escort for the rest of the war.

The Navy was equally behind with its people. In mid-1943 it suspended its traditional practice of rotating officers from one type of duty to another. Anyone trained and experienced in anti-submarine warfare was to stay in such duties permanently. Ultimately, the Navy's people were its best weapon.

• • •

To borrow another Churchill description, the Battle of the Atlantic was a "war of groping and drowning, of ambuscade and stratagem, of science and seamanship."[5]

It was into that battle that I stepped.

---

[5]Morison, page 11

✪ ✪ ✪ ✪ ✪ ✪ ✪ ✪ ✪ ✪ ✪ ✪ ✪

Figure 20: **German torpedo.** Members of a U.S. Navy boarding party jettison a damaged torpedo from the captured U-boat U-505. American torpedoes looked similar (Figure 247). The leader of the recovery boarding party, Lt (jg) Albert David from the USS Pillsbury (DE 133), received the Congressional Medal of Honor. (See page 222.)

Chapter 1

Ensign, USNR

The train to New Orleans was crowded with soldiers, but I was oblivious to them. I had other things on my mind.

I pulled out my orders and took another look. I read them again and again, slowly.

"Ensign George P. Sotos USNR, hereby detached from all duties on the USS Nitro (AE 2). Proceed and report to the Commandant Eighth Naval District in New Orleans for duty as the executive officer of the PC 476."

Why did I have to keep looking at those orders?

The answer: Things were happening to me so fast they were very hard to believe.

Just 16 months earlier, in November 1940, I had been a 20 year old aspiring baseball player and senior at the University of Chicago, heading toward a career in law.

And now, I was ordered to be the second in command of a brand new war ship, the PC 476.

During that 16-month period I had earned a commission as an ensign in the U.S. Naval Reserve and completed an eleven month tour of duty (mostly training) on the USS Nitro, a huge Navy ammunition ship.

I remembered well the strange feeling I had when the large motor launch stopped at the foot of a long gangway on the port side of the big gray vessel.

1. Ensign, USNR

"This is the Nitro, your ship, sir," said the launch coxswain. "Good luck."

"Thanks," I said, wondering how badly my nervousness showed.

Spic and span in my new dress blue uniform and carrying my heavy sea bag, I found it hard to be erect and military as I finally got to the top of the steep gangway.

I dropped my sea bag, faced aft and started to salute the colors. "Request permission to come aboard," I started to say. Then I noticed no one was there.

In a few minutes, a short, chubby, almost fat, middle-aged man in a black turtleneck sweater, khaki pants, soiled black shoes, wearing an officer's cap and with a sagging pistol belt at his side, walked rapidly toward me.

"What can I do for you?" His wrinkled, strange looking face broke into a smile.

"Request permission to come aboard, sir," I said, and saluted smartly.

"Sure, come aboard, you already are though," he answered, waving a salute at me.

"Reporting for duty, sir," I said.

"For duty or as a passenger?" he asked.

"For duty, sir." I handed him a copy of my orders. He studied them for a while and, without looking up, said, "Welcome aboard, you'll be sorry. ... Are you a Naval Academy graduate?"

"No, sir."

"Harvard or Yale?"

"No, sir."

"You didn't go to Princeton did you?"

"No, sir."

"That's good, I don't like those smart-aleck kids."

"I'm a graduate of the V-7 officer candidate program."

"The what? Oh, what the hell, it doesn't make any difference. My name's Holidan, Lieutenant Junior Grade (Lt jg). That's why I have these silver bars," he said, as he withdrew two metal Lt jg bars from his pocket and rolled them around in his hand.

A third class petty officer strolled up. He, too, was wearing a pistol belt. "Can I help you, Mr. Holidan?"

"This officer's reporting aboard for duty."

"I'll log him in, sir, and get one of the stewards from the wardroom."

He took my orders and made an entry in the ship's log. It was April 20, 1941.

"I'll also notify the executive officer," said the petty officer.

"Right, What department you going to work in?" asked Holidan.

"I don't know, sir," I replied, "I've never had duty aboard a ship before."

"That's a good one," smiled Holidan. "Here I've got over twenty-five years at sea. I was a gunner's mate during the war (World War I). Then I went to sea in the merchant marine. I've got Master papers."

"You have, sir?" I was quite surprised at the conversation.

"Doncha believe me?"

"Yes, sir, I certainly do."

"Well, I'll prove it." He pulled a folded parchment out of his wallet and opened it for my inspection. "There ya're. Any ship, any ocean."

While I was too flustered to read the fine print, I did see the words "any ocean" and was immediately impressed, but still quite puzzled.

"You know what rank they gave me?"

"No, sir."

"A damn lieutenant junior grade. That's why I wear this sweater." And some sweater it was! – a black turtleneck that covered the entire upper half of his very ample body. There was no insignia of his rank anywhere.

"They shoulda given me at least a lieutenant commander rank," he continued angrily. "The Merchant Marine officers are getting shafted. I'll be dammed if I'll wear those little silver bars."

A white-jacketed steward had picked up my bag and was headed for a doorway. "Shall I follow him, sir?" I asked.

23

1. Ensign, USNR

"You sure as hell better if you want a place to sleep."

After about three months I better understood Mr. Holidan and felt sorry for him. An ugly man, with several prominent warts on his face, he was known throughout the ship as "Mumbles," because he never spoke loud enough to be heard clearly. A further disconcerting characteristic was his habit of rolling his eyes whenever he spoke directly to anyone. The older officers considered him incompetent and the younger officers treated him with harsh contempt.

I followed the steward as he walked ahead of me about thirty feet, turned into a passageway and then opened a door leading into what I could see was the officers' wardroom. We walked around a large dining table into a narrow passageway with staterooms on either side.

"I believe this is your room, sir," he said as he set my bag down. "Mr. Sheridan is already here."

I didn't say anything, figuring that Sheridan was my roommate since he apparently had the lower bunk.

"Are you ready to meet the exec now?"

"Thanks, yes."

He led the way back outside the wardroom, up a short ladder, and then knocked on a door that I could see was below and behind the ship's bridge.

"Come on in."

The steward opened the door, revealing a short man sitting at a desk. He turned towards us and I could see the lieutenant commander insignia on the collar of his open necked khaki shirt.

"Commander, this new officer just reported aboard for duty."

"Good, thanks Ray."

Ray turned and left. The exec looked at me for a second. "Welcome aboard young man, I'll talk to you later." He dismissed me with a wave and turned toward the papers on his desk.

A couple hours later he sent for me. He introduced himself as Lieutenant Commander Milner, offered me a cup of coffee, and immediately made me feel at home. He asked me a few questions about my training and then told me that Ensign Hunnewell would be in touch with me and explain my duties. I left his cabin convinced that I was lucky to have him as my exec. As I got to know him however, that view changed somewhat.

A tall young officer with sparse blonde hair greeted me when I returned to my room. He was picture perfect in his khaki uniform, and I sensed this was Ensign Hunnewell even before he introduced himself as the "bull" ensign.

"That means I'm the senior ensign aboard this ship," said Hunnewell. I got the sense that he was responsible to the exec for the six ensigns aboard the Nitro, even though he didn't say so explicitly.

He told me that, as an ensign under instruction, I would rotate among the ship's departments at roughly two to three month intervals. The deck department would be first, then engineering, ordnance, and navigation. At the same time I would stand junior officer of the deck (JOOD) watches on the bridge. I was expected to meet certain qualifications in every assignment.

He took me around and introduced me to all the other officers. He also explained many of the details of daily life aboard the ship. He told me where I would sit at the wardroom table for all meals.

"Make sure you read the plan of the day first thing every morning. That's how the exec runs the ship," he said.

"Also, when we are alone you can address me as Jim and I'll call you George. But on deck and about the ship you will always address me as Mr. Hunnewell or Ensign Hunnewell."

After the first few days I was pretty much left alone to perform my initial duties as a deck division officer. In that capacity I soon found out that my mentor was a chief petty officer named Graham who ran the division, and indirectly watched over and taught me what I needed to know. In subsequent assignments I wasn't as lucky with my chief petty officers. They just didn't match Graham's qualifications. He was our top Chief Petty Officer when it came to hands-on knowledge of his job. He knew his men well, teaching and delegating responsibility with a confident, pleasant, but firm demeanor, in a way that made follow-up

1. Ensign, USNR

supervision unnecessary. He made the deck department, with its vast number of tasks, a shining example of a proud, efficient navy ship. And at the same time he indirectly taught me a great deal about going to sea.

For the most part, I found each new assignment interesting and challenging. However, I learned that an ensign under instruction on the Nitro was about as low as one can get in the officer chain of command. I had very little responsibility, and, at first, even less authority. It was fun. But there was a downside. No matter what we were doing, there was always this sense of danger posed by our very volatile cargo.

Also, "under instruction" meant just that. I was expected to learn some specifics in each department to which I was assigned. For example, when my engineering department assignment was over, I had completed hand-drawn schematics which showed the complete run of every pipe in the ship. Included were the pipe's contents (salt water, fresh water, oil, etc.), direction of flow, and the location of every valve in the pipeline. I became very knowledgeable about the entire ship and in the process become acquainted with all the sailors who ran the engineering department.

I still have those schematics. (See Figure 27.)

I had the same experience in the deck department and quickly learned that the vast amount of paint supplies we carried were almost as volatile as our ammunition.

I learned how to store anchor chains in the huge chain locker and how to avoid the serious dangers of carelessness when dropping and picking up the anchor.

But, of course, the ordnance department, which was responsible for the thousands of tons of ammunition that were our routine cargo, was the most important, as well as the most dangerous department. Although we had large numbers of specially constructed storage holds, called magazines, each with a special sprinkling system, where every manner of ammunition and explosives were stored, handling, maintaining and securing that cargo was by far our most intense and continuing concern.

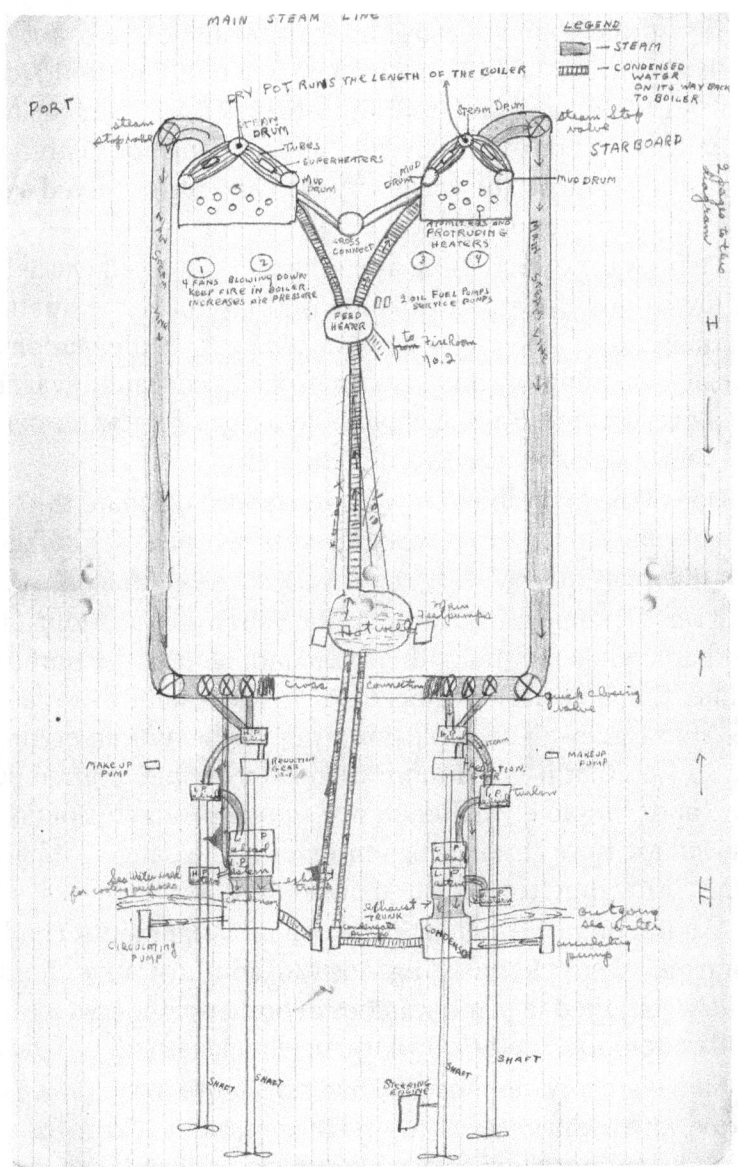

Figure 27: **Schematic of USS Nitro's main steam line.** This two-sheet drawing shows two boilers (top) that send their steam down port and starboard steam lines to turbine and gear systems that drive the propellers (extreme bottom). The boilers are fed from condensers (bottom) that are cooled by sea water. Multiple other shipboard systems can be similarly diagrammed. In reality the Nitro had just one propeller.

1. ENSIGN, USNR

If just one shell got loose in a magazine it could not only crush a man, it could initiate a chain reaction that could easily destroy the ship and probably any others nearby. The sensitivity of the crew to our extremely volatile and dangerous cargo was readily apparent by the way everyone carefully observed safety precautions day and night, especially for fires.

There was no such thing as a minor fire. A small waste basket fire from a discarded cigarette butt got the same attention as a major fire. The entire crew would go to battle stations so that all fire equipment and personnel would be readily available. Whenever an ammunition cargo hold or magazine was open all smoking on the ship was prohibited.

One of the first things I saw when I reported aboard the Nitro was a bronze plaque that was affixed to the side of a bulkhead near the quarterdeck.[1]

It was in memory of an ammunition ship, the S.S. Mont-Blanc, that had collided with another merchant ship in the harbor of Halifax, Canada, on December 6, 1917. The resulting fire caused the largest man-made explosion prior to the atomic bomb. It was so vast that it killed more than 2000 people, injured 9000 more and completely flattened two square kilometers of northern Halifax. It was a sobering reminder of the dangers inherent in the Nitro's much larger cargo of ammunition.

In addition to the regular instructional assignments, I had division officer duties consisting mostly of administrative chores. I was also required to stand watches in port and underway where I had to demonstrate practical use of what I learned.

And, like every new ensign, I had my share of problems. They started with the navigator's top enlisted assistant, Norm Skyzanski, the chief quartermaster. I had been assigned as assistant navigator under instruction. But in addition to not liking reserve officers, especially inexperienced ensigns like me, Skyzanski was convinced that I had dropped and damaged one of his sensitive,

---

[1] The quarterdeck is the deck area where the gangway is located when in port. It is usually in the midships area.

precision sextants.

Early one morning, after the navigator and Skyzanski had already shot their stars, I decided I was ready to take star sights. I removed the precious number two sextant from its case, asked a seaman to mark the time for me when I took the sights, and with the seaman I walked importantly out on the bridge wing. It was still dark but sunrise was beginning to show in the eastern sky and the horizon was very sharp. I had no trouble identifying stars I would shoot. (Figure Figure 30.)

I took my sights as I had seen the navigator (Lieutenant Commander Thompson) and Skyzanski do it. Ordinarily, I would then wait until the navigator left the chart room so I could get access to the single available chart. Mr. Thompson was a very quiet man who rarely spoke to anyone but Skyzanski and the captain. He was all business and very quick in his work. Even though I was the assistant navigator he rarely spoke to me. I was lucky to receive even a nod when I saluted and said, "Good morning, sir."

Skyzanski was still in the chart room, computing the ship's eight o'clock position for the navigator's morning report to the captain.

"Get a good fix this morning, Chief?"

"Our fixes are always good, Mr. Sotos."

And indeed they were, I thought as I saw their five-star pinpoint fix on the chart.

"I'd like to use the Hydrographic Office 214 publication (H.O. 214 pub) for this latitude Chief, so I can work out my fix."

"Sorry, Mr. Sotos, I have strict orders from the navigator that no one but he can use the H.O. publications."

"But as his assistant, I'm supposed to do a day's work in navigation. That exclusion doesn't apply to me, does it?" I asked with a little anger.

"I'm sorry, sir," Skyzanski's voice was firm and not a bit sympathetic, "it does include you."

"How am I supposed to work out these star sights?"

29

1. ENSIGN, USNR

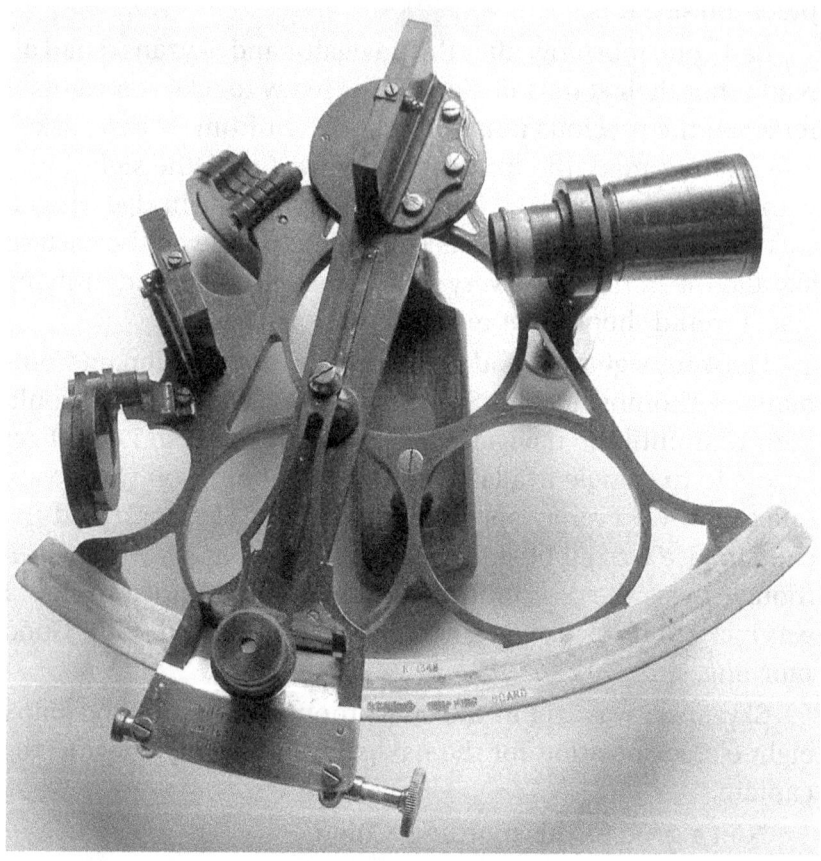

Figure 30: **My sextant.** A sextant measures how far up in the sky a particular star is. So long as the stars are correctly identified and the time is accurately known, measuring the elevation of three stars allows calculation of the the observer's location anywhere on earth. Before electronic location systems were invented, it was the standard tool for navigators at sea and in the air. The sextant has a movable mirror (at top) that feeds light into the small telescope mounted on the side of the instrument. The observer looks through the eyepiece of the telescope at a star, and then adjusts the mirror so that the star moves down to kiss the horizon. The star's elevation, in degrees, can then be read from markings on the bottom rail of the sextant. This sextant, made in 1918, still works.

"I was told to give you this." He handed me a thin black booklet titled "Dreisonstok Tables of Navigation."

"What's this?"

"It's the book Mr. Thompson wants you to use."

"But, I've never seen this book before."

"The instructions are in the book, sir."

I examined the small book briefly. "Is this your idea or the navigator's?"

"I take orders sir," and he paused, "Just like you do. You can ask the navigator yourself, if you like."

"I sure as hell will," I thought, but didn't say anything as the navigator walked in. I had not yet exchanged even a single word with him, but he had apparently heard part of my conversation with Skyzanski.

He got right to the point. "Mr. Sotos, in the Merchant Marine the officer of the watch does the navigating. That's different from the Navy where it's a full time job for a senior officer like me. Frankly I think it is a waste of an officer's time, but since I am on active duty in the Navy and assigned to this ship, that's the way I'll do it. But you, Mr. Sotos, are going to learn how to navigate the same way I did as a young officer in the Merchant Marine.

"Navigation is a simple task, but the Navy has turned it into a full-fledged production, with a staff of quartermasters doing all the detail work. You're going to learn how to do it all by yourself, just as I did.

"That book by Dreisonstok is the same one I had to use when I first started and I want you to use it, O.K.?"

He could see I was stuck for words. As I hesitated he added quietly, "Remember, that little book is your bible. Forget all the navigation they taught you in that Officer Candidate School and learn how to navigate with that little book."

I stammered a feeble, "Yes, sir," and started to walk out of the chart room.

"Just one more thing. I'm the only one on this ship who knows how to use that little book, so don't bother Ski with any ques-

1. Ensign, USNR

tions. Come right to me if you get stuck."

"Yes, sir," I answered a little more strongly and left the chart room. Needless to say, I was shook up by this turn of events. Mr. Thompson wasn't my idea of the friendly mentor I would run to if I had any questions.

But I had no choice. I didn't work out my star sights that morning or for quite a few mornings after that. A few days later Jim Hunnewell saw me pouring over Dreisonstok. He told me that all the other officers had been permitted to use the H.O. 214 publication.

"Are you on Skyzanski's shit list?" he asked.

"I don't know. Guess I must be."

"Here's a piece of advice for you. The navigator backs Ski up all the way, and Ski hasn't been wrong yet in his eyes."

But, whoever made the decision, it turned out to be a blessing in disguise for me. Though Ski and Mr. Thompson left me alone and never asked me any questions, they couldn't help but see my steadily improving fixes on the chart. In a month, using Dreisonstok, I was as proficient and fast in taking my star sights, recording my own time, and computing my fixes, as were the navigator and Ski using the H.O. publications.

While the three of us were on the bridge every morning, taking sights at the same time, it was a full month before the navigator started answering my morning salutes with a verbal "Good morning," instead of a routine nod. But other than that, our social interactions remained at a zero level until our arrival at the Bremerton, Washington, Naval Shipyard some time later.

With everyone from the captain to the lookouts searching the darkness ahead, I was the first to make the landfall on Cape Flaherty. I didn't realize it at the time, but being the first to make a landfall sighting was a major achievement on the Nitro. My sharp eyes, and knowledge where to look, were beginning to diminish Skyzanski's reign as the first one to call "Light ho" in seeing navigational lights.

After daybreak that same morning, as we steamed up the Straits of San Juan de Fuca toward Bremerton, I was busily taking bearings on the prescribed shore navigational aids and shouting them to Chief Skyzanski who, with the navigator watching over his shoulder, plotted them on the channel chart.

Suddenly, just after I had finished a round of bearings, Ski shouted, "Mr. Sotos, that was a bum set. Give me another round."

I was puzzled. I knew the bearings had been good, but I quickly gave him another round which he plotted.

At the suggestion of the navigator, which I overheard, and with an air of tolerant, respectful disgust, Ski came out on the bridge wing to take the bearings himself. I moved over and watched as Ski shouted the bearings in to the navigator, who quickly plotted them.

Apparently not satisfied, the navigator himself, muttering some unintelligible words, came out on the wing of the bridge, took a round of bearings and returned to his plotting board.

Ski picked up the phone, "Engine room, this is Ski, have you slowed our speed?" After a second or so, he turned to the navigator, "It's not down there, sir."

A strange, bewildered look on his otherwise very confident face, the navigator told the officer of the deck (OOD), "We're only making good 11.5 knots when we should be doing 14.4. It's not the current – you had better ask the captain to come up here."

The navigator again came out on the wing, took the bearings and went through the same routine. He was standing there shaking his head as he studied the chart, when the captain stepped on the bridge.

At the same time, the bridge talker received a message from the foc'stle (the most forward part of the ship's main deck): "We have an unusually large bow wave. Are we standing into shallow water?"

"Stop all engines," ordered the captain.

"Damn, look at that!" They all heard the leadsman shout from his small platform that stuck out from the side of the ship. From this platform he could freely swing and lower a line, with a heavy lead piece at its end, down into the water to check the channel depth. This vantage position gave him a clear view of

33

1. ENSIGN, USNR

the ship's most forward part, the stem that cuts through the water.

Rushing to the starboard wing of the bridge we all saw him pointing down at the sharp stem.

The first lieutenant joined him on the platform as we watched. Almost immediately the bridge received an excited report from the foc'stle talker. "There's a very large fish stuck athwartship on our bow. Looks like a large whale. The first lieutenant recommends you back down and shake him loose."

"All back two-thirds," ordered the skipper.

As the ship gathered sternway we all saw the water near the bow turn red as the wounded whale slid off the stem and disappeared. The whale, by slowing the ship's forward speed, had made the bearings appear wrong, when it was actually the expected position of the ship that was wrong.

A ship as big as the Nitro can't dawdle around in a channel – even one as large as the Straits of San Juan de Fuca. We never saw the whale again and were soon beyond the reddish water. It all happened quickly, and I immediately started taking bearings again as we headed for the shipyard.

The day after our arrival in Bremerton, I was alone in the chartroom studying a well-known navigation book by Bowditch, when the navigator walked in.

"You like going to sea, Mr. Sotos?"

"I'm not sure yet, sir."

"You seem to take it pretty well."

"Thank you, sir."

"Never mind that sir stuff. I see you've learned how to use Dreisonstok. I'll bet you're the only ensign in the Navy who knows how to use it. You can make that your personal copy if you like. It's the one I used when I was your age."

"Thanks, Mr. Thompson."

"You're doing fine, George, better than any of the others. Keep it up."

By the time I recovered from the unexpected compliment, the navigator was gone. I felt a warm glow of pride as I realized what had happened. And I sensed that Mr. Thompson, too, was very proud of his teaching experiment.

"That hard-headed Swede has never complimented anyone on this ship," remarked the exec, when he heard about Mr. Thompson's compliment to me.

Figure 36: **USS Nitro (AE 2).** Pierside at Balboa in the Panama Canal Zone, 1938. The house-like structure near the front of the ship is part of the pier.

Vital Statistics
Type: Pyro-class ammunition ship
Displacement: 10,600 tons (loaded)
Length: 482 feet
Complement: 226 enlisted, 21 officers
Draft: 21 feet 11 inches
Speed: 17 knots

Chapter 2

Fire

The ear-piercing, shrill whistle of the boatswain's pipe suddenly split the air on the morning of our second day in Bremerton. It was followed by shouts of "Fire! Fire in the paint locker. Fire in the paint locker!"

Everyone within earshot was galvanized into action as the alarm spread throughout the ship. No questions! A fire, any fire, on an ammunition ship is the worst nightmare come true. For us, if not contained promptly, a fire in our paint locker meant that over 5000 tons of various types of the most sensitive explosives could cook off, and create an explosion that would make memories of the Nitro and the shipyard itself.

The paint locker was the Nitro's favorite location for a fire drill, so I wasn't alarmed at first. But when I got to the foc'stle and saw the billows of heavy smoke pouring out of the paint locker entrance hatch, my heart rate escalated.

The fire party was already busy at the scene. Several men had donned gas masks and were inside the paint locker pulling special smothering chemicals with them. Others had charged up the fire hoses and were wetting down the exterior of the locker, which was actually a good-sized compartment.

During drills, I had been in charge of the fire party. But never did I confront an actual fire. Fortunately for me, when I got to this fire, Mr. Martin, the first lieutenant, was already there and

2. Fire

giving orders to wet down everything around the paint locker to make sure nothing cooked off.

It didn't take me long to realize that I was well out of my water.

When we drilled, the extent of my duties had been to look on, in what I hoped was a proper supervisory manner, as the leading boatswain's mate mustered the men and checked the equipment they carried. We had never fought an actual fire.

I suddenly discovered that being an ensign in charge of a fire party didn't mean a damn thing unless I knew how to fight a fire, and I certainly did not.

No one bothered with me and I was grateful for that. No one noticed my quiet withdrawal to the quarterdeck area where I was suddenly flattered by a question from the chief on watch. "Have they found the source of the fire yet?"

"Yes, it's an electrical fire," I replied. I had overheard this information when on the foc'stle.

Apparently this was the first information from the scene because the chief promptly called the engine room and told the people there.

The quarterdeck phone rang and the chief answered it. "Yes sir, yes sir, just a minute sir," he turned to me. "Will you please take this? It's the Captain of the Yard's office."

"Yes, sir," was my first remark into the phone.

"This is Lieutenant Commander Muldoon of the Captain of the Yard's office," I heard a worried voice ask, "Where is the fire?"

"In the paint locker."

"Is it out yet?"

"No, sir."

"Is it close to any ammunition?"

"Yes, sir," I said, thinking of the smoke engulfing the ammunition kept in special lockers topside near the guns, ready for quick use.

"How close?" There was alarm in the voice.

"The smoke is covering the ready lockers."

"I mean your cargo ammunition," the relief in Muldoon's voice smothered his irritation.

"Rather far."

"How far?"

"One deck above and two holds forward. There sure is a lot of smoke there though," I added, as I saw new billows pour out of the hatch.

"Not under control yet, huh?"

"No sir, sure doesn't look like it."

It took about five hours, one man overcome by smoke, and help from the shipyard fire department, to put the smoldering fire out. During that time everybody on the base, including the commandant's office, had called. The Nitro gave the shipyard a real scare.

Once the news was out that the Nitro had a fire, I suspect there was a quiet exodus from the shipyard.

The flammable paint materials had been kept wet and were quickly removed from the paint locker. And, except for extensive damage to some electrical wiring, the incident was soon behind us.

While they never said anything, I think it was with some relief that the Bremerton people saw us depart the next day.

The Nitro was one of two ammunition ships in the Navy. The other was named the Pyro. Our mission was to supply good ammunition and pick up old ammunition from naval bases and ships all over the world, wherever the Navy was posted.

So we traveled a lot. On each trip we would cover every U.S. port where there were naval forces.

Our next stop down the west coast was the Mare Island naval shipyard near San Francisco. It was quite a thrill to sail beneath the beautiful Golden Gate Bridge en route to the shipyard. The weather was pleasant and we saw many recreational boaters.

We passed a medium size, sleek looking pleasure cruiser that seemed to be drifting. Looking down at the cruiser I could see its two female occupants, both wearing bathing suits, shouting for help, motioning that they couldn't start their boat engine.

2. Fire

In response to the captain's order that we assist them, we stopped and lowered a small motor launch in the water. At the time I was the JOOD and I went to the main deck and told the three sailors in the boat crew to assist the occupants of the boat, and meet us later in the shipyard, which was visible a short distance away. They saluted smartly and headed for the drifting boat.

In less than an hour we were moored to a dock and all of us without duty assignments soon were heading for colorful Vallejo and its numerous bars.

It happened that there was also a British cruiser undergoing repairs in the shipyard. Britain was at war with Germany and this particular cruiser had been damaged in action somewhere in the Mediterranean and sailed around to our west coast for repairs. Among the many rumors about the cruiser was that she had arrived with a flooded compartment containing twenty five dead men sealed within. This and other stories had given the cruiser and its crew an almost legendary reputation.[1]

It was mid-1941, well before anyone even dreamed about an attack on Pearl Harbor, and an American sailor was just an American sailor. The combat veterans from overseas were something special to the girls in Vallejo, and the Brits made out without half trying, much to the chagrin of the Americans who were left out in the cold. Nevertheless, they kept drinking and trying.

The second day in port I was in the duty section and was the OOD. Early that morning, the chief boatswain's mate came to me and reported that the boat we had sent to help the drifting plea-

---

[1] After the war, I learned that the name of the British cruiser was HMS Liverpool. Attacked in the Mediterranean by Italian torpedo bombers in October 1940, she lost her bow. She was towed to Alexandria, Egypt, where she was fitted with a temporary bow, and then made her way to the Vallejo, California shipyard where they built and attached a new bow. She was being repaired there when we stopped in Vallejo. While the Liverpool lost 3 officers and 27 crew in her fight with the Italians, there was no mention, as was rumored, of any sailors still being in a flooded compartment when she arrived in California. See Wikipedia: HMS_Liverpool_(C11)

sure cruiser the day before still had not returned to the Nitro. He and I left the ship, and walked to the end of the pier where we could look in the area we had last seen the boat. Sure enough we sighted it right away. Our boat and the one that had been in distress were anchored together at the edge of the channel about a half mile away.

"Send another boat over there and bring them back here," I ordered.

Within the hour the chief boatswain's mate had his boat and the three sailors back on the Nitro.

I confronted the sailors and told all three, "You are on report for failing to carry out orders. You are restricted to the ship until further orders. Do you understand?"

All three acknowledged that they understood and said nothing more, obviously expecting some sort of disciplinary action.

That morning, the captain held mast (men are brought before him on the bridge for possible discipline) and I explained the charges against the men. They said that they worked a long time on the boat engine, but couldn't fix it. However, they gave no excuse for not returning earlier.

I thought the captain would award them some sort of punishment. Instead he referred all three to a summary court martial to be convened by Mr. Thompson.

The remainder of that day was quiet, but toward evening it became so foggy that neither the bow nor the fantail could be seen from the midship quarterdeck, where we stood our watch.

About eight-thirty in the evening, the shore patrol brought three sailors back to the ship. All three were drunk. They had been picked up in a waterfront bar for fighting, not an unusual occurrence. Twenty minutes later, the shore patrol returned with six more of our sailors, all drunk and accused of fighting with British sailors.

I instructed all of them to go below and turn in. They all went below so cheerfully that I quietly complimented myself on the way I handled it.

2. Fire

For the next couple of hours everything was quiet until the shore patrol showed up again with four more sailors. They were drunk and also accused of fighting with the British sailors.

To my surprise, all four had been in the group escorted aboard earlier and whom I had assumed were below in their bunks.

I immediately wanted to put all four in the ship's brig, but the senior duty officer, Mr. Thompson, said no. "Make sure they get in their bunks this time and put a watch over them until they fall asleep," he instructed.

About an hour later after the guard reported that the men had fallen asleep, I decided to make a routine inspection of the mooring lines up forward, which were still enshrouded in fog. As I approached the bow, I heard some whispering that seemed to come from the dock. Looking over the side I caught a glimpse of two men shinnying their way down the bow line toward the dock.

This time Mr. Thompson agreed that we should put them in the brig.

Early in the morning on the third day, what remained of the fog wasn't enough to keep us in port, and we were underway for San Diego. Just after we had passed beneath the Golden Gate Bridge and it was safe for me to leave my station at the ship's stern, that's when the whole ship suddenly became very quiet.

The silence was hard to believe at first. But it was especially noticeable when we no longer heard the nearby, very noisy ship's ventilation exhaust system. It was so deathly quiet we could even hear voices from as far forward as the bridge.

Of course, I had no idea what was happening. However, an older boatswain's mate first class standing nearby, immediately knew what it was. "We've lost power!" he shouted. "We're dead in the water."

He was right. We had lost all propulsion and electrical power and were literally at the mercy of the elements. Luckily there wasn't much wind, but there is a strong current under the Golden Gate Bridge and it soon took charge of us.

I didn't realize how serious a problem it was until we floated over a channel buoy that, fortunately, missed our propellers.

After fifteen minutes we regained propulsion power and headed safely out to sea. Later I learned that one of our condensers had salted up, causing us to lose power. Few of us appreciated the operation of the condensers at that time but I, for one resolved to find out more, and I did.[2]

Later that day Mr. Thompson convened the summary court martial for the three men I had placed on report.

The men had Ensign Sheridan, my roommate, as their defense attorney. They pleaded not guilty to disobeying orders.

The men testified that when they got to the boat there was nothing wrong with the engine, there was nothing to fix. The girls just wanted some company. And they admitted freely that all three decided to remain with the girls and would probably still be there had not the chief boatswain's mate come after them.

Mr. Thompson found all three not guilty, and that was the end of it.

Later I asked Mr. Thompson if he would mind telling me the basis for his decision. "I thought they were out and out guilty," I said.

"Were they now?" he asked.

"Sir, they disobeyed their orders."

"What were their orders?"

"To help the occupants of that boat and return to the ship."

"Well, that's exactly what they did."

"I don't understand, sir."

"It's a matter of interpretation."

"Many people, and I am one of them, would conclude that those men did assist the girls. The only issue here is the form of

---

[2] The condenser is part of a heat exchanger. It is a bank of steel tubes that uses sea water to cool exhaust steam into water for reheating by the boilers. Sea water salt crystallizes on the tube surfaces and, if not cleaned regularly, will disrupt the heat exchange that provides propulsion steam to the ship's turbines.

2. Fire

that assistance. Technically, or rather physically, they did provide assistance that was requested. Had you phrased your orders to them to return if they couldn't repair the boat engine, my decision might have been different." Then, as a smile tried to take over his face, he said, "I agree that in a strictly moral sense they probably should have returned when they discovered the engine was O.K. But, I had what I considered reasonable doubt to that effect, hence my decision. Perhaps as you gain experience you might agree with me. That's it, young man."

I was frustrated, but I was learning that everything isn't black and white. However, incidents of that type were a very small part of my education aboard the Nitro.

Our next stop was San Diego, where we picked up 250 Marines for transport to the east coast. We were soon on our way to our next stop, Panama.

The buoys and ranges which mark the Pacific entrance to the Panama Canal complex make it as easy to enter as driving a car down a well marked street. Then, before transiting the canal itself the Nitro moored to a dock in Balboa for a few days. Balboa is the port city on the Pacific side of the canal. During this time we all got a chance to wander around the nearby small town of Panama City, but it was a rather quiet place and there wasn't much to do. The officers' club extending out over the water was an especially relaxing place to drink and dine, and that's what we did.

The transit through the Isthmus of Panama reminded me of a boat ride down the Chicago River. The mass and nearness of the huge cliffs felt like the skyscrapers rising steeply from the banks of the Chicago River. But then it changed. Alligators, awakened by the ship, suddenly discarded their log-like appearance and slid silently into the canal. Tropical birds of different colors and sizes flew around the ship.

The locks themselves, and our movement through them, was like a high school lesson suddenly taking place before my eyes and I couldn't get enough of this living history.

If some one had told me, at that time, that I, a brand new

"Ninety Day Wonder"[3] would, in four years, command a destroyer escort and actually pilot my own ship through that same Panama Canal, I would have called him crazy. But, as you'll see, it happened!

On the Atlantic side of the Panama Canal all the activity is centered in the small town of Colon. It was there that I received my first shore patrol assignment along with one of our passengers, a new Marine second lieutenant.

It was three in the afternoon when we reported into shore patrol headquarters. I was wearing my dress white uniform and the Marine his khaki. Both of us had donned the familiar S.P. brassards (shore patrol arm bands) on our left upper arms. Since we were inexperienced, the senior shore patrol officer assigned several veteran enlisted petty officers to us. They were to precede us as we patrolled our area. We were to intervene only if it appeared that the petty officers couldn't handle a situation with their authority.

The patrol started to get both interesting and educational in the early evening after most of the sailors and marines had streamed ashore.

Both the Marine and I were wide eyed when we entered the Cocoanut Grove section. Everywhere we looked we saw prostitutes, and, just behind the girls, their "store front" cubicles.

About ten feet by eight, each cubicle contained a bed, a dresser with a homey familial picture in a pleasant frame, a wash-stand, a nice rug, and normally a little dog of some local breed. Also, a chair, which, when the door was open, would be on the sidewalk directly in front of the cubicle.

The price ranged from fifty cents to two dollars, depending on looks, age and bargaining astuteness. There were colorful remarks for all the sailors and especially the shore patrol officers

---

[3] "Ninety day wonder" refers to graduates of a special three-month Navy "V-7" program that awarded qualified young men an officer's commission (with the rank of Ensign) in the U.S. Navy Reserve. Normally, four years at the Naval Academy or four years in a college Reserve Officers Training Corps (ROTC) program was required for a commission.

2. Fire

like ourselves. These remarks and gestures are among the most colorful and vulgar in the world. Anything and everything was available by merely showing the color of the American dollar.

The business girls, and to them it was a business, were rough, tough and alert. A good number of them were quite pretty.

They had no qualms about rolling a sailor, and the drunker the sailors were, the more the girls pursued them. Arguments, knifings, and brawls were not rare. Some men, disappointed, would refuse payment, and unless the shore patrol got there first, the local populace would work the Americans over before sending them off to jail.

Only an inexperienced stranger or a very drunk fool ever refused to pay one of the business girls. It was a deadly serious transaction for the girls, who did not take their work lightly.

As we walked slowly through the crowds the girls, sitting in their chairs just an arms length away, would make lewd gestures and pretend to grab at us as prospective customers. They were constantly talking and, in their spiced up broken English, would try to convince passers-by that they were the best.

About a third of the doors were closed, indicating that business was being transacted. However, a closed door was no assurance of privacy. Always out for as much money as they could get, the girls or their friends sold "peep show holes," where, for a dime or a quarter, observers could watch the unsuspecting customers.

It was a wild part of the world and a slip could ruin a life. There were other risks, besides the known high rate of venereal disease.

Some local characters, in a sleazy tavern, got a glimpse of a boatswain's mate's roll as he was paying for his drinks. They instructed an emaciated looking girl to work him for some drinks. Quite drunk, he was an easy target. He didn't notice that she was picking up his change until she pocketed several bills in her brassiere.

The boatswain's mate got sore and reached for his money. She bit him and he slugged her hard. As she fell to the floor the local characters jumped him, beat him up and took all his money.

When the Panamanian police arrived, the boatswain's mate was just struggling to his feet, but the girl was on the floor, still unconscious.

Even though the boatswain's mate was a passenger on the Nitro, we could not persuade the Panamanian police to release him to us. Instead, they took him to jail – a Panamanian jail – where, not only was he out several hundred dollars, he was facing an assault and battery charge. Worse yet, the girl was in the hospital suffering more from her run-down health than the blow from the boatswain's mate.

Almost as bad as the punishment he was facing, was his stay in jail. Girls, boys, women, men, old hags, drunks, bums – it made no difference what age, sex, or color – they were all thrown into the one giant jail cell. There was no privacy for any of them at any time. The fact that the toilet facilities were out in the open was apparently startling only to us. We had to leave him there. Ultimately the Nitro transferred his records to the local U.S. Navy command and sailed without him.

Our night of shore patrol duty was by no means over yet.

One way to prevent trouble, the Marine and I had been instructed, was to make ourselves conspicuous. That is what we were doing in a small night club that advertised a floor show.

The master of ceremonies was cracking some dirty jokes, and, accustomed to the shore patrol, was ignoring the two of us as we stood conspicuously off to the side of the raised stage, the Marine on one side and I on the other.

Suddenly a tall, very pretty young white girl from Costa Rica, voluptuous and curvy with long dark hair, walked out on the stage. She wore a beautiful blue evening dress.

She didn't waste any time. To the music of the "Bolero," which had started quietly and gradually in the background, she slowly started to dance across the stage from one side to the other.

Then very gracefully, to the tremendous roar of a full house of sailors, marines, soldiers, local Panamanians, merchant sea-

2. Fire

men, and many others, she started, in perfect timing with the slowly increasing tempo and volume of the Bolero, to remove her clothes.

It didn't take a special messenger to tell me that I was about to witness, close aboard, a really professional strip tease dance.

Unlike the master of ceremonies she did not ignore either the Marine or myself. But, to our embarrassment, she made us a part of her show.

I realized she was concentrating her performance in three sections of the large stage. First she would spend a few minutes in the center facing the audience and smoothly removing an article of clothing. Then she would dance away from center all the way to one of the sides so that she was almost in front of either the Marine or myself, always in perfect rhythm with the booming drums of the Bolero.

The embarrassment, discomfort and urge to leave my post, for some reason, disappeared after the first round of laughter subsided. She was such an entrancing combination of beauty and grace, that even as she danced in front of us it seemed that, after the initial laughter, few people even saw us.

Thankfully she took more of a shine to the Marine than to me, and practically provided him with a one man show. He was the first, and, it turned out, the only one, to see her completely nude!

The Marine and I easily had the best seats in the house and we both joined the wildly applauding crowd when she finished.

"That was some show. We'll never get another duty assignment to match this one," smiled the Marine.

"Boy, she was a beauty, too," added one of the petty officers as we left the club and resumed our patrol.

The two petty officers were ahead of us by about a hundred yards as we walked through the crowded streets. About an hour later, just after we had returned to the Cocoanut Grove, we heard what sounded like eight or nine shots. Everyone on the street stopped and the air suddenly became silent as we all looked in the direction of the gunfire.

"What do we do now?" I asked the Marine.

"Guess we go see what's happening," he answered hesitatingly.

All four of us, now together, had run about fifty yards in the direction of the shots when suddenly the crowd thinned and we came face to face with two uniformed Panamanian police, guns drawn and pointing downward. The policemen said nothing, but it was obvious that no one was allowed to pass them.

We stood there watching them silently as we debated our next move. Suddenly, a fast moving jeep skidded to a stop alongside us. Its occupants, an Army major and a Panamanian police official, beckoned to us.

"Get the hell out of this area and send all the soldiers, sailors, and Marines back to their stations. You got that?" shouted the major. At the same time several more jeep loads of military police (MP's) and SP's arrived to help carry out his orders.

In an hour the streets were clear of American military. We later learned that a drunken soldier and a Cocoanut Grove businesswoman had been in an altercation that turned into a riot. No one had been hurt except the soldier, who had been slashed.

A few days after we left Panama, the medical staff held short arm inspections. By the end of the day, at least seven or eight men were placed on the "sick list" with suspected venereal disease.[4]

We continued on to Norfolk, Virginia, where we off-loaded the Marines and picked up some old ammunition.

Our next stop was the major ammunition deport at Iona Island, New York, in the Hudson River. It was there, during cargo operations, that one of the questions almost all of us had asked ourselves was finally answered.

What would happen if, during cargo operations, we dropped one of our 16-inch projectiles? These were the largest shells we carried. Battleships fired them.

---

[4] Penicillin was not available in those days.

2. Fire

I was among the first to see the answer – not because I was alert or on the ball – but because I was the in-port officer of the deck, and my station was at the quarterdeck about 20 feet aft of the cargo hold that was working the 16" shells.

I watched as our winch man lowered his sling into the cargo hold and then I saw him start to raise it. His wide, strong, rope cargo net cleared the top edge of the cargo hold, and I could see a huge 16" projectile nestled securely in the net.

As every good winch man does, he paused at the end of his uptake phase well clear of the cargo hold and above the ships gunwales (its side). He then started to swing the entire load out over the side of the ship, above the concrete dock where some stevedores were hard at work.

As he did so, the projectile rolled to the side of the cargo net. It hung there for an instant, yet seemed secure, as he stopped the swing. But then it suddenly slipped over the edge and fell, nose first, about twenty-five feet down onto the concrete dock.

I never saw people scatter so fast in my life. I didn't follow them because I was the OOD. It was a lonesome feeling, standing there with the quartermaster and boatswain's mate of the watch, wondering if that projectile was going to explode.

Mesmerized, we watched the huge projectile hit the concrete dock, nose first, and roll slowly off the dock into the net stretched between the ship and the dock for just that purpose.

It was a full two hours before the civilian stevedores were all back on the job. And each one carefully examined the four-inch hole in the concrete where the projectile had struck.

There was never any danger of an explosion since there was no explosive in the projectile. But no one knew that, except perhaps for the chief in the cargo hold who was supervising the operation.

Yes, I was scared. And when I think about it, I can still see the point of that projectile hitting the concrete dock.

From Iona the Nitro went back south to San Juan, Puerto Rico, a sunny, pleasant, easy-going place where we were going to unload some more ammunition. As luck would have it, I was again the in-port OOD and enjoying my watch on the quarterdeck.

About an hour after the unloading got underway, I was surprised to see Chief Gunners Mate Collins march a strapping, shirtless, perspiring, and visibly frightened Puerto Rican stevedore to the quarterdeck. He was prodding him in the back with a forty-five caliber pistol.

"Do you know how to use this gun, Mr. Sotos?" Collins' lips were trembling with anger.

"Yes."

"Here take it. It's loaded and the safety is off."

"Shoot this sunofabitch if he moves an inch–shoot him!" He handed me the pistol and headed for the exec's room.

A few minutes later Collins and the exec stormed out of the passageway and relieved me of both the pistol and the thoroughly frightened Puerto Rican who hadn't moved an inch.

The report, as I later entered it in the log, was that Collins had discovered the Puerto Rican smoking a cigarette in a black powder cargo hold.

```
Refer to:
AE 2                    U. S. S. NITRO
                                          Coco Solo, C.Z.,
                                          December 12, 1941.
2nd Section Duty.
4th Section Duty.
                        ORDERS OF THE DAY

0545 - Call BMs and MAA.

0600 - Reveille.

0630 - Breakfast.  Open hatches # 2A, 4A, and 5.

0715 - Commence cargo operations.
       Muster on stations.

1200 - Dinner.

1300 - Turn to;
       Sweep down.
       Continue as in forenoon.

1600 - Sweep down.

1700 - Supper.

1800 - Empty all trash cans.



                                          E.J. MILNER,
                                    Lieut.-Comdr., U.S.Navy,
                                        Executive Officer.


NOTE:  Attention is invited to the fact that the Bureau should have
       on file a correct beneficiary slip of each man. All men should
       make certain that the slip in their service record is correct.
```

Figure 52: **What war?** Five days after the attack on Pearl Harbor, the only unusual feature of the daily plan aboard the USS Nitro was a reminder for crewmembers to have a correct "beneficiary slip" in their record.

Chapter 3

Load the Guns

When I first went to sea, I was an eager young ensign, perhaps too eager. I read the books about what young new officers should do and, of course, I tried to apply what I learned. That's not always a good idea because most of the sailors you work with haven't read those books. So I made the mistake of trying to apply that "book learning" at the wrong times and in the wrong situations.

This included simple things, like telling a first class gunner's mate that he wasn't wearing his uniform correctly when he reported for an "in port" quarterdeck watch with me. Or, reminding a first class boatswain's mate (who probably knew more about Navy customs and traditions than I did) to return a salute smartly when he was welcoming a Navy visitor aboard.

I really don't remember how many of those incidents there were. But I do remember the way I discovered it was a problem, because it really shook me.

It occurred about three months after I had reported aboard the Nitro. We were alongside the pier in San Pedro, California, and I was the in port OOD.[1] The telephone rang and I picked

---

[1] The officer of the deck (OOD) in port is the captain's direct representative. He has the same authority and responsibilities as the OOD on the bridge underway. However, because the ship is in port, the duties are primarily administrative. In port OODs on the Nitro were primarily the junior officers.

3. Load the Guns

it up, answering smartly, "USS Nitro quarterdeck, officer of the deck speaking."

There was a slight pause, then a very soft and sweet voice asked, "Can I speak to the executive officer?"

The exec, also known as Shorty for obvious reasons, was still aboard.

"Just a minute, please."

"All right honey," she responded as I frantically motioned to the enlisted petty officer to show me how to connect the call to the exec's stateroom. We finally made the connection and rang his room but there was no answer.

"I'm sorry, miss, but he's not answering."

"Oh, please keep trying."

We tried again but still no answer. The caller simply didn't want to hang up. She started to engage me in a friendly conversation, which included the exciting and interesting information that she was a member of Sally Rand's Nude Ranch. Had I seen the show? Of course I was interested and probably asked for more information. Then I suggested she call back later. Still calling me "honey," she hung up.

I thought that was the end of it.

But ten minutes later she called back and this time when we rang the exec's room he answered.

We had kind of a switchboard there at the quarterdeck, so I knew when they were no longer talking, about twenty minutes later.

No sooner had they ended their call than Shorty called the quarterdeck and told the enlisted petty officer to send me to his room immediately.

"He's hot about something, sir. You better get in there."

Well, he sure was hot. He had been in the shower and was just half dressed when I entered his stateroom.

"You damn red ass reserve ensign," he shouted. "Who the hell do you think you are! I don't remember the rest of his words, but the implication was that I was flirting with the girl who had called him. At first I was too frightened to say anything. When I did try to respond he blew up. He really got angry and told me I was in the Navy for three months and trying to run it. He told me to stop bothering the petty officers, they knew ten times as much as I would ever know. "You're just a red ass reserve ensign. Stop trying to run this ship!"

He didn't even tell me to leave, I just stood there, dumbfounded, not knowing what to say as he turned and went into his bathroom.

As soon as he left I did too. When I went out to the quarterdeck the petty officer on watch with me knew that I had been chewed out. And of course he told others.

Later that day, after I had been off watch, Ensign Hunnewell came in to see me. He had heard about the blast the exec had given me and asked what had happened.

I told Hunnewell everything I remembered, but I couldn't understand what had pissed him off.

"Shorty is hot tempered. He also listens to the senior petty officers. Something else must have been bothering him. He'll forget about it. Just stay away from him for a while."

But as far as Hunnewell knew, I was the only one he had ever called a "red ass reserve ensign." And for a while that name stuck to me like glue even though all the other ensigns were also Naval Reserve.

I didn't need Hunnewell's advice to steer clear of the exec. For the next four months, if I saw him coming down the port side toward me, I would cross over to the starboard side to avoid him.

During meal times with the officers in the wardroom, I carefully avoided any eye contact or verbal exchanges with him. In fact I stayed so clear of him I didn't speak to him at all for those four months.

He broke the ice by coming to see me in sick bay. I had bruised my leg badly and it had some type of infection. The doctor put me in bed and kept me there for a week until it healed.

When the exec came by to see me he was very pleasant. He told me to take it easy and get well. But, while he never used it

3. Load the Guns

again, my fellow officers wouldn't let go of the "red ass" label.

I did take away a lesson from this incident. The exec's attitude toward the senior petty officers reinforced my own personal experiences in working with them. For the rest of my naval career I treated them with great respect, never repeating the slips of my first few "red ass months."

We left San Pedro, made a quick stop in San Diego, and headed for the Panama Canal's Pacific port of Balboa. We were scheduled to arrive in Balboa on December 7, 1941, to pick up some old ammunition. Then we were to transit the canal into the Atlantic, enroute to Norfolk, Virginia, our home port.

Jim Hunnewell was the OOD and I was his JOOD the morning of December 7, 1941. It was about 1000 (10 am) and we were about 100 miles from Balboa. The weather was perfect. The sky was a pretty blue. The sea was as flat as glass. We had the ocean to ourselves and there was a light pleasant breeze that kept us cool. It had the makings of a beautiful, restful, and peaceful Sunday.

The captain was sitting in his bridge chair chatting quietly with the exec when the bridge phone rang. I quickly picked it up.

"Bridge, Ensign Sotos," I said.

"Is the exec there?" It was our communications officer.

"It's for you, Commander. It's the communications officer, sir," I said to the exec.

He walked over and I handed him the phone.

"What is it Mel?' he asked.

I could hear Mel saying something excitedly.

"O.K., slow down bring it up here," said the exec.

He handed me the phone and turned towards the captain. "Something hot, sir. Mel is bringing it up here."

In less than a minute Mel, a chubby, normally slow moving, talkative, friendly and pleasant lieutenant was on the bridge. Breathing heavily from his quick ascent, he brushed by me and handed a message to the exec.

The exec said something like "Oh my God," as he glanced at the short message and handed it to the captain.

After reading it quietly several times the captain got out of his chair and said. "Come with me," as the exec and Mel followed him to his cabin.

On the way the captain handed the message to Hunnewell. "Enter this in the log," he said.

Normally Jim would hand the message to me and I would make the entry in the log. This time, as we both read and reread the messsage, he didn't hand it to me.

I read the message but for an instant its contents didn't really register with me.

"JAPAN HAS ATTACKED PEARL HARBOR. REPEAT. JAPAN HAS ATTACKED PEARL HARBOR. THIS IS NO DRILL. REPEAT THIS IS NO DRILL. EXECUTE WAR PLAN 43."[2]

Jim was just as dumbfounded as I was. He didn't say anything to me or anyone until he had made the entry in the ship's log.

There was no formal announcement to the crew about the start of the war. There were no ship's loudspeaker in those days and the only announcements we normally heard were from the boatswain's mates to carry out events scheduled in the plan of the day.

It seemed that everyone on the ship knew it as soon as we did. Some knew even before we did. The radio shack always had a few sailors hanging around it, reading news bulletins that our radiomen would copy and post on their bulletin board right outside their door.

When I got off watch I joined the large number of sailors that had gathered outside the radio shack. The radiomen were posting news bulletin after news bulletin and that's when I really learned what the beginning of World War II was like.

---

[2] I am not sure if that is the correct number of the war plan. I had never seen or heard of the war plans.

3. Load the Guns

> **U. S. NAVAL COMMUNICATION SERVICE**
> N.C.S. 387   SRS
> USS NITRO
>
> **INTERCEPTED PRESS**
>
> 105 BULLETIN SECOND ADD 103 WASHINGTON DEPARTMENTS STATEMENT SAID HULL READ JAPANESE REPLY AND QUOTE IMMEDIATELY TURNED TO JAPANESE AMBASSADOR AND WITH GREATEST INDIGNATION SAID COLON EYE MUST SAY THAT IN ALL MY CONVERSATIONS WITH YOU BRACKET JAPANESE AMBASSADOR UNBRACKET DURING LAST NINE MONTHS EYE HAVE NEVER UTTERED ONE WORD UNTRUTH STOP THIS IS BORNE OUT ABSOLUTELY BY RECORD STOP IN ALL MY FIFTY YEARS PUBLIC SERVICE EYE HAVE NEVER SEEN DOCUMENT THAT MORE CROWDED WITH INFAMOUS FALSEHOODS AND DISTORTIONS DASH INFAMOUS FALSEHOODS AND DISTORTION ON SCALE SO HUGE THAT EYE NEVER IMAGINED UNTIL TODAY THAT ANY GOVERNMENT THIS PLANET CAPABLE UTTERING THEM UNQUOTE
>
> SANFRANCISCO BT LEAD ENEMY PLANES RETURNED TO GOLDEN GATE FROM THEIR OFFSHORE LURKING PLANG ARLY TODAY AND SANFRANCISCO BAY AREA LAT IN DARKNESS UNDER AIR RAID ALARM TENSELY AWAITING POSSIBLI ATTACK STOP IT SECOND VISIT OF NIGHT STOP EARLIER ARMY REPORTED SOME THIRTY SHIPS APPARENTLY BENT ON RECONNAISSANCE WINGED CLOSE TO HARBOR ENTRANCE AND OVER OTHER PORT ON CALIFORNIA STOP ALL CLEAR SIGNAL FOLLOWED THIRD ALARM COMMA AT TWO THIRTYNINE AM COMMA BY HOUR AND THERE NO IMMEDIATE INDICATION WHENSER RAIDE AGAIN FROM OVER THIS STRATEGC AREA OR INTERCEPTED BY UNISTATES SQUADRONS STOP ARMY INTERCEPTOR PLANES FOLLOWED FIRST QU IN SQUADRONS BUT UNABLE DETERMINE WHERE THEY FINALLY WENT STOP NAVY THEN TOOK UP SEARCH FOR PLANE CARRIER PRESUMABLY LURKING OFF CALIFORNIAS COAST AND POSSIBLY FIVE OR SIX HUHDRED MILES AT SEA

Figure 58: **Wild news dispatches.** The top bulletin reports Secretary of State Cordell Hull's meeting with the Japanese ambassador hours after the attack on Pearl Harbor. The bottom reports thirty enemy airplanes over San Francisco during one of three air raid alarms sounded in that blacked-out city in one night. Only the top bulletin was true.

We couldn't believe what we were reading in those bulletins. I made copies of a number of them, as in Figure 58.

We arrived in the Balboa anchorage late in the afternoon of December 7, 1941, immediately presenting the local authorities with a major problem.

A loaded ammunition ship is the last thing any one would like to have in his back yard at the beginning of a war. They had us anchor outside the harbor for a few hours while the captain went ashore to confer with the Senior Officer Present Afloat

(SOPA), the captain of a cruiser.

Finally we were instructed to go alongside the dock and finish our business as quickly as possible.

We started cargo operations immediately after mooring to the pier and worked until it was too dark to see. All during cargo operations different people came aboard and asked us to take packages of all sorts back to the states for them. It was clear they expected to be attacked.

It was a very gloomy atmosphere.

We darkened the ship and turned in. Darkening meant that we had to make sure that no lights were visible topside. That included, of course, no smoking topside after dark.

It was very hot and most of us slept on deck. Air conditioning was not even a dream for ships in those days.

I had fallen asleep in a cot near the fan-tail (the ship's stern).

Shouts of "General quarters, general quarters," and the shrill piercing whistle of a boatswain's pipe followed by more shouts of "Man your battle stations, man your battle stations" suddenly awakened me.

I didn't know, or care about, the time, but it was still very dark. Groggy from sleep, I hesitated for a few seconds before jumping out of the cot and heading for my battle station. Fully clothed and with my shoes on (no one had undressed), I ran forward on the starboard side for about fifty feet to a ladder leading up to the boat deck, and to the two 3"/50 anti-aircraft guns, for which I was the gun control officer.[3]

The gun crews had slept alongside the guns and, when I got there, both mounts, including the telephone talker, were fully manned.

---

[3] The term 3"/50 – pronounced "three inch fifty" – refers to a gun that fires a projectile 3 inches in diameter out of a barrel 3x50 or 150 inches long. The 3"/50 had a horizontal range of about 12,000 yards and a ceiling range of about 21,000 feet. The projectiles weighed approximately 13 pounds and varied in length from about 9 to 13 inches, depending on the type (illuminating, armor piercing, anti-aircraft proximity fuses, etc.). Our 3"/50 ammunition had to be hand loaded and hand rammed (pushed into the open breech).

3. Load the Guns

"Report guns manned and ready," I ordered, and the talker repeated it to the bridge. That's when we all saw a wide, brilliant, searchlight beam cut the darkness from our bridge.

Pointing skyward, just forward of the port bow, it wobbled back and forth searching for a target. Then we saw three or four more searchlights from other ships pointing skyward in the same general direction.

Suddenly from the opposite side, low and broad on the starboard beam, we heard the loud roar of an airplane engine.

Before we could even see where it was, the roar stopped as though squelched, and for a few seconds we heard and saw nothing. Then from that general area, we heard a shout over and over again. "Hey on the ship, give me a hand, give me a hand, send me a boat."

"Can anyone see where he is?" The talker repeated the question from the bridge.

My starboard gun captain, who had the sense to bring binoculars, quietly pointed to a spot in the water broad on the starboard beam and said, "I see him. He's standing on the wing of the plane and waving his arms."

My talker repeated that information to the bridge. "They see him and are sending a boat," he reported.

In almost the same breath my talker shouted, "Bridge reports unidentified aircraft on port bow."

"Shall we load the guns sir?" It was the lead ammunition passer.

"Yes, load the guns," I ordered without thinking.

"Can't open the ammunition locker. It has a lock on it."

"Only the captain can give that order," said Warrant Officer Ridge, who had just arrived with the keys.

"He's too busy. Open the locker," I ordered. Ridge refused.

Urged on by the searchlights that seemed to be focusing together on a still unseen target, I didn't hesitate. "Break it open," I ordered, as Ridge, muttering something about going to see the captain, turned and left.

The sailors had the ammunition locker open in seconds and withdrew rounds for each of the two guns.

Dark as it was, we could plainly see the live ammunition. For most of us, especially me, it was the first time we had ever seen the real stuff up this close. All our gunnery drills had been with wooden shells which we loaded into a dummy mount that had a breech. That was the extent of our knowledge about these guns.

"Shall I take off the lead seal?"

I took a closer look and saw a smooth cap that covered the nose of the foot-and-a-half long shell. The cap was held in place by a lead seal circling its edge. Fully convinced we were about to be attacked from the air, I ordered "Remove the seals,"

As soon as the seals were off I was asked, "What setting do you want on the fuse sir?"

At the same time we all heard the faint hum of an airplane engine, high off the port bow, where the searchlight beams seemed to be converging.

"Set three seconds on the fuses and load," I ordered with excited confidence in my own authority. Then I added, "Report when on target."

Fortunately neither gun reported on target, because just after we had loaded both guns my talker shouted, "Bridge says to secure from battle stations, it is a friendly commercial airliner."

"Christ," I thought to myself, "that was really close."

"Unload the guns," I ordered.

The starboard gun captain quickly opened the breech, removed the shell, and without any orders, walked to the side of the ship and threw the shell overboard.

The port gun captain had his hand on the breech lever about to open it, when Ridge, who had returned with the captain, shouted, "Don't open that breech."

I started to protest, but the captain stepped up ahead of Ridge and asked, "What the hell is going on here?"

Again I started to say something and Ridge interrupted. "Captain, we have a loaded gun. We can't unload it through the breech."

61

3. Load the Guns

"I know Ridge, I know," exasperation, surprise and disgust colored the captain's words.

"Mr. Sotos, point that loaded gun skyward and keep it that way. Set an around the clock watch on it and make sure no one comes near it. We will unload it through the muzzle when we are out of the canal. Do you understand my instructions?"

"Y-Yes sir," I stammered, not quite sure of myself, as the captain turned and left.

I told the port gun captain to set the watch and let no one near the gun. Then the crews of both guns who witnessed the whole thing shuffled off the boat deck leaving me there with Ridge.

"Dammit, I told you that only the captain can order guns to be loaded, but you wouldn't listen," he said, as he picked up the broken locks.

"It's a Bureau of Ordnance regulation that you shouldn't unload a gun through the breech, it might go off when you do," he continued.

I was grateful in a strange way that he waited until most of the sailors had left before he tried to straighten me out. Then as I was leaving, a messenger came to me and said that the captain wanted to see me.

I felt like two cents as I slowly walked toward the captain's cabin. The ship settled down after the battle stations alarm and everyone was crawling back into his bunk. I looked at my watch. It was 04:30.

"Come in," said the captain in response to my gentle knock on his door. "Have a seat young man."

He was sitting in a chair by his desk. I sat down quickly but stiffly in the first chair I could find near the door.

"Ensign Sotos, do you know what you did wrong today?" he asked quietly and with an unexpected lack of animosity that made me less apprehensive.

"Yes sir," I answered quietly. "Mr. Ridge told me."

"Good, I'm sure you learned a valuable lesson this morning." He paused, and in a pensive tone added, "We all have. Ridge is your friend, he's a fine warrant officer with experience that none of us have. Until you have been here a lot longer it would pay you to listen to what he says."

"Yes sir," I responded.

"O.K. George, you've had a full morning. Go get some sleep."

I didn't know he even knew my first name, but nothing he could have done would have made me like him more than I did at that instant. I left his cabin, went to the gun mount for a look at the watch stander there, then to my cot where I quickly fell asleep.

The next morning we all awakened to the sober reality that we were at war. That really didn't mean much, at the time, since we just continued with our daily routine.

It turned out that a regularly scheduled airliner was the cause of last night's battle stations alarm. A little homework would have precluded the need to go to battle stations, and also would have avoided loss of the fighter plane that rose from a field on the opposite side of the bay. Its pilot had suddenly sighted the Nitro's tall, unlighted masts, and crash landed in the water to avoid hitting us.

Had he hit the Nitro the resulting explosion might have plugged up the Panama Canal for a long time.

The pilot – the one who had yelled at us from the water during the night – was not hurt, but his plane was a total loss.

I didn't see a ship go through the canal in either direction for the next two days. Then suddenly we got underway and made a routine transit through the canal into the Atlantic ocean.

Except for the wild, exaggerated messages we continued to pick off the airways, the war was not only thousands of miles away from us, it was getting harder for us to understand what our role might be.

The one thought that stuck in my mind was the incredible good luck we had in not being in Pearl Harbor when the Japanese attacked. Exiting into the Atlantic, we took a few minutes to unload our 3"/50 gun through the barrel. The battle stations gun crew manned the gun just as we would at battle stations. Making

3. Load the Guns

sure there were no ships in the area, we trained the gun forty-five degrees on our port bow, elevated it about thirty degrees and reported ready. When the captain, who was standing nearby, nodded to me, I ordered "Fire!"

None of the entire gun crew, including me, had ever seen the guns fired. Now, having fired one of our big guns, we no longer had that rookie uneasiness about shooting.

With just one shot, I felt like a veteran. And even though everyone on the ship knew that I was responsible for the loaded gun, the embarrassment I had previously felt turned into a status symbol. I was probably the best-known of the six ensigns on the Nitro.

We really were cut off from any reliable news about the war, obtaining all our information solely from intercepted radio traffic. The information we did receive was all bad.

The news remained so bad we couldn't believe it. In addition to our massive loss of ships and men at Pearl, we read that we were suddenly at war with Germany and Italy as well as with Japan.

But when the sea is calm, the sky is a sunny blue and the ship has a gentle following sea, the impact of the war simply didn't jump out at me despite the crazy messages that were circulated about the ship.

The presence of two escorting destroyers did help to bring home the seriousness of our situation and change our daily routine.

Coming into Panama, the exec had qualified me to stand a top watch. That meant I would be the Officer of the Deck (OOD) underway, a very responsible job and one to be very proud of achieving.

But now that was changed. I was assigned to stand a newly established watch as gunnery control officer, with responsibility for using the guns quickly when so ordered.

I was disappointed, but not too much, since the gunnery control assignment was a very responsible job. Also, I had the written qualification as OOD in my file and on my record.

We immediately settled down to a new routine as we headed for our home port of Norfolk: blacked out at night, gun crews on watch around the clock, with an escort on each bow. Nosing around, patrolling, twisting, and turning, the escort destroyers reminded me of a couple of sniffing bloodhounds.

Reassuring as they were, the two destroyers ahead on our bow made us think that the German submarines were all around us.

Repeated discussions, throughout the ship, on what had happened to the fleet in Pearl Harbor were hard to avoid. The frantic type of messages we had received on December 7th continued as the only outside news we were receiving.

Then reports of German submarine activity and sinking of ships in the Atlantic started to come in. At the time, we didn't examine these reports to see how close we were to the submarine activity.

It was in my capacity as gun control officer, on our second night out of Panama, when I took over the mid watch (midnight to 0400), that I noticed our escorting destroyers seemed to have disappeared.

There was no radar on any of the three ships. In fact, in those early days we had not even heard of radar. So the station-keeping of the destroyers was based purely on how well they could see the Nitro and how accurately the Nitro observed the turns and times of the zig-zag plan we were all following.

Because the screening destroyers made me very comfortable, I made it a habit to keep my eye on them. No matter how poor the visibility, I had developed a knack with my binoculars of seeing either the destroyers or their tell-tale wakes. So, when I came on watch and failed to see them, I reported their disappearance to Ensign Hunnewell, who was the oncoming OOD.

Finally, when neither Ensign Hunnewell nor Lieutenant (jg) Holidan, whom he was about to relieve, could see the destroyers, Hunnewell decided to inform the navigator.

The navigator called Ski, our chief quartermaster, and they both immediately came to the bridge. The two of them then

3. Load the Guns

went over our zig-zag track from the current time back to when we had last seen the destroyers on station.

They discovered that three hours earlier, at 9:00 PM, Lieutenant (jg) Holidan had ordered the wrong course change. He, and Ensign Hoover his Junior Officer of the Deck (JOOD), had ordered the ship to zig when it should have zagged.

Even though the captain and navigator were awakened and told about the course changes as they were made, they were half asleep and had no way of knowing if the reports were consistent with the zig-zag plan.

And by now we were hopelessly separated from our escorts.

The navigator personally informed the captain, so none of us witnessed his reaction.

When he arrived on the bridge, the captain was obviously angry. But he said nothing to Lieutenant (jg) Holidan, except for pointing out to him on the chart when and where he ordered the wrong course.

We learned that later in the day he sent for Mr. Holidan, but none of us ever found out what transpired between them.

There was, however, no doubt that Mr. Hollidan had later taken it on the chin. It was a really tough one. An older man in his fifties, with many years in the Merchant Marine, he had pulled himself up by his bootstraps to earn a Merchant Marine ticket to command any size ship in any ocean. The Navy's decision to award him only the rank of lieutenant (jg) was an affront that made him a perpetually angry, disgruntled man with no real friends on the ship.

He was unusually crestfallen and silent the next few days, and none of us even mentioned it to him. One immediate result was that the navigator, who made up the OOD watch list, saw to it that Mr. Holidan no longer stood any OOD watches after dark.

As for the two destoyers, not wanting to break radio silence, we continued our trip to Norfolk, zig-zagging alone.

Losing our escorts was not the end of our problems. About a hundred miles from Norfolk, the condensers in the engineering plant salted up so badly that we had to stop all engines in order to prevent the boilers from being permanently damaged. We remained stopped, floating at the mercy of the wind and sea, praying that no U-boats were in our area. After four hours the engineers completed repairs and we continued zig-zagging on our way to Norfolk.

After our arrival in Norfolk, in late December 1941, we had a chance to read newspapers, listen to the radio, and read our mail. It was then the impact and seriousness of the war really hit me.

The mail from my family, especially my sister Virginia, was almost hysterical. They knew the Nitro was scheduled to go to Pearl Harbor, but they didn't know when. And while we were not on the list of ships sunk at Pearl Harbor, we had been reported earlier as sunk in the Pacific.

Virginia had written many letters to me which, because of the confusion in the Navy, had remained undelivered, and despite all her efforts she could get no news of the Nitro.

There's no doubt this lack of information caused more suffering to my family than it did to me.

In port, I called immediately and they were elated to hear from me. Virginia also asked if I would be returning to school after my year of active duty was completed, as had been the arrangement when I signed up in the Naval Reserve. I really didn't have any official information about my status, but without discussing it, both of us knew I wouldn't be coming home for a long time.

Figure 68: **Depth charge racks on USS Janssen (DE 396).** Two racks are seen on the stern of the ship. The depth charges themselves are also visible in the racks, as large cylinders. They roll off the rack and drop into the water. Destroyer escorts like the Janssen were built to fight submarines. See Figure 198 for more about this photograph.

Chapter 4

U-Boats

The start of the war didn't significantly alter the Nitro's job or its schedule. Newfoundland was added to the northern leg of our trip out of Norfolk, and there was an increase in the number of depth charges and torpedoes in our cargo.

One afternoon, while still in Norfolk, the British battleship HMS Royal Sovereign entered port and tied up at our dock, just opposite us.

Our communication officer asked me to hand deliver an urgent radio message to them.

I had never been aboard a British ship or any foreign ship, for that matter, and welcomed the opportunity to deliver the message.

The gangway on the huge battleship had been secured for just a few minutes when I jauntily started up. About halfway up the gangway I heard a clipped British order snap everyone in sight of the quarterdeck to "attention." At the same time I saw a sailor at the top of the gangway, with a boatswain's pipe in his mouth, start piping someone aboard. I stopped dead in my tracks, looked behind me to see who was coming aboard, and saw no one. Getting a little flustered and not knowing what to do I just stood there and saluted. An officer on the ship beckoned me to come aboard and I suddenly realized the honors were being rendered to me. The poor boatswain's mate blowing on the

4. U-Boats

pipe ran out of breath before I got to the top of the gangway. I could see that I had ruined his performance. Still, somewhat embarrassed, I went between the two side boys and introduced myself to the Officer of the Deck.

I looked, felt, and acted like a scared young ensign and tried to hand him the radio message so I could leave. However, he would not take it, instructing me to proceed to the signal officer's quarters and deliver the message personally. He sent a sailor ahead to show me the way.

As I started through the ship I naturally looked about and was surprised at the careless housekeeping appearances. It was obvious that they did not pay as much attention to cleanliness as we did on the Nitro.

Eventually we located the signal officer in the wardroom where I handed him the message. Opening it he read aloud. "Twenty aircraft arriving Norfolk Naval Air Station 1400 today." It was an information message to insure that the British did not mistake the planes for enemies and start shooting. Thanking me for the message, the signal officer confirmed my amazed suspicions by inviting me to have a drink of scotch before I returned.

I stayed for so many drinks that I lost count. The drinks were not very strong and I managed to stay sober. They sent an invitation to the other officers on the Nitro who promptly came over. The party proceeded at a very jolly pace and was very enjoyable. The most amazing part of the entire affair, to me, was the young British enlisted Marine who served the drinks in the wardroom. Dressed in khaki shorts, he walked about the wardroom with a tray containing a bottle of scotch, soda, water, some ice, and glasses. When someone asked for a drink, he would stand on one leg, lift the other leg up, bending it so that the foreleg (thigh to knee) was parallel to the deck. He would then place the tray on this impromptu serving table, and mix and serve drinks with both hands while standing on one leg. I marveled at the length of time he could maintain the position and also the dexterity with which he served drinks without swaying or moving a muscle in his legs.

Though the appearance of their ship was not up to Nitro standards their hospitality and conviviality certainly exceeded ours. After several hours, observing several of their older officers getting a little drunk, I blurted out the question that had been on my lips: "How do you operate the ship at sea with so much drinking going on?"

The stern answer accompanied by a frown from one of the older officers was, "We voluntarily refrain." Later, as I heard of the ship's war time experiences, I concluded that "on or off the wagon," it was a fighting ship with a fighting crew.

We learned later, unofficially, that the Royal Sovereign had carried Prime Minister Winston Churchill across the Atlantic to visit with President Roosevelt.[1]

I left the British battleship and my new found friends late that afternoon and was again piped ashore.

A few days later we left Norfolk, rendezvoused with two destroyers just outside Thimble Shoals Light and set course for Newfoundland.

Of course we zig-zagged, but by now we were getting quite good at it.

It wasn't long before we started to receive radio reports about ships being sunk, some right ahead of our projected course. We also began to receive Morse code SOS distress messages from ships that had been hit and were about to be abandoned before sinking. We never went to provide assistance, probably because we were never the closest ship.

Two distress signals, when plotted, were hard to believe; one was fifty miles astern and the other was a hundred miles ahead! I had the feeling that there were more U-boats than there actually were.[2]

---

[1] Records published later show that Mr. Churchill and high ranking members of the British military met with President Roosevelt and U.S. officials in Washington from December 24, 1941 to January 14, 1942. Their conference was code named ARCADIA. The State Deparment's records are available at: `http://bit.ly/1d7W42T` See also Bercuson.

[2] Morison estimates that only 12 U-boats at any one time were responsi-

4. U-Boats

The snow, ice, and heavy weather we ran into added to our troubles. We hoped it bothered the U-boats, too.

The first depth charge attack by our escorting destroyers scared the hell out of us. It was a cold gloomy day, not far from Cape Race, which had been the scene of several sinkings and had earned the name "Torpedo Junction."[3]

"Flag hoist on the DuPont," shouted one of our lookouts. Before the signal man could train his glasses on the destroyer's signal flag, the OOD and quartermaster had read it, and the OOD had ordered the general alarm plus full right rudder and emergency full ahead to turn sharply away from the DuPont. At the same time he yelled, "Inform the captain."

The DuPont's flag hoist said she had an underwater contact and was going to attack.

Watching the scene from my gun station, which had been manned and ready in record time, I saw and heard my first depth charge attack. (See Figure 73.)

Large, massive geysers of water flew skyward in a string of successive rumbling explosions, as the Nitro, in a hard right turn, leaned to starboard and shuddered ever so slightly as she picked up speed.

The other destroyer, now on our port quarter, had already completed a sharp right turn and was heading toward us at full speed to get ahead of and screen us.

The Nitro engineers poured on the steam as we reached 17 knots and slowly left the DuPont behind us.

Excited and scared as I was, I couldn't help but wonder, "How did the DuPont know they had a submarine? What would hap-

---

ble for the many sinkings off the east coast in the first half of 1942 (Morison-I, page 128).

[3]Cape Race is about 110 miles south of Argentia. It is the first landfall on the North American continent for ships arriving from Europe. Its radio station was the first to hear the Titanic's distress message. It coordinated the rescue actions and was the source of all news about the Titanic. It was also the site of the first Marconi wireless station and the site of of one of the most powerful lights in the world. – www.stats.gov.nf.ca/aboutUs/

Figure 73: **Depth charge explosion.** Two depth charges, dropped from a PC boat (see Chapter 5) have exploded simultaneously.

pen if we did get torpedoed? Is it true that if the explosion doesn't kill us the freezing water will? Did our special construction insure that we can sustain several torpedo hits without sinking or blowing up? Has the DuPont actually sunk an enemy U-boat with all those depth charges?" These and many other thoughts flew through my mind as I stood by my guns, ready to start shooting if the submarine did surface.

The more questions I asked myself, the shakier I got. It was frustrating as hell to not know what was going on, and to be so helplessly dependent on the destroyers.

As we stood there, watching the DuPont disappear out of sight and the second destroyer overtake and get ahead of us, I

4. U-Boats

got the very unsettling feeling that I needed to get off the Nitro and onto a ship like the DuPont – one that could fight back. As much as I liked the Nitro, I made up my mind to ask for a transfer to the destroyer Navy as soon as I could find out how to do it.

It is strange but, as you will read later, I didn't have to request a transfer.

The rest of the trip included several submarine scares and depth charge explosions, plus snow, cold, ice, day and night battle stations, until, finally, we reached Newfoundland.

Here again, after we went ashore we were greeted with, "Sure glad to see you, we heard that you were sunk." After a number of these "happy" greetings I began to get the feeling that they were expressing an unconscious wish that this particular ammunition ship was somewhere else, rather than in their back yard.

The naval base at Argentia, Newfoundland was a small one. It was at the edge of a bay that could accommodate a number of ships. But because they didn't have much in the way of piers, all the large ships had to park in anchorages.

The entrance to the anchorage was several miles wide, a width that dangerously exposed ships there to both the sea and enemy U-boats.

In really bad weather, a ship could get underway, go further inland and anchor in the lee of one of the many mountains in the area. But, in order to land and receive supplies, a ship had to anchor near the naval base and take its chances against the U-boats.

While there was no record of any U-boats entering the bay and taking a shot at a ship (as occurred at Scapa Flow, in Scotland, in 1939), the exposure and the steadily increasing U-boat activity in that region was getting to the captains.

The captain of a Navy oiler, anchored not too far from the Nitro, complained that there was diesel oil floating alongside his ship and it wasn't from his tanks. The implication, of course was that it was from submarine diesel engines.

As a result, the assembled captains from four or five ships decided to institute a boat patrol across the entrance to the bay.

The Nitro and one other ship were selected to share the patrol responsibility, with the Nitro drawing the midnight to six a.m. patrol. Eager for some type of action, I volunteered to be the officer in charge of the Nitro's patrol boat, which turned out to be a large open motor launch with no protection from the elements.

The boat crew consisted of three sailors and myself. We were armed with machine guns, 45 caliber pistols and "Very" signaling pistols (a type of flare gun).

The machine guns were provided in the event a submarine attempted to sneak in on the surface. Our orders were to fire the flares if we detected anything like a submarine trying to enter the bay.

Fortified with several thermoses of hot coffee and some sandwiches, we relieved the other boat at midnight. They reported everything quiet, but exceptionally cold. And, it being winter in Newfoundland, they were right about the cold!

Our patrol was uneventful. There was some moonlight, so the visibility was pretty good. There was no wind at all and the water in the bay was so flat that we would have detected anything that cut the surface. But it was a very, very frigid six hours – bad enough to freeze the coffee in our thermos – and we were all stiff from the cold when our patrol was up.

While the bay itself was quiet, the reports of submarine activity in the region gave the impression that the ships in Argentia harbor were, indeed, being targeted by U-boats. That afternoon some of the ships left the anchorage for safer, less exposed berths.

The enemy activity reports steadily increased the Nitro's unpopularity, and we were practically alone in the anchorage, unloading our cargo to the naval station with lighters (flat bottom barges that are towed back and forth by tugs).

Sailors, civilians and all personnel involved in unloading the Nitro worked hard, long, and very quickly to complete their task.

4. U-Boats

When the time came, there was little doubt that the people in Argentia were happy to see the Nitro depart.

We did know that there were a number of U-boats nearby. Two days after we arrived in Argentia, a Navy PBY patrol aircraft sighted one on the surface not far from Argentia. He attacked it and reported "Sighted sub, sank same."

The brevity of his report caught the interest of the Naval Communications system and the civilian media from coast to coast, and the incident became famous in the annals of anti-submarine warfare.[4]

We learned later that many of the alarms at Argentia were due to a short-circuited submarine warning device that warned of submarines that weren't there.

As I got older and smarter I realized that the odds were against U-boats sneaking into the Argentia harbor. The channel leading to the harbor, a long and tortuous one, is especially dangerous in bad weather when visibility is poor. It's a problem that occurs all too frequently from sudden snow storms in that part of the world.

An experience related to me by Captain Fred Wollseiffer, USN, for whom I worked in 1952, illustrates the seriousness of navigating that channel in the winter months. Captain Wolseiffer commanded the USS Wilkes in 1944, two years after that destroyer's involvement in the below incident.

The story he told me started on February 25, 1942, just two weeks after the Nitro had departed from Argentia. The destroyers USS Truxton (DD 229) and USS Wilkes (DD 441) were escorting the large supply ship USS Pollux to Argentia when they were caught in a vicious winter storm in the channel leading to Argentia harbor.

The three ships were one behind the other in column formation as they tried to navigate the channel. Visibility caused by the heavy snow storm was poor. None of the ships had radar.

---

[4]In reality, the U-boat got away. Morison-I, page 154.

There is no more unsettling feeling in the world than to be on a ship in a narrow channel among big rocks and mountains in bad weather with poor visibility. You can't see the rocks or the mountains, but the charts tell you they are there. You can't see any channel buoys. You can't anchor. All you can do is to keep track of the water depth, take it slow – but not so slow as to be controlled by the wind and currents – and just plod ahead and pray.

It was early in the morning when an officer on one of the destroyers, I believe it was the Wilkes, was standing in front of a wash-basin mirror shaving when the mirror, cabinet, and all, started to move toward him. That was his first indication that his ship had run aground and hit something.

His ship was not the only one that ran aground. The Pollux and the Truxton were in the same fix! All three had run aground in the driving, freezing winter blizzard.

After being smashed against the rocks for some time, both the Pollux and the Truxton sank, while the fortunate Wilkes managed to back off and get clear.

The men abandoning the two sinking ships found themselves in a brutal mountainous region. In their attempts to escape, many of the men tried to climb the side of an ice covered mountain and literally froze to death, their bodies sticking to the side of the mountain. It was a very gruesome incident, but one which forever identifies the dangers in that area. A total of 203 men died.

Even worse, the tragedy occurred in a remote area and it was the local villagers who battled the elements and helped save many at the scene by bringing them out of the cold into their homes. Some 186 men survived this wild unforgettable tragedy.

Remarkably, 71 years later, on February 25, 2013, the anniversary of the disaster was formally observed in Newfoundland by the citizens of the small city of Saint Lawrence, the home of many of the rescuers.

My main point here is that the navigational hazards of that channel plus the tricky weather in that region probably did a lot

4. U-Boats

to keep adventurous U-boat captains out of Argentia.

One of the happiest persons aboard the Nitro when we left Argentia was me. I had received radio-dispatch orders to a PC boat. This was a new type of Patrol Craft, about which I knew nothing, except that it was built to chase enemy submarines. And to my amazement the orders read that I would be the executive officer – the second in command of the ship.

I couldn't believe what I read, and asked the radio man to check the message and see if I had it correctly. He confirmed that it was correct.

The other officers were equally impressed, and I guess we were all puzzled. Jumping from being an ensign-under-instruction to second-in-command of a small ship was highly unusual. I was so happy I never thought any more about it. But I did realize that, in spite of the mistakes I had made on the Nitro, they must have given me a top-notch evaluation.

Being ordered to the PC boat was as though some one in the Bureau of Naval personnel had heard and granted my wish.

Our return to the United States was much like the trip up. By now we were accustomed to the nearby reported sinkings, distress calls, depth charge attacks, and the terrible weather.

Accustomed is really the wrong word. The continued bad weather in the North Atlantic and the occasional depth charge attacks made by our escorts kept us nervously on our toes, but reading a distress message was far worse. No matter how hard I tried, I couldn't stop myself from visualizing what was happening to the people who sent the message. One look at the ever-present, wild, freezing waves, the frustrating knowledge of our helplessness to provide any assistance, and our complete inability to protect ourselves, made the situation almost unreal and depressingly hopeless.

We actually welcomed the terrible North Atlantic weather, for the very reason that the more it tossed our huge ship around, the less the danger that a U-boat could get a decent shot at us.

And, of course, I had an ace in the hole. I had orders to a submarine-chaser, so my days of going to sea in a large, priority, sitting duck target were coming to an end.

I didn't think then that actually seeing a torpedoed and burning ship could be much worse than helplessly reading the desperate pleas for assistance we were receiving. I found out later how wrong I was.

Because of the value, criticality, and volatility of our cargo, the Nitro was always well protected. We didn't venture outside of a port without an escort, and our escorts dropped a lot of depth charges. Yes, we were frightened, but we never did see or get hurt by the enemy.

Although the war and the activities around us occupied most of our waking hours, we began to get used to life at sea under these conditions. We even started to go to sleep in pajamas instead of with our clothes and shoes on. We started to find again time to examine the particular part of the world we were in. The "Grand Banks" area was especially interesting. War or no war, we observed many fishing boats plying those fertile fishing grounds. Tremendous schools of fish, small whales, and fish of unknown types, even to old salts, seemed to abound in this area. Our old friends the porpoises were with us constantly.

I couldn't help but wonder as I watched the small fishing boats, just what made those fishermen choose that occupation. The weather in the Grand Banks area is anything but good for most of the year. To see their small, hardy fishing boats tossed around like corks when the weather got rough made me wonder if they ever doubted the logic of their choice.

Mr. Thompson, who knew a lot about them, said none of them ever got wealthy, yet they kept coming back. We all knew that every year one or two of those fishing boats never made it back home.

Then, when the weather wasn't giving them a bad time, the Navy would sometimes mistake their small silhouettes for U-boats, especially at night. None were actually sunk, but they were subjected to intense searches because we suspected U-boats might be hiding among them.

4. U-Boats

We couldn't help but grudgingly admire the toughness of these fishermen.

We made a stop in Portland, Maine to offload some ammunition and then went on to Norfolk.

In spite of my happiness at getting orders to a submarine chaser, I had mixed feelings about leaving the Nitro. I hadn't realized how close I had become to the other officers.

Being detached from the Nitro was almost as sad as leaving home. Shorty, the exec, who had originally labeled me as a "Red Ass Reserve Ensign" called me into his stateroom, offered me a cup of coffee and told me he was genuinely sorry to see me go. I had begrudgingly admired the rough, harsh speaking, stormy exec but, somehow, had received the impression that he didn't know I was alive. Surprisingly he told me I had come a long way and wished me luck in my new assignment.

The navigator, Mr. Thompson, called me into his room and told me that I was a smart, tough, fine young officer and that he would miss me. He then gave me a small mahogany box and told me to open it. It contained a professional sextant with all the parts needed for professional use.

"George," he said, without any emotion, "this is my personal sextant that I no longer use. It's an old one but still useful. I want you to have it to remember your navigating days on the Nitro."

I was stunned and for a minute didn't know what to say. It was a beautiful sextant, which, seventy-two years later, I still have. I started to thank him and he cut me off and said, "Good luck, George and don't forget us."

I simply hadn't realized how seriously he had approached his job as a mentor for young officers. While I had always admired and respected him, I suddenly realized his strong quiet demeanor hid a genuine warmth and considerateness.

Then he said, "Let's go," and I followed him into the wardroom where the other officers were assembled.

That's when I realized they were almost like brothers to me, how happy I had been, and how much I had learned aboard the Nitro.

Later, after I returned to my room, the thought of being on a ship without these men began to give me some qualms.

I was starting to pack all my stuff into a seabag and suitcase when two sailors knocked on my door.

"Here's your cruise box, Mr. Sotos." said one of the sailors who I knew worked in our machine shop.

They deposited a large, newly built, rugged looking wooden cruise box in the entranceway. They opened the top to show me the expansive interior, wished me good luck, and shook my hand as I thanked them and left.

I was examining the locking hasp and small brass plate on the front of the box that said "Ensign George P. Sotos USNR," when Hunnewell walked in.

Like Mr. Thompson, Hunnewell, was invariably "all business." A Harvard graduate, and commissioned from its Reserve Officer's Training Corps (ROTC), he truly cared for the Navy. He was an excellent, meticulous teacher and role model for his five subordinate ensigns.

More than the others, I was the recipient of his corrections and tips. The latter ranged from wardroom etiquette (don't ask for seconds until the exec has done so or passed) to practical advice (carry a small pocket notebook and always write down anything a senior officer asks you to do; keep notes on all assigned duties, appointments and important information).

At first I thought he was joking about the notebook. But he handed me one and told me to use it. I fully expected him to check it once in a while. It took me a while to get used to him, but not only did I learn a great deal from him, I formed a friendship that lasted long after I left the Nitro. I still carry a little notebook in my pocket.

"Rather nice, isn't it?" said Hunnewell. "You can thank Shorty. He ordered it for you. After you fill it, ask the stewards to have it shipped to your next ship. It's a rather nice tradition and saves a lot of wear and tear when transferring from one ship to another."

He was right. The box held everything I had, including my books, my folded sea bag, sextant, extra uniforms and other cloth-

4. U-Boats

ing. It reduced to one small suitcase the things I needed for my trip home.

It is, indeed, a splendid Navy tradition. I used that box for the next 30 years. And today, 72 years later, somewhat beat-up, it sits in my basement, still holding several old uniforms.

It was February 8, 1942. Most of the officers and some of the enlisted men I worked with were at the gangway to see me off. I didn't have tears in my eyes when I walked down the gangway for the last time, but as I walked down the dock to the cab they had called for me, I felt my eyes getting moist.

Figure 84: **PC 476.** Shown refueling from the USS Long Island off the coast of Florida, circa 1942.

Chapter 5

PC 476

I had about six days leave and enjoyed a wonderful reception when I got home in Chicago. It was clear I was no longer the "Kid Brother."

The war had changed the way my family looked at me. They gave me a lot more credit for things than they should have. Anyway, it was a short visit. The worse part was saying goodbye, especially to my mother.

I was soon on the train toward New Orleans. The train was full of soldiers and it seemed the war was right on our doorstep.

The soldiers were raising hell on the train. A couple of them had removed the small signs from the ladies' and men's rooms and had switched them. They were sitting there waiting to see what would happen.

I kept dozing off and reflecting about my months on the Nitro, so I never did find out what happened.

Over and over again, I mentally walked through the jobs I had on the Nitro and wondered which ones helped the most in getting me assigned as the exec of the PC 476.

My best guess was the officer of the deck and navigator qualifications. But I had serious doubts that they were enough to warrant a second-in-command job.

I gave up trying to figure out the Navy's reasons for making me an exec, and concentrated on catching up on my sleep.

5. PC 476

In New Orleans, I rented a room in a house in a quiet area across the Mississippi River from the Algiers Naval Base.

I had never been to New Orleans and it didn't take me long to find the French Quarter and its friendly bars. They were packed with Army second lieutenants. To my surprise, I was the only one in a Navy uniform. They didn't bother with me.

I spent most of the evening listening to juke boxes blare out the song, "Just Remember Pearl Harbor," and watching second lieutenants compete for the few girls that wandered in.

The bars started to thin out about midnight and that's when I left and caught a cab. Much to my surprise, I forgot the address of the house where I had rented the room. I remembered the street name but not the address.

The cab driver, who seemed to be in a hurry to get rid of me, dropped me off in what he said was probably the right area. But he was wrong. I started walking.

After about fifteen minutes I unknowingly wandered into a cemetery. It was enveloped in some kind of mist, which I had mistakenly assumed was a fog. Not knowing, at first, that New Orleans has above ground cemeteries full of monuments and statues, I had a scary few minutes before I figured out where I was. I wasted no time getting out of there.

After about another half hour of walking and looking, I was lucky enough to recognize my building. Needless to say, when I crawled into my bed it wasn't with happy memories of New Orleans.

I should have known when I reported to the Naval base the next day that things would be screwed up. A very uninformed young officer, after many phone calls, managed to find out that my ship was berthed some distance away, at the Todd Shipyard.

I returned to my room, packed my bag, and told the landlady I would be leaving in the morning.

Eager to get started the next day, and curious about my new ship, I got up early and hailed a cab for the shipyard. The cab driver was friendly and talkative. He wondered how many more patrol ships were headed for New Orleans.

It was about eleven in the morning, on March 1, 1942, when the cab dropped me off at the foot of a large pier in the Todd Shipyard, about a twenty minute drive from the naval base. I was spic and span in my full dress white uniform with my sword hanging by my side. I guess my perception of the importance of my status as second in command made me think that was the correct uniform.

Was I wrong!

I was the only Naval officer in sight. In fact, I was the only Navy man in sight. The pier was full of shipyard workers going back and forth, working the many ships that were tied up on either side of the huge pier.

I finally stopped a yard workman. "Do you know where the PC 476 is moored?" I asked.

After looking me over, as though he had never seen a Naval officer in full dress whites, he smiled and said, "Sure do, son. It's right over there." And he pointed to the left side of the pier, toward a huge green transport ship.

"No," I exclaimed. "It's a PC boat not a transport." "Look carefully, son," he smiled again. "See that small piece of wood sticking about a foot above the port gunwale (the left side) of that transport?"

I followed his finger as he pointed and indeed saw the small stick. "Yes, I see it."

"Well son, that's the top of your little ship, the PC 476. She's moored outboard of that transport," he said kindly – almost sympathetically.

"Thanks," I said as I grabbed my sword with one hand, lifted my suitcase with the other and started walking halfway down the pier to the transport's gangway.

After some difficulty I boarded the empty transport, which was still under construction and full of obstacles, crossed over to her port side, and looked downward over the gunwale.

It was my first glimpse of the PC 476.

I could see the entire little ship, from her high bow that flowed smoothly down her flush deck for about 173 feet, to the stubby

5. PC 476

stern that terminated abruptly about four feet above the surface of the water.

A solid-looking, compact steel ship, "She looks almost like a little toy boat that has been abandoned and left snugly alongside this much bigger ship," I thought to myself. She was so much smaller than the Nitro, that I couldn't make a reasonable comparison.

After finding my way four decks down on the transport, with my sword dangling at my side, I finally found a small gangway – actually a wide flat board – that I used to cross over to my ship.

The quarterdeck watch that I thought should have greeted me was strangely absent as I stepped precariously down from the narrow gangway, still guiding my sword with my right arm and carrying the suitcase in my left arm.

"It's not the way I expected to report aboard," I thought as I visualized the helping hands that were always available on the Nitro.

As I stood there waiting, I reflected on how fast things were happening to me. Just a few weeks ago I was a junior officer on the veteran, well disciplined, regulation USS Nitro. Now here I am, just three months past my twenty-first birthday, and I'm the executive officer of a PC boat that doesn't even have a quarterdeck watch.

I began to feel a little foolish standing there all dressed up. There had been no one there to return my salute as I came aboard. That's when I noticed there wasn't even a flag flying anywhere on the ship. That should have told me the ship was not in commission and that a watch was not required. But I was so eager I didn't make that connection.

I was beginning to get a little nervous about my new assignment and wondered what I should do next.

I suddenly realized also, that as of now, the absence of a quarterdeck watch was my responsibility.

I decided to take a look around. With my sword still bumping against my leg as I walked, I wondered if I would ever learn to wear the damn thing properly.

I was puzzled at not seeing anyone. I went down to the mess hall aft, and noticed that it had been used and not cleaned up. I walked to the engine room hatch but decided not to go down there because it was too dark.

I wandered forward and that's when I heard some voices coming from the small pilot house.

I walked inside the compartment behind the pilot house, went up three steps and found myself in the center of the pilot house looking at the little ship's large steering wheel, right in the center of the pilot house.

The deck was littered with cigarette butts and the pilot house was full of smoke.

Off to the left, sitting on four tall stools and standing around a large chart table, bedecked with money and cards, were five bare-chested and barefoot men.

So engrossed were they in their game, none of them noticed me. Finally one of them, who had apparently laid down his cards earlier, looked up and saw me.

"Hi," he said cheerfully.

"Good morning," I answered as formally as I could.

The man nodded, glanced briefly at my uniform and dangling sword, shrugged his shoulders and returned to studying his neighbor's cards.

Mildly upset at the cold reception, I retreated from the pilot house, convinced that these men were not sailors.

I walked around the deserted topside, went back in every compartment except the engine room, and saw no other sign of life. Nor did I see anything that resembled the sea-going appearances of the compartments we had on the Nitro. It just didn't look like a ship of the U.S. Navy. Those men were not dressed like sailors. Nor, when they saw an officer, did they act like sailors.

"Perhaps," I thought to myself, "this is the informal destroyer Navy I've heard so much about."

Finally, still not sure of myself, I decided to go back to the pilot house. The group had not moved, and, as before, only casually noticed my arrival.

5. PC 476

"Are you men sailors?" I asked sharply.

"Yeah," came the answer from within the cigarette smoke, "What-aya want?"

"Well, my name is Sotos, Ensign Sotos, and I'm assigned to this ship. Where is everybody?"

"Damn if I know," someone grunted.

"I think it would be a good idea if you all got on your feet and let me know what is going on around here," I said clearly and forcefully.

Surprised at the strength of my own voice, this time they all took a good look at me and started getting to their feet.

It didn't take me long to realize that I was younger than all of them.

Propelled by my slow but effective start, I continued, "Who's in charge here?"

"I am," said a medium sized man of about 35.

"Come on outside with me." I said to him. "The rest of you can go back to your card playing for the time being."

We both went out of the pilot house door and he followed me to the main deck.

"I'm Ensign Sotos," I said, "I have orders to be the executive officer. What's your name and rate?"

"Boatswain's Mate First Class Hart," he answered.

I felt very relieved, a first class boatswain's mate! All the boatswain's mates on the Nitro were top men who ran not only their divisions, but the entire topside of the Nitro.

"What ship did you come from?" I asked.

"Oh, I haven't been assigned to a ship in fifteen years. I finished up my first enlistment on the Arkansas." His voice was certainly not that of a rugged boatswain's mate.

"Did you make first class on the Arkansas?"

"Oh my, no, I was discharged as a seaman first class and received all my promotions in the Naval Reserve. I've got a small business in Chicago, and except for a few cruises, this is my first sea duty since I left the Arkansas."

"You mean you have never had sea duty as a boatswain's mate?

"That's right." He paused a moment. "To tell you the truth that's what has me a little worried. I'm not too proficient at this deck business. But there's a seaman in there who just came from a destroyer and he seems to know what it's all about."

My surprise and disappointment must have shown in my eyes, but it didn't perturb Hart. "How about the rest of them?" I asked.

"Two of them are like me, reserves. And two, the cook and an engineer, are regular Navy. The cook's name is Greenwald," Hart spoke the name contemptuously. "He just came from a battleship. He's regular Navy and has twelve years active duty."

"Where are the other officers?" I asked.

"I don't know anything," he answered. "I don't even know what's supposed to happen next. The five of us were sent to Bay City, Michigan, and told to stay aboard and ride the boat down the Mississippi while she was being towed. Yesterday they tied us up down the stream. Then this morning they moved us in here. We've just been sitting here waiting for something to happen."

"How have you been eating and getting paid?"

"Oh, they put enough food aboard to last a long time, but that Greenwald sure stinks as a cook. We ought to get rid of him."

I suddenly felt very discouraged. "Do you know where the officers' quarters are?"

"Yes sir." It was the first time he said "sir" and it stood out like a sore thumb.

He led me through the officer's wardroom and into a small berthing area right behind it. There were two small rooms on opposite sides of a narrow passageway. One had a single bunk and a single metal desk (for the captain). The other, same size as the first, had a double bunk and two small metal desks. The rooms were small, about five and a half feet by eight feet and the bunks and desks were attached to the bulkheads. A single washroom with a head and a really small shower was located just aft of the captain's room.

5. PC 476

Hart watched as I inspected both rooms. "Are you the captain?" he asked. Then he caught himself, "No, you said you were the exec."

"Do we have any log books aboard?" I asked.

"No sir, I haven't seen any and no one said anything to me."

"Well, I think we had better set a watch," I said. "Knock off that poker game. Tell the men to get into a working uniform or a dress uniform. Set up a watch at the gangway. They know how to stand a watch and keep a log don't they?"

"I think so, but I know they ain't going to like it."

"You let me worry about that end of it," I responded.

He started up the ladder and then stopped. "Pardon me, what kind of a uniform was that you wanted the others to wear?"

"A complete working uniform, or a dress uniform if they don't have dungarees"

"But we all have our dungarees on now."

"A complete working uniform requires a shirt also, do you understand?" I said pointedly looking at his bare chest.

"You mean wear shirts all the time?"

"Yes."

"It's pretty hot in this climate and especially aboard ship," he hedged.

"Don't stand around and argue with me. See if you can get it done."

After he left, I sat down in the exec's room, the small room with the double bunks. There was so much to think about and so much to do, and at the same time, I wasn't quite sure what to think about or what to do.

There were no books I could refer to, no instructions, no officer or office ashore where I could go for help. Hart had mentioned that he had heard that someone at the eighth Naval District headquarters was wondering what shape the PC 476 was in. If they came by to ask me, what would be my answer?

Overwhelmed by the whole thing, I just sat there and tried to figure out where I should start. I felt as though the whole ship was sitting right on my shoulders, and my experience with the leading boatswain's mate had only made things worse.

I was getting depressed about the whole setup and felt frustrated. I found a notebook pad and started writing a list of the actions I had to take.

About a half hour later there was a knock on my door. I looked up and was surprised to see a sailor dressed in regulation whites with his hat squared away and a guard belt around his waist.

He was holding my suitcase. "Sir, this was on the quarterdeck." he said, and placed it in my room. Also there's a draft of forty-five men on the dock – the rest of our crew. They're waiting to come aboard."

"Where's Hart?"

"He's down below trying to find his uniform."

"Do you know where to put these men?"

"Yes sir, there's five or six first class and some other rated men among them."

"Good, show them where to go."

"Aye aye, sir," he answered smartly.

"Wait a minute," I called after him. "What's your name?"

"Lincoln, sir."

"Are you the seaman who came from the destroyer?"

"'Yes sir," and he appeared proud when he said it.

"Very well, thank you," and he was gone toward the quarterdeck.

A bright ray of sunshine, I thought to myself. He at least looks and acts like the sailors on the Nitro.

I had my head down at the desk, still wrestling with my list of things to do when I heard a knock. It was one of the five sailors I had seen in the pilot house, but he was fully dressed in regulation dungarees and was holding his white hat.

"Captain," he started to say, and then corrected himself, "Sir, I'm the ship's cook."

"You're Greenwald?"

"Yes sir," surprised to see that I knew his name. "I'm ship's cook first class Dave Greenwald and I need to talk to you."

5. PC 476

"Sure, go ahead."

"Sir, we've got about forty five men who just came aboard. It's going to take me some time to feed them. I didn't know there would be that many."

"Neither did I." I hesitated, not knowing what to tell him.

He continued, "I'll need some help in the mess hall and the galley, and Hart needs to know that he's got to assign some people to help."

"Have you asked him?"

"Yes sir, but I don't think he's going to give me what we need."

"Do you have any one else helping you?"

"No, sir, just me as of now," and he didn't look too happy.

"It's about lunch time now, how long will it take before you can feed them?"

"At least an hour and a half if I get the help I need right now,"

"Do you have the food?"

"Yes sir,"

"Trays, knives, and forks and all the equipment you need?"

"Yes sir, I just need the help. The mess hall hasn't been cleaned in a week."

"I guess you know I just came aboard and haven't had enough time to set things up," I said, wondering what to do. "I'll tell Hart to give you all the help you need."

Then I had an idea. "Suppose I let everyone go on liberty as soon as they want today, except for those who you need to get ready. We can make it up to them later. You think that might help?"

"It might, but I think most of them will wait and eat first before they go ashore." He paused, "But if I can get an idea of how many will stay aboard to eat, that will help."

"O.K. I'll get Hart and get him going. I'll tell him to find out how many will stay aboard and get you the help. Then, I'll come down to the galley in about twenty minutes to see if you have everything you need."

"Thank you sir." I could see he felt better as he turned and left. I also had the sense that he was a responsible ship's cook and that I could depend on him.

Hart didn't seem too excited to help Greenwald. I gave him orders that he should announce liberty starting now, to expire at 0800 the next morning, excepting the one-third of the crew he would assign to a duty section. I would work with the leading petty officers to set up a permanent organization.

"How many duty sections will we have?" he asked.

"Three," I answered, "but we'll settle on that tomorrow."

I also told him to let me know in five minutes how many men would stay aboard for lunch, and to tell Greenwald, too. Then I told him to come back in twenty minutes and both he and I would go to the mess hall and tour the ship to see how things were going. I reminded him that he was the master-at-arms on the ship, and an orderly and effective mess operation and assistance to Greenwald was part of his responsibility.

By an hour later Hart and I had finished inspecting the mess hall, which was full of sailors just starting lunch. Everything was orderly and clean. I was pleasantly surprised and complimented Hart. I think that lightened him up a little and he felt more like the master-at-arms.

As planned, the whole crew, except the duty section, went ashore that night. We didn't issue liberty cards because we didn't have any, but things turned out O.K.

The next morning I called all the leading petty officers into the wardroom and gave them instructions as to how I wanted the morning quarters for muster conducted. I told the senior petty officers in each rating that they were the department heads for the time being and would accept full responsibility for the men assigned to them and their particular parts of the ship.

The muster went off without a hitch. Learning there were no absentees made me feel a little better about our prospects.

After muster, I called the leading petty officers into the wardroom again for another meeting. They were as curious about the situation as I had been the previous day and assumed I knew

5. PC 476

all the answers. The cook wanted to know how and where he got food. The engineers wanted to know when and where they should fuel, and if they could light off and test the ship's generators and main engines. The storekeepers wanted to know who would pay us and when – a lot of the men were flat broke. The pharmacist mate wanted to know where and when he would get his medical supplies. The quartermasters wanted to know the operating schedule so they could make sure to put the latest updates on the relevant charts.

Even Hart warmed up, asking if he could start cleaning up the ship, then immediately asking what time liberty started. After telling then to go ahead and do as much as they could, based on their own experiences, I dismissed them.

I continued adding to my list of the previous day in order to make a trip to the headquarters eighth Naval district for answers. The top question on my list was when will the captain report aboard?

Our two recently arrived yeomen were busy checking service records and making up receipt forms for the men we received. I had asked them for a list of the men who came from sea duty and those who came from inactive duty. The totals were amazing. Out of the fifty-three men aboard only nine had extensive sea duty.

I felt quite alone and a bit scared. I almost wanted to go up to the most experienced of the nine, a grizzled, dignified first class machinist mate named Harris who had sixteen years service, and unburden all my problems to him. While I was sitting there, feeling sorry for myself, who should knock on the wardroom door, but Harris.

I was happy to see him. He reminded me of the first division chief on the Nitro who had really been my mentor on that ship. I felt very comfortable with an experienced leader in charge below decks and had just told Harris that, when he politely asked for a transfer. When I realized he was serious, I couldn't contain myself. I told him he was the most experienced man on the ship and that we all looked up to him and needed him badly.

Then, with tears in his eyes, he said that was the problem. He had all these responsibilities but he didn't know anything about our diesel engine main propulsion plant. His entire career had been in steam ships and he couldn't understand how he was sent to a diesel ship. His very young second class motor machinist mate, just out of the diesel school, knew so much more than he did that it was very embarrassing.

"I'm simply too old to start learning about diesels," he said. "I don't know a damn thing about them and I don't know where to start."

I was visibly crushed and he could see it. I told him I couldn't go to sea without him and asked him to think it over. I think the strength of my reaction affected him and he agreed to withdraw his request. There was no doubt he could see the relief in my eyes when he agreed to stay.

Thankfully, and to his credit, he never repeated his request to me and remained aboard as the leading engineering chief.

✪ ✪ ✪ ✪ ✪ ✪ ✪ ✪ ✪ ✪ ✪ ✪ ✪

Figure 98: **Loaded K-gun.** This K-gun on the USS Willis – similar to the ones on the PC 476 – fires a depth charge out to the side of the ship, thus widening the depth charge pattern. The weapon's name derives from its partial resemblance to the letter "K." The upper right arm of the K is the cylindrical, pipe-like structure, extending up and to the right in the photograph, holding the cylindrical depth charge at its end with a chain strap. The back of the K is the short, stubby, vertical, oblong looking pipe, which is the chamber for the propellent that explodes and tosses the 300 pound depth charge out to the side. There is no analog to the bottom arm of the K. Racks of depth charges are visible behind the K-gun. The white lines along the rim of each depth charge are used to set the water depth that will detonate the charge.

Chapter 6

Near Miss

Clearly, I was not prepared for the exec's job or for most of the other tasks that fell into my lap over the next few months. Of our crew of 55 men, who trickled aboard over the next few weeks, most were reserves. The learning process was challenging, tough, and often dangerous.

The first time we tried to put our motor whale-boat in the water, our leading seaman (Lincoln, the destroyer sailor) narrowly averted a serious injury. Under his guidance, the men had used our center-line boat boom to winch the boat up free of her cradle. The next step was to swing the boat boom and boat outboard to port, before lowering it into the water. This was done after much shouting and swearing. But it caused the PC boat itself to list (lean) heavily to port and for some reason all the men holding the line, except Lincoln, let go. The boat dropped about six feet into the water, flipping Lincoln over and onto his back as he held onto the line. He was lucky to come away uninjured. That was the first time I ever heard one sailor call others, "f... feather merchants" (a snide term for civilians).

I took seriously the admonitions to strip the ship of hazards that could prove dangerous in combat. This included stacks of papers and other inflammables, so I ordered the two yeomen to box all the records, forms and papers and place them in the bilges. It was an excellent way to eliminate the administrative

6. Near Miss

chores that I really didn't know much about anyway. The yeomen, who knew better, thought I knew something they didn't, and were happy to comply. However, when the storekeeper said he needed some of those papers to make sure we got paid, I rescinded my order.

Our captain, Lieutenant Junior Grade William Meyers, and our engineering officer, Roy True, reported aboard about two weeks after I did. By that time the ship was pretty well organized and ship shape, and neither of them had any idea about my growing pains.

It was a great relief to see our new captain. Although more experienced than me, and a graduate of the Naval Reserve Officers' Training Corps (NROTC) program, it was a big jump for him. His last job was as navigator on a large Navy cargo ship.

The engineering officer, Roy True, who became my roommate, was completely inexperienced. He had never been to sea before. He had been sent direct to engineering school after graduating from college. Shipboard life to him was brand new and he was just learning to adapt.

But problems of adaptation were not confined to the engineering officer.

Even though the 476 had been moved around a lot to pick up supplies, ammunition and fuel, it was always by tugboat or with the help of tugboats.

On March 18, 1942, we were scheduled to depart New Orleans. Our destination was Key West, Florida, where we would undergo anti-submarine training before heading to the war in the Pacific. We were now the commissioned United States Ship (USS) PC 476.

Designed to hunt and destroy enemy submarines, the people in Key West were going to teach us how to use this little ship as the designers envisioned. And it was indeed a little ship. We displaced just 450 tons. It felt like a rowboat when I compared it to the Nitro's fully loaded displacement of 10,000-plus tons.

Constructed on an assembly line at Defoe, Michigan, our ship was 173 feet long, or about one third the length of the Nitro. We were armed with a dual (air and surface) 3"/50 gun, four "K-guns" (each of which could launch a 300 pound depth charge out to the side), two stern depth charge racks which held 8 depth charges each, and three 20mm guns. About 5 knots faster than the Nitro, the 476's two large diesel engines could probably reach 20 knots (about 23 miles per hour) in smooth water.

While the 476, with its sonar gear, was a powerful little sub hunter, what about the submarines it was designed to hunt?

Neither I nor anyone else on the 476 knew much about the U-boats, except that they were sinking ships at an alarming rate off our east coast. It was only well after WWII ended that information about them was available to officers like myself.

The German workhorse submarine early in the war was the type VII U-boat. It was 211.6 feet long, had a surface top speed of 16 knots (8 knots submerged), maximum surface range of 4,300 nautical miles (90 nautical miles submerged at 4 knots), displaced 745 tons submerged, and could withstand water pressure at depths of about 656 feet before being crushed. It carried 11 torpedoes. As a rule, when compared with large cargo carrying ships, U-boat skippers considered PC boats small targets of low value. They apparently preferred to surface and sink them with their powerful deck gun, designed specifically for that purpose.

The good news was that PC boats seldom found themselves confronting a U-boat alone. Air support or other supporting ships were almost always nearby. By the end of the war (May 1945) the type VII U-boat had progressed through seven variants (Types VIIA through VIIF). Each variant was a major improvement over its predecessor.

The latest variants displaced 1,099 tons submerged, had an operating range of 6,500 nautical miles, a snorkel (which permitted intake of oxygen while cruising submerged near the surface), a crush depth of 820 feet, as well as other technological advances like radar and radio direction finding equipment.

Knowledge of the U-boat's capabilities would have been helpful to the captain of an attacking ship. For example, knowing the U-boat's "crush" depth would influence the depth at which an

6. Near Miss

attacking ship would set its depth charges to explode.

Although we did know that a U-boat was more powerful than our PC boat, we also knew we were not pushovers with our depth charges and option to ram.

A small group of friends and wives were standing on the dock to see us off. As was my responsibility, I had monitored a checklist that tracked each department's readiness to get underway. It was now complete, so I turned to the captain, saluted smartly and reported, "All departments report readiness for sea, sir."

"Thanks, George," he said pleasantly and walked out to the starboard side of the pilot house which was the side closest to the dock.

"Engine room standby to answer all bells," he ordered.

"Engine room reports ready, sir."

"Standby your lines," he ordered. Then in a few minutes, "Take in lines four, five and six."

"Lines four, five and six in, sir," came the response. "Take in line two."

"Heave around on line 1."

"Line two in, sir."

"Heaving around on line one, sir."

Of course, looking down from our small pilot house we could see everything that was happening, but it sure did sound good to hear the reports. You'd never know it was our first underway fully loaded and that we were on our way to join the war.

We saw the heavy strain on line one as the bow moved slowly in toward the pier and our small stern, bucking the Mississippi current, moved out toward the center of the river.

The small crowd on the dock was quiet and somber as they waved to us. There were only a few wives and kids, but we all felt the seriousness of the goodbyes.

"Take in lines one and three, all engines back one-third," ordered the captain. Almost immediately the engines came on line with a small roar and we started moving.

But we didn't move out into the river. The strong current pushed our stern back in and we slid slowly downstream against the pier.

"All stop."

"All engines answer stop, sir."

"All engines ahead one-third. All ahead two-thirds."

"Engines answer two-thirds."

Our backward momentum stopped. Then we started to slide forward toward our old berth as we hugged the dock and scrapped some paint off our freshly painted starboard side. Thankfully, it was a big long pier.

"All stop."

"All stop, sir"

We were right back into our old position. The small puzzled crowd stopped waving and just watched as we put over lines three and one to hold us against the strong current.

We repeated the same maneuver. Except this time the captain ordered two-thirds backing power. But the same thing happened and once again we were back in our original berth. By now the small crowd was not sad but some of them were smiling as they waved.

"George, get me Knight's seamanship."

I left the bridge, hurried to the captain's room and retrieved that well-known bible for seamen.

On my way back to the bridge, on the port side, the captain of a small tugboat who had apparently been watching our efforts, steamed close by and beckoned to me.

"Throw me a line and I'll pull you out young man."

I looked at the captain who had crossed over to the port side.

"No, thanks," said the captain, too embarrassed to say yes.

Sensing the captain's embarrassment, the tugboat skipper motioned to me to come as close as I could and he moved almost to touch us. Cupping his hand to his mouth so that others could not hear him, he said, "Tell your captain to put the rudder hard left, back your outboard engine and go ahead two-thirds on your inboard engine. That'll do it."

6. NEAR MISS

I thanked him and went up to the captain and repeated the advice quietly so that no one overheard me.

The captain waved to the tugboat skipper and followed his advice.

The maneuver moved our bow into the stream and the strong current caught it, whipped us away from the dock and out into the river. It happened so fast that the small crowd on the dock almost didn't get a chance to wave goodbye.

We were on our way. Our next stop was Key West.

It felt good to be underway after so long in New Orleans, with all our logistics and readiness problems behind us.

The captain kept her at two-thirds (twelve knots) as we threaded our way out of the busy New Orleans area into the more confined, but less busy, part of the river heading toward the Gulf of Mexico.

After we had cleared the busy area and were well into the narrower part of the river almost by ourselves, the captain said, "Take over George. I'm going below for a while." He had read the memo from my exec on the Nitro qualifying me to stand top watches. But he didn't know I had never stood one, and I didn't tell him.

So, he left me up there in control of our little ship as we steamed down the Mississippi.

I ran into problems almost as soon as he left. The river is not straight. On the Nitro my orders to the helmsman were always something like, "Come right (or left) with so much rudder, steer new (previously planned) course so and so."

Well, that wouldn't work in this portion of the Mississippi, because the river was winding and we had to constantly change course. I adapted by using a steady stream of orders like "Come right (or left) ten degrees rudder steer so and so." The helmsman, less experienced than I, responded well and that's the way we sailed merrily down the river.

I knew enough about the rules of the road to remain on the right side of the river. What I didn't know, and learned the hard way, was that there are times when that rule does not apply.

In the distance I could see the top-most part of a ship's mast moving across the tree-line. As we got closer, it turned out to be a huge green monster of a troop transport ship of about 25,000 tons on my port bow, steaming toward me. We were 450 tons. You can easily visualize the difference.

I could see we were both approaching a large bend in the river. He was coming up river and we were going down river in the opposite direction. Cautious as I was, I hugged the right side to give him plenty of room, expecting him to remain on his right side of the river.

The bend in the river ahead of us would require him to turn right about eighty degrees while I was approaching the bend. At first, all we could see was his huge superstructure moving up river into the bend. I really wasn't concerned because the river was wide and I knew if I hugged the right side of the river we would pass, port to port, (left side to left side) well clear of one another.

But I was wrong.

He began making his right turn into the bend, but he didn't stay on his side of the channel as I expected. We were now about two miles apart. He was well into the center of the channel and moving steadily over to my side at about ten knots.

I didn't know what to do. He was really crowding me. But I stuck to my side as we closed rapidly toward one another. (We were making about 14 knots, and he was making about 10.)

Suddenly, I realized that if I didn't move left he would hit me. He obviously felt the same way because he sounded four sharp blasts on his horn – the danger signal!

It was an easy maneuver for me. "Left ten degrees rudder, steer new course one zero zero," I ordered.

The helmsman needed no more prompting. He could see the monster bearing down on us head-on and quickly swung the rudder over. After a few agonizing seconds, our ship started turning to the left, away from and clear of his track, so that we would pass each other, not port side to port side as I had expected, but starboard to starboard.

6. NEAR MISS

All eyes in our pilot house were on the transport. Drawing closer and closer, the actual passing alongside her lasted just a few seconds but scared the hell out of me. It was so damn close I could see the rivet heads on the looming steel side of the transport zipping past at a relative speed of about 24 knots.

But for some reason, I felt a huge sense of exhilaration afterwards. Perhaps it was the thunderous roar of the soldiers who were crowded on the top side of the transport, looking down on our sleek daring PC boat.

Still shaking inwardly, I looked back and wondered why he persisted in staying on what I thought was my side of the channel.

Even though I knew better, things happened so fast that I never had time to report it to the captain. He never heard the four blasts from the transport and never learned about my mistake.

It was indeed a mistake – almost a tragic one.

Common sense should have told me that it was impossible for the transport to remain on the right side during his turn. Big as he was, his turning circle was not small enough to permit him to turn sharply and remain on the right side. He needed to be on my side during a portion of the turn.

I learned subsequently that at sharp river bends big ships are required to maneuver that way.

With the euphoria of that near miss, I immediately created another serious mistake. I increased speed to 15 knots (standard speed) and watched with excitement as the huge wake we made cascaded toward the river bank.

What I didn't know, until weeks later, was that our wake had indeed cascaded into the river bank and smashed a number of pleasure boats moored in a marina. It was then that I learned about a federal law prohibiting high speeds in that part of the channel. The Navy was billed $25,000 for the damages.

Unsettling as it had been, there were advantages to sailing on a river. Everyone, except Lincoln (the destroyer sailor) and Morgan the pharmacist mate, was seasick an hour after we left the protection of the Mississippi and entered the Gulf. It was a strange seasickness because the sea was smooth except for long swells.

By the time we entered Key West, two days later and without incident, most of us had our sea legs, but not much food had been consumed.

Figure 108: **Heavy seas aboard PC 451.** But not so heavy as to deter the sailor at upper left.

Chapter 7

Aground

Our sonar personnel, the captain, and I spent our first two days in Key West aboard the PC 451, a well known school-ship for the Fleet Sound School based there. We eagerly learned, for the first time, how to use our anti-submarine sonar equipment.

We were then ordered to the Submarine Chaser Training Center (SCTC) in Miami, which was just getting started.

We left Key West late one afternoon and expected to arrive in Miami the next morning.

As luck would have it, we ran into a terrible storm that turned what should have been a pleasant 175-mile trip into an unforgettable nightmare.

In no time at all, everyone was deathly seasick, except for our Pharmacist Mate Second Class Morgan and Seaman First Class Lincoln – the same two who did not get sick during our first voyage.

A ship our size didn't ride through the waves. It rode up and over, with the "over" usually accompanied by a thudding drop down the other side of the wave.

The height of the waves probably exceeded 40 feet – an estimate, since measuring the actual wave height was the last thing on our minds. But it was a sound estimate. Our main mast rose about 40 feet above the water, and its top was well below the wave crests when we were in a trough.

7. Aground

The fierce wind was so mixed with the sea that we couldn't tell whether it was wind-driven spray or hard rain that kept hitting our small pilot house. We warned all hands to stay off the topside. We locked ourselves in the pilot house and secured all hatches leading below. There was nothing to do but stay in a bunk or wedge yourself in a corner with your slop bucket close at hand.

After about six hours of pounding and rolling in the sealed up ship, the air down below, and even in the airtight pilot house, began to smell pretty bad. To make the stench worse, the water in the toilets flowed the wrong way and became flooded and useless.

As the waves got bigger our little ship was tossed from wave to wave, only to fall heavily, with mast-shaking thuds into the bottom of deep mountain sized troughs. I say "mountain sized" because there was no way we could see over the tops of the waves. That was possible only when we were at the top or nearing the top of a wave, just before we cascaded down the other side.

At first we could see the huge waves ahead of us as we looked out the pilot house port holes. But as the storm raged on, visibility worsened until we couldn't even see the massive waves that were engulfing us. Although we were all still seasick, that seemed to matter less and less as the upended slop buckets kept the pilot house deck wet and the air oppressive.

Seasickness seems to affect everyone differently, except for the one common denominator of vomiting. But even that has a wide range of differences. While this is not the most pleasant subject for any narrative, no account of life at sea in a vicious storm is complete without it.

For myself, my feelings ranged between anger at my inability to control my stomach to wondering how much time it would take for my stomach to empty itself. And then, what would my stomach do when it had emptied all its contents through my mouth?

If one is really seasick, and stays seasick for five or six hours, the stomach will indeed empty itself. But the stomach convulsions do not stop when the stomach is empty. They simply become dry. That is, very little exits from the mouth and one enters a stage called the "dry heaves."

Although uncomfortable, the "dry heaves" are a lot easier to tolerate than the wet heaves. And the urge to do nothing but lie down somewhere, which accompanies the "wet heaves," is lessened somewhat.

Another item of some interest is that when you reach the "dry heave" stage very little in the way of stench seems to be bothersome. For me, stench was almost always a trigger for the wet heaves. Unfortunately it is very difficult to avoid stench on a small ship in bad weather.

Certain foods, or even conversation about food, could also be a trigger. For me, pork, or the smell of pork, was a guaranteed trigger. Other people must have been similarly affected, because most ships I was attached to rarely served pork at sea.

Some hardy souls tried to eat at meal time. I would munch on saltine crackers. Other men would try dry toast. But we rarely had regular meals when in a storm. It was too rough on the cooks trying to control the pots and pans. And sometimes even the oven itself would move. Eating with a knife and fork in heavy weather wasn't all that easy and only men like Lincoln and Morgan did it. For most of us, the cooks would prepare simple sandwiches. Overall, eating is not a priority on a PC boat in rough weather.

Some men simply give up and quit when they get seasick. They are capable of lying in their bunk and nothing else. Fortunately we only had three or four in that category. All the others, including myself and the captain, maintained varying degrees of productivity. But it was a rare person who would eat a meal when seasick.

When 95% of the crew is seasick there is not much noise from the people themselves. Most are silent as the noise of the waves crash around us. But occasional conversations do occur.

"I wonder where we are?" The question, part of a conversation between the quartermaster striker (apprentice) and a sea-

7. Aground

man, floated up from the small navigation desk just below, but integral with, the pilot house.

"Yeah, I wonder where the hell we are," echoed Lincoln, the helmsman. He had been on the wheel for most of the last four hours. It had been Lincoln, two hours earlier, who first reported that the gyro was out of commission. And he had been trying to steer by the spinning magnetic compass ever since – an almost impossible task.

It wasn't the magnetic compass that worried me. We hadn't done our homework and calibrated it as we should have, so we really didn't know how reliable it was. I have since read that there is no magnetic deviation in the Bermuda triangle, where we were. But I wonder if that's really true.

The heavy seas that tossed us around like a cork could easily have been the cause of the magnetic compass' wild oscillations. Nor did I have sense enough to get worried when the gyrocompass went out.

Instead, it was Randolph's refusal to obey an order from the captain to come down from the crow's nest, for his own safety, that rang the alarm in my head. His frightened voice seemed to wake us all up to the seriousness of our situation.

Randolph was a quiet, young black sailor and the last person in the world I would expect to refuse to obey an order, especially one designed to assure his safety.

Funny, I thought to myself, "I wouldn't stay a second in that small, cramped perch." The crow's nest was a cube-shaped metal enclosure attached securely to the mast, about ten feet above the top of the pilot house, with a small slit enabling the occupant to see. Because it was up so high, with every plunge and roll of the ship it swung wildly all over the sky, giving Randolph the roughest ride of anyone on the ship. "Somehow, that scared sailor thinks he is safer up there."

"No sir. I'm not coming down." Even above the screaming of the wind against the pilot house, everyone inside could hear the fear in his voice. "I'm just not climbing down this mast and that's it!"

"O.K." muttered the captain, "let him stay there."

About the same time I was trying to replace our injured sonar operator. In addition to being deathly seasick, he had forgotten to hang on during a big roll and was tossed out of his chair, injuring his knee. I was trying to replace him with Morgan, our pharmacists mate second class. But Morgan, was not happy about his new duty.

"I don't give a damn what the Geneva Convention says about you not being required to perform combat duties," I said. "I'm ordering you to sit in that chair and operate that sonar machine. And if you hear an echo you yell 'contact, contact.' Do I make myself clear?"

"You know I am required to report this violation to the Chief of Naval Operations, don't you?" he replied.

"I don't care who you report it to. For the remainder of this trip you are now the sonar operator."

"What if someone else gets hurt and needs me?"

"We'll cross that bridge when it happens. But right now you sit in that chair and start rotating that hand-wheel." I could see he was angry. I was surprised and bothered by his reaction but I was too seasick to spend any time worrying about it.

But nevertheless he sat down and confronted the hand-wheel and what appeared to be a complete vertical pinball machine. The hand-wheel controlled a pointer on a large compass rose. At regular intervals an underwater blast of sonar sound waves would be emitted in the direction selected by the pointer. We couldn't hear the blast. But we did hear a loud ping every time the sonar blasted out. At each ping, lights would dance around the compass dial.

"Just turn that dial every fifteen degrees and search from beam to beam," I instructed. What Morgan didn't know was that my knowledge about the machine and its operation was limited. I had received a couple of days training aboard the PC 451, but in these heavy seas our sonar machine was not operating like the one on the PC 451.

7. AGROUND

The idea was that if the underwater sonar blast encountered anything (especially metal) it would send an echo back to the machine. This would indicate there was something out there – perhaps a U-boat.

More importantly, it let anyone under the surface know that we were there and that we constituted a danger for them. That part made the pinging reassuring.

When I explained all this to Morgan he settled down and seemed to lose his anger.

"Why me?" he asked.

"Because you're smart, we need someone here we can depend on, and you don't get seasick," I answered. That really placated him, and he went to work.

I knew I made a wise choice as I watched Morgan sit in that chair for the next 5 hours. Of course he took a few breaks, but he took charge and remained glued to the machine during the remainder of the entire rough trip from Key West to Miami. His comfortable chair was secured to the deck, and while books, charts, pencils, ashtrays, and other loose gear slid back and forth, Morgan was oblivious to the bad weather and stuck to his job. The machine had many echoes but we soon figured out they were caused by the turbulent water.

I was the navigator. They had told me on the Nitro I was a qualified navigator. But no one ever taught me how to shoot a star sight from a rolling, lurching, bouncing, rough riding bucking bronco like the PC 476.

In the first place, rapidly moving dark clouds covered the sky most of the time. I was lucky to even acquire a star in my sextant and when I did, the horizon was so dark and fuzzy I had no confidence in my sights. The captain, a more experienced navigator, also tried, but his luck wasn't much better. Once we were swallowed up into that massively dark storm, getting any kind of a position was hopeless.

Then we encountered another serious problem. Waves breaking on deck, plus the ship's violent lurching, tore loose the depth charges we had secured on deck. That was when I really started to worry. Until then my trust in the ship designers from the U.S. Navy Bureau of Ships had been so consuming that I thought we were impervious to real danger from the heavy seas.

Depth charges are explosive-packed, 300-pound metal cylinders about a foot and a half in diameter and about 2 feet long. The PC 476 normally had 16 of them secured on deck, ready to be dropped on submarines on command. Half were on rails at the sternmost part of the ship, where they were rolled into the sea, and the rest were mounted on stubby, special-purpose, mortar-like guns that blasted the depth charges out and away from the side of the ship. The guns got their name from their shape, which resembled the letter K (Figure 98).

When the depth charges tore loose from the chains that held them on the K-guns, and when others in depth charge racks came out of those racks, my confidence in the Bureau of Ships started to waver.

"Are the charges set on safe?" asked the captain.

"Yes, sir," I responded to his worried question.

Three minutes later an explosion we heard – and felt – made a liar out of me. Someone had goofed!

"Full speed ahead," shouted the captain.

He didn't have to tell me why. We weren't making much headway, and at times we even slid backwards.

We quickly learned that full speed into those mountainous waves might be worse than sitting next to an exploding depth charge and, just as quickly, the skipper slowed to ten knots.

I went out on the port wing of the pilot house. Wedging myself into the corner I looked aft. It was still dark but I could see the depth charges rolling around and then, one by one, going overboard. I braced myself several times because I could see that we really weren't moving away from the charges fast enough to avoid damage. But luckily, unlike the one that had exploded, the rest were, indeed, set on safe. And there were no more explosions.

However, I could see that there was one depth charge stuck or wedged beneath the starboard depth charge rack. No matter

115

7. AGROUND

how we rolled or pitched it stayed there.

Soaking wet, I went back into the dark pilot house and told the captain that all the charges except one were gone. "And the one that is left isn't going anywhere." I assured him.

The fact that I had the guts to go outside, stay there and get that information, and the information itself, must have impressed him. His soft "Thanks, George," told me that whatever anger he surely felt earlier had dissipated.

"I see a ship! I see a ship!" It was Randolph's shouting voice coming out of the crow's nest voice tube.

I jumped to his voice tube. "Where? Where?"

"Over there, over there," he shouted his voice full of excitement.

We knew he was pointing somewhere. But none of us could see him. Even if we had gone outside of the pilot house to look up at him we wouldn't see any part of him. He was inside that cubicle with only an opening for his eyes.

"Where the hell is it?" I yelled into his voice tube. "Which side of the ship?"

Suddenly he recovered. "One point on the port bow. A big black ship over there. Do you see it?"

The captain saw it first through his glasses and the porthole just in front of him. Then I wedged myself between the compass stand and a porthole and saw this big blur that was blacker than the night sky behind it. He was about 4000 yards away and not always visible to us as we slid down into the mountainous troughs.

"Challenge him!" ordered the captain (the challenge was a light signal encoding two or more letters; the recipient would respond to it with specified letters).

No one moved.

"It's not safe on the signal bridge," I said quietly.

"Oh yeah. I'll swing the ship around and we'll parallel him. Tell everyone to hang on."

I grabbed the ship's microphone speaker. "Attention all hands, attention all hands. We are going to make a full turn to port and will probably be leaning way over. Hang on."

"Starboard ahead full, port back two-thirds. Left full rudder. Stand by for a big roll," shouted the captain.

"Yes sir," responded the suddenly alert helmsman, spinning the wheel to his left with one hand, while hanging onto an overhead beam above his head with the other hand. Just as quickly, the quartermaster moved the engine order telegraph levers to send the captain's orders to the engine room. The engine room immediately acknowledged the orders.

"Rudder is left full sir."

"Port answers two-thirds astern. Starboard answers full ahead sir."

For a brief instant I was so proud of their response I almost forgot my seasickness.

For a few minutes she straightened up. Then, in a slow jerky motion with the sea fighting us every inch of the way, we could feel her coming left. Suddenly, a hard bump the full length of the starboard side told us we were turning and the raging sea was coming at us on our starboard beam. It pushed us hard, and into a terrible hanging roll that I thought was the end.

But no. With water smashing over the top of the pilot house making us feel like we were a submerging submarine, she kept turning to the left.

The captain, wedged rigidly against the pilot house bulkhead, had his binoculars glued to the big black ship. Suddenly we could all see that ship was now on our starboard side.

"All ahead two-thirds, steady as you go," he ordered. We all felt the sea behind us as it picked us up and hurled us forward – a far smoother ride and far less frightening than heading into those mountainous seas. We still rolled and pounded but far less. And the sea was now pushing us, not smashing into us.

The signalman carefully opened the pilot house door on the port side, now in the lee (away from the wind), and waited a few moments with the door open. Convinced it was safe, he went out, scrambled up the ladder to the searchlight, raised the big ship and sent a challenge.

7. Aground

We all saw the welcome blob of light from the massive black ship as he answered our challenge.

"Challenge O.K., captain." shouted the signalman.

"Good. Ask him his position."

When the response came back I plotted it. Neither the captain nor I believed him. It showed us 70 miles east of our expected track.

"Ask him what course he is steering now." The answer came back: "275."

"Ask him where he is going."

"Miami," was the answer.

"Tell him thanks."

"Follow that ship," the captain ordered.

It was about four a.m. when we picked up the lights of Miami. The storm had abated a great deal but the downwind course was our savior. Even though we still rolled and seemed to skid forward, it was a pleasant ride compared to what we had previously experienced.

We watched our huge guide enter the channel and slowly disappear from our view.

By now I had the harbor entrance charts on the chart table and told the captain we were heading for the Miami Ship Channel.

"O.K." he answered.

It was strange, I thought. A few hours ago we were fighting for our lives in a raging storm and now we are in smooth waters heading for the well illuminated and cheerful Miami coast.

My navigational fixes, even without a working gyrocompass, placed us right in the middle of the entrance to the Miami Ship Channel. And I so told the captain.

He nodded his head but I knew he didn't trust me.

"Captain, I'd keep on the right side of the channel. There's a big rock on the southern edge of the channel."

Again he said nothing.

The different lights on the shoreline were confusing me and I was not getting good fixes.

"I think we better move right to stay clear of that rock."

I knew he heard me, but he remained silent.

Suddenly the mast started to shake violently.

Randolph screamed, "What the hell is going on?"

I stepped out to the port wing of the pilothouse and immediately saw that we were no longer moving - even though the engine order telegraph indicated both engines were going ahead two-thirds.

The shaking became very violent and suddenly the captain and I both knew – we were aground!

"All stop," yelled the captain.

Then almost immediately, "All back two-thirds."

In a few seconds the mast started to shake again as Randolph screamed. But the ship didn't move.

"All stop. Aw shit!" muttered the captain as he walked over to the chart table.

The quartermaster took his time and plotted several fixes. One of them placed us right on top of the large rock about which I had earlier warned the captain.

"Oh shit!" he said again as he looked down at the water.

None of us said anything for a while.

"Get on the harbor frequency and ask them to send a tug out here to pull us off."

"Yes sir," said the radioman, who had come to the pilothouse.

The radioman twirled some knobs and tried to raise someone by voice transmission. He kept asking for a response but there was none. Then he went into his small radio room and tried to raise someone with his hand key. Still no response.

The captain was growing angry. "Can't you raise anyone?'

"No sir. Not a beep."

"Jesus Christ, don't they know there's a war on. Hell, the Germans could come in here and shell the whole place and they would never know what hit them," he muttered angrily.

None of us said anything. Especially me. I was the navigator and I knew that I had blown my job. I should have been much more forceful in warning him about the rock

7. Aground

After studying the harbor chart, I realized that there was probably a southerly set that would push us to the southern edge of the Main Ship Channel where the rock was. The set was caused by another channel (the Malloy Channel) that flowed into, and merged with, the Main Ship Channel just ahead of the rock.

I really felt miserable, envisioning all kinds of possible disciplinary actions coming my way.

"Shall we try the searchlight?" asked the quartermaster.

"Yeah. Go ahead."

The quartermaster went to the signal bridge and aimed the searchlight toward what he thought was the harbor entrance control building. But no response.

We sat there for a few minutes wondering what to do next, when we suddenly felt the ship swing clear.

We hit the rock at 0450 in the morning and by 0500 we were no longer stuck on it. I don't know if it was a rising tide or sheer luck that moved us off the rock, and I never spent the time to find out.

We went ahead at one-third speed on our starboard engine. The ship shook even at that speed but not enough to force us to stop.

By signal light, we asked a passing tugboat to contact the harbor master for us. He did, and a short while later a small tug came out to help us.

Up to this point we really hadn't looked at ourselves. But now, as we moved toward our pier, daylight was breaking and we could readily see the mess we were in. There was debris all over the topside, especially the piles of canvas at the stern. The depth charge, the only one of 16 that was left, was still wedged under the depth charge rack. And none of us felt like lifting a finger to start cleaning up.

Finally, with the assistance of the tug, we tied up alongside a big dock in downtown Miami.

After the grounding, the captain hadn't said a word all during the short remaining trip. I could feel his pain, since I also felt like hell. I told him I was going to order an all hands muster of our crew on the dock to make sure we still had everybody.

He didn't say anything but just went below to his room.

A few minutes later, some of us still woozy, we stood in ranks on the dock and counted heads.

Over and over we counted, checked and rechecked and each time we came up short. Two men were missing.

I told the crew to sit on the dock while we searched the ship – which we did stem to stern several times.

I found the captain sitting at his desk when I reported the names of the two missing men.

"Are you sure?"

"Yes sir. Can't find them."

He started to get up when the boatswain's mate of the watch burst in. "We found them! We found them!" he shouted.

"Thank God. Thank God," said the captain quietly but emotionally as he sank back down in his chair.

I, too, was relieved – and then angry. "Where the hell where they?"

"They were seasick, couldn't stand the stench down below, and were afraid to stay there. They came topside before the storm got too bad and tied themselves to some stanchions just aft of the whale boat. They covered themselves with some heavy tarps we had secured there. I think they passed out and rode out the storm under there."

He kept talking rapidly. "One of the guys who went back there to take a leak over the side stepped on the tarps. And that's when he heard them moaning."

"Are they O.K.?"

"Doc (our name for the pharmacists mate) says they are O.K."

One of the two, let's call him Roger, promptly sent a personal letter to the President of the United States. "I can't stand it aboard this little ship," he wrote. "I want to serve my country but I must be transferred to shore duty, anywhere. If I am not transferred to shore duty I will desert and ruin my life and my family name."

7. Aground

Roger's letter was forwarded to us by the Navy department for action. We weren't told what to do. Roger was a quiet, sincere young man who decided that he could not and would not stand the rigors of sea life on a PC boat. About a week after receiving the correspondence we transferred him to a shore station. In spite of the beating received by all our men, Roger was the only one who quit.

We started to clean up the ship while the captain went ashore. He came back in about twenty minutes with a couple of officers, including Commander McDaniel, head of the new Submarine Chaser Training Center (SCTC) the Navy was setting up in Miami.[1] He and the captain went through the ship as I tagged along.

There was a huge dent where a monster wave had hit the pilothouse. The platform for gun one had been pushed back and the gun was now useless. The explosive that would detonate that lone remaining depth charge had been removed, and the unarmed depth charge was now sitting on the dock. The large oven range in the mess hall – sliding back and forth as the ship rolled – had done a lot of damage before the range itself was secured. It was too early to know if it was still usable. All the living compartments, including the officer's quarters, had water in them, primarily from the back-flow of the toilets – which were also useless.

The stench below decks was almost unbearable and the engineers were making efforts to rig blowers and circulate outside air into the ship.

The only part of the ship that was not damaged was the engine spaces. Initially, gear had broken loose, but it was quickly secured and the engine spaces fared pretty well.

Two divers reported that the blades of the port propeller were badly damaged. While the starboard propeller only had some sizable nicks on one blade, both main shafts, they reported, were O.K. Other than the propellers, there was no other damage. The

---

[1] Morison-I, pages 213-233.

entire bottom had not touched the rock and it was still in pristine shape.

Arrangements were made for us to enter a marine railway drydock. About five days later, when the replacement propellers arrived, a tug came alongside to take us there.

As luck would have it, the tug towed us through the same channel used by the fancy yachts and powerboats for which Miami is famous. That included some sections through very populated areas. The banks became lined with people who watched us quietly.

The demeanor of the people watching us made us realize how bad we looked. It was obvious that they felt sorry for us. There was no waving and cheering. The sad plight of the U.S. Navy was reflected in the astonished but sympathetic looks we received from the onlookers, who were just a few feet away on the banks of the narrow channel.

By early afternoon we had been pulled out of the water and repairs started.

It didn't take long to get the ship cleaned up and by 5 p.m. we started liberty for two-thirds of the crew. The captain and engineering officer went ashore. The captain told me he would be back in the morning.

I stayed aboard until after dinner when I took a cab into downtown Miami. The grounding was still very much on my mind and I felt rather bad no matter where I went, or what I did.

When I returned about 10 p.m. to a strangely quiet ship. I asked the quartermaster of the watch where his messenger and everyone else was?

He hesitated at first and then said, "They are all across the street."

"Does that include the duty section?" I wasn't sure I had heard him correctly.

"Yes sir," he answered, knowing full well there was something really wrong here.

"Who gave them permission to leave the ship?"

He didn't answer.

7. Aground

"Who gave them permission to leave the ship?"

"I, I don't know sir." He stammered.

"You mean you and I are the only ones aboard this ship now?" I said, my voice rising in anger and surprise.

"What's across the street?"

"The bar. Marty's bar."

"Why didn't you go too?"

He could tell it was a sarcastic question but as I waited for an answer, he said, "I have the watch."

Angry as hell, I turned around, walked off the ship and headed for Marty's bar. I had seen it as I entered the small shipyard.

I was still very angry and ready to raise hell and order all the sailors back to the ship when I opened the door and walked in the bar.

But I stopped by the door and hesitated. The place was full of people, including a large number of sailors from the PC 476. It was easy to distinguish them because they all still wore their dungaree working uniforms.

I was dressed in my service dress white uniform so I stood out like a sore thumb. A few of my sailors noticed me. They stopped talking as they put their drinks down.

In just a few seconds it was no longer a raucous noisy bar room as I became the focus of attention.

Still angry, but also a little nervous, I walked toward a large group of my sailors and was about to order them back to the ship. I had an uneasy feeling that I was about to make a mistake. I had learned on the Nitro that an officer wading into a group of sailors who are drinking, as I was about to do, was a bad idea. But I was too deep into it to stop, as I tried to find the right words to order them all back to the ship.

Suddenly, our leading engineering petty officer, Harris, appeared by my side. He put a friendly arm around my shoulder and guided me away from the group to a spot at the bar.

Surprised and puzzled at this action by our most senior petty officer, a man for whom I had an enormous amount of respect, I relaxed a little.

"Mr. Sotos, I know we shouldn't be here. But things were O.K. on the ship and we haven't been here long. I suggest you have a short drink with me and go back to the ship. Then I'll bring every last one of them back."

It didn't take me long to realize that he was giving me a good steer. Ordering a bunch of half drunk sailors out of the bar wouldn't have set well with them or with all the other people who were now watching us.

"Thanks, Harris," I said quietly. "I'll have a beer. And then I added softly, "I'm really disappointed that you let this happen."

He didn't apologize. He merely said, "Yes sir, I know. But I'll get them back with no problems."

Harris waited as I quickly finished my beer, got off the bar stool and headed for the door. He remained seated as I left.

I could hear the noise start up again almost as soon as I walked out the door. I returned to the ship and went straight to bed.

In the morning we had our normal "quarters for muster," and there were no absentees. I never mentioned the incident to the captain or to Harris, nor did Harris ever bring it up.

The captain returned about 10:00 and our daily routine continued.

We were in the dry-dock for just two days. Changing the propellers was almost like changing wheels on a large truck. The second night I remained aboard and everything remained quiet and orderly.

Once out of the dry-dock, we learned that the Miami SCTC was not yet ready for any customers, so we were soon underway for Key West.

All during these days I kept expecting to be arraigned for a court martial or some type of disciplinary action for my culpability in the ship's grounding. For some strange reason neither the captain nor I ever mentioned it between us.

Nor did anyone else ever mention it. There was never an investigation. Nothing. We never even saw an official dispatch or a letter notifying anyone of the grounding.

7. Aground

I never took any action to learn any more about any part of the experience. I didn't even try to determine why the gyrocompass went out so quickly, or who failed to set that single depth charge on safe.

I just kept my mouth shut and kept hoping that it would never come up again. And it didn't! In fact, this is the first time since it happened 72 years ago that I have mentioned it.

Figure 128: **Smoke screen.** Looking aft, as the USS Willis lays a smoke screen during a training exercise.

Chapter 8

A Failure to Communicate

After a smooth trip from Miami we returned to Key West in the early afternoon of April 26, 1942, where we would complete preparations and training for duty in the Pacific.

A few hours earlier, the USS Sturtevant (DD 240), an old four stack destroyer, had left Key West by a different route: the northwest channel. That channel is used by ships coming from or going to New Orleans, as we had on March 20, when we first arrived in Key West.

Later that evening we were surprised to receive a report that the Sturtevant had been torpedoed and sunk not far from Key West.

About an hour after the torpedoing report, our quarterdeck watch reported that there was a great deal of activity on the Key West Harbor fuel pier, which is at the entrance to the small harbor. When he said that the activity included a large number of ambulances, I decided to see what was happening.

When I got to the fuel pier Navy people were bringing in survivors from the Sturtevant. I talked to the lieutenant in charge to see if we could provide any assistance but he said no.

It was not a pretty sight to see boatloads of survivors, one after the other, almost all coated with black oil. A number were injured and 15 had died. Most were moving under their own power, but they were obviously exhausted and needed help dis-

8. A Failure to Communicate

embarking from the motor launches which brought them in. Soon the ambulances were filled and heading to the hospital. I watched the grisly, unusually quiet rescue operation continue under the lights well into the night.

I wonder how those survivors would have reacted had they known their ship was not sunk by a U-boat.

Shortly after leaving port, the Sturtevant was rocked by an explosion at her stern. All her sonar equipment was knocked out, but she was still seaworthy. Assuming the ship was under torpedo attack, the captain maneuvered and dropped several depth charges to discourage his attacker.

Minutes later the ship was rocked by two more large detonations which caused major flooding. She sank in 60 feet of water.

In a sad twist of fate, the source of the explosions was the USS Miantonomah (CM-10), a U.S. Navy mine-laying ship that had berthed intermittently alongside the Sturtevant in Key West Harbor. Her minefield, laid just weeks prior to the Sturtevant's departure from Key West, was unknown to the destroyer's navigator and captain.

The PC 476 had used that same channel when it first arrived at Key West. Apparently the mine field had not been laid then or the PC 476 luckily went through without hitting a mine. The sinking of the Sturtevant was our first knowledge of the minefield.

Unbelievably, our Navy, through a failure of common sense communications, killed 15 sailors and lost a first line destroyer. Even harder to believe, in the next three months the same minefield sank three merchant ships: the Gunvor, the Basiljka, and the Edmund Lukenbach.[1]

The Sturtevant sank not far from the entrance to Key West Harbor. All during the war, and for many months afterward, she sat on the bottom, her mast sticking well above the water's surface for every ship entering Key West to see. She remained a vis-

---

[1] Morison-I, p. 136. He mis-attributes the cause of Sturtevant's sinking.

ible daily monument to the inept communications in that part of the U.S. Navy.

We spent most of the short time we had in Key West with our instructors on the PC 451 school ship, and became close friends with them. A day before we were to leave for the Pacific, Bob Norman, the exec of the 451 and my counterpart, dropped by to chat. We were having coffee in the wardroom, just the two of us, when he suddenly said," George, how would you like to swap jobs with me? You don't seem to be too happy about going to the Pacific."

He was right on that score. I had mentioned to him that it was a long way off and probably meant that I'd never get any leave to go home until the war ended – if it ever did.

"No way," I said. "I've invested too much in this ship and crew, and I want to stay with them."

To my surprise, he suddenly became emotional. Dropping to his knee, he said, "Look, on bended knee I am begging you to swap with me."

Embarrassed and puzzled, I hesitated. "Wait a minute Bob, what are you doing?"

"On bended knee I am begging you to change jobs with me. I have to get to San Diego (the PC 476's assigned home port) or I'll go mad."

"But Bob–"

He interrupted. "George, I'm engaged to be married in San Diego and the only way I can get there is as exec on your ship. It's the only way. I've been stuck here in Key West for a year and there's no other way out. I have to get there or I'll go nuts. Please, please, I implore you – swap with me."

"The 451 is a really good ship." He continued quickly. "You'll like it. I know. You're single. You don't really care what ship you are on. You told me so. You said you wanted to stay in the Atlantic. Here's your chance. And you'll actually be saving my life."

I still couldn't believe what I was hearing as he kept pushing and pleading.

8. A Failure to Communicate

In a moment of sympathetic weakness I said, "I will never request a transfer from the 476 but if I was ordered off I wouldn't fight it."

That was all he needed. "I've already spoken to your captain. He said if you agreed to the swap he'd go along with it. And you will go along with it, won't you?" he pleaded.

"How about your captain?"

"He wants to help me. He knows I can't get out to San Diego any other way." He paused. "And he knows I am going bonkers unless I get out there."

"Why don't you take leave and go there?"

"My captain has authorized leave over and over again. But the squadron commander's policy prohibits it, except for emergency leave. And no matter what I say, they don't think I have an emergency."

I started to think seriously about the swap. I knew his ship. It had been in commission for over two years and was the star of the Fleet Sonar School. I could learn everything about antisubmarine warfare and start getting involved in the war on patrols right here out of Key West. And besides, I wasn't too anxious to go to the Pacific. That ocean is huge and my experience on the Nitro in the Pacific did not bring back happy memories.

He saw me start to weaken. "Okay, George? O.K.? Please. Please!"

"Okay." I said only half sure of what I was doing.

He jumped to his feet, hugged me and near shouted, "Thanks, thanks. I don't know how to thank you." And then, before I could change my mind, he was gone.

Left alone with my thoughts, I had many regrets about agreeing to leave this crew to whom I had become attached. Deep down, I was glad I said Okay and escaped the Pacific. But, still, I wondered if it was the right decision.

My skipper had been more than fair to me, and though I believe he was happy with the way I ran the ship, I knew the grounding would always be on his mind. And I could see that for him it was a good swap. He would get an older exec who had much more experience, especially on PC boats.

I told my captain what happened and yes, Bob had already talked to him. He had some kind words for me but I could see that he was satisfied with the swap.

Because of the 476's impending departure, he said he would arrange the transfer with a phone call to the Navy Department.

The next day I received despatch orders from the Navy Department to transfer to the PC 451 and assume duties as the exec. Then on April 27, 1942, I said my goodbyes to many of the crew waiting at the gangway and I walked sadly off the PC 476.

I crossed the dock and reported aboard the PC 451.

A few days later, with mixed feelings of regret and excitement about my new ship, I watched the 476 steam out of Key West on her way to the South Pacific.

Figure 134: **PC 451.** One of the first PCs built, PC 451 was the only one with a raised forward bow section. All other PC boats had a flush deck.

Vital Statistics
Type: Patrol craft (submarine chaser)
Displacement: 374 tons
Length: 163 feet
Complement: 65
Beam: 20 feet 9 inches
Speed: 18.8 knots

Chapter 9

PC 451

Even after I reported aboard the PC 451, I kept waiting for some official action on my role in the grounding of the PC 476. It preyed on my mind for several months but nothing happened, and soon I had other things to worry about.

Ten days after I reported aboard, the 451 was off the coast of Florida hunting for a U-boat that had just sunk three ships.

I was not aboard, but, as the captain told me later, they were lucky to acquire an underwater contact (it's always a combination of luck and skill) and proceeded to attack it several times.

After the second attack, it appeared that the target was broaching (coming to the surface), so they prepared to engage it.

"Load Gun One," the captain had ordered. This gun was just forward of the pilot house, so everyone heard the breech slam shut behind the 3"/50 shell.

"Ready One," the gun captain had responded.

But when the U-boat did not surface, the 451 attacked again with 16 depth charges. The gun crew all rushed to the starboard side, where the contact was, to see the charges explode.

When the vibrations from the first explosion hit the ship, the unattended gun went off. The shell went straight ahead, over the anchor winch. It tore off the winch's canvas cover and went into the water ahead of the ship.

9. PC 451

The gun captain turned around just in time to see the gun recoil.

"Gun One, one round expended. No casualties," he shouted as his crew came back to the mount.

As cool as the gun captain was, there was no doubt that the 451 was in a life and death battle with one of Hitler's deadly U-boats. The captain was too busy pressing the attack to worry at that moment about the errant gunshot.

Was the U-boat destroyed?

We can go directly to a postwar book written by famed U-boat ace Peter Cremer for the answer. Cremer, one of only three senior U-boat commanders to survive the war, was the captain of the U-333, which the PC 451 had detected and attacked.

Cremer writes:

> It was 6 May, 1942. ... Lifted off the bottom and saw a steamer. But at the same time much finer sounds were reaching our ears at seconds' intervals: the ping-ping-ping-ping of an asdic sonar... with which a pursuer was on our trail. My periscope was still only patched up (from a previous encounter) but so much I could recognize at once: on the flat calm surface coming towards me with foaming bow wave. It was the PC 451.[1] ... I lowered the periscope and went at once to 20 metres, ... the first depth charge crashed, making us stagger. The hydroplanes failed, the boat went down by the stern, on its knees as it were, and for a few terrible moments tried to break surface, bow-first and show itself. We were just able to prevent that by flooding, but overdid it so that the boat sank like a stone to the bottom.

---

[1] Cremer incorrectly calls the PC 451 a Coast Guard vessel. She was transferred from the Coast Guard to the Navy before the war started.

> ... These old depth charges of the Americans...
> were not precisely accurate, ... Diving tanks and
> oil bunkers were torn open, ... Depth gauge and
> rudder indicator came loose, the engine-room tele-
> graph broke, the diesel air supply mast was leak-
> ing... The minutes became eternity... And the en-
> emy would not give up.[2]

Luckily for the U-333, after 15 hours the PC 451 and two other attacking ships gave up their attack, allowing the U-boat to survive and limp home. U-333 went on to do considerable damage to the Allies until the British sank her in July 1944, when Cremer was not commander.

I was not aboard during this attack because, unfortunately, five days earlier I had been sent to Miami as the supervisor of a small liberty party. It was a group of four of our outstanding sailors that the captain wanted to reward with some well deserved rest and recreation.

Early on Sunday May 3, my captain telephoned and told me to round up the sailors and get back in a hurry. The ship had been ordered out even though it was a maintenance period.

"Hurry. I'll delay as long as I can," he said.

I knew why he would try to hold the ship up until we got back. One of the sailors with me was Bowman, our top sonarman, if not one of the best in the Navy. He had an uncanny ability to identify unseen underwater contacts and an even better skill at locating and following them. Anytime he was on the sonar "stack" we all felt that the target was as good as dead. He was the key member of our attack team.

But on that Sunday morning Bowman was tangled up with a very pretty young blonde girl who wouldn't let go.

I made a mistake. I trusted him when he said he would join us. He didn't. We waited and waited for him. When the blonde

---

[2]Cremer, pages 72-74.

9. PC 451

finally let him loose it was too late. We arrived in Key West about a half hour after the ship left.

Had Bowman been aboard and on the sonar stack when the 451 attacked the U-333, the odds are great that the U-333 would have, indeed, been destroyed. Captain Cremer never knew that a tenacious, voluptuous young blonde was instrumental in saving his life on that eventful day of May 6, 1942.

I tried to discipline Bowman, one of the most popular and well liked sailors on the ship, but he was acquitted at his summary court martial on the grounds that my order to him was not sufficiently explicit to be construed as a direct order. The verdict did not upset me, I liked him, too.

As things turned out, I didn't know how lucky I was to be on that ship. The 451 proved to be a wonderful ship. The crew was top notch, most of them experienced professionals. The young captain, Fred Kellogg, was a full lieutenant about four years older than me. He was a terrific ship handler, an even-tempered leader, and was well liked and respected by the crew. Not only that, he was a real expert on anti-submarine warfare and the personal protégé of our all powerful squadron commander, known as "Bulkhead."

I didn't know it at the time, but Bulkhead established all the policies for the growing number of ships permanently attached to the anti-submarine school. This included the iron clad personnel policies that prevented Bob Norman, who engineered my swap to the 451, from getting leave so he could get married.

Bulkhead was disliked for his rigid personnel policies and by almost everyone in the squadron who had to do any business with him. That did not include me for a long time, since I had very little contact with him. But, as I explain later, it turned out he really put the screws to me.

As is true of most hard-headed commanders, however, Bulkhead got the job done. There is little doubt that he ran the best anti-submarine school in the entire U.S. Navy. Indeed, at a time when the U-boats were having a field day on our east coast, it was in large measure Bulkhead-trained sailors and officers who

Figure 139: **Target practice.** Ensign Sotos taking target practice on the PC 451 off Key West.

helped turn the tide.

Our ship had two full time jobs. The first was as a school ship. We would take officers of all ranks, including admirals, to sea for a day and guide them in practice combat runs against our own submarines. Except for not dropping actual kill weapons, the runs were as close as one could get to the real thing.

In the fifteen months I was on the 451 we trained hundreds of attack teams for the Navy's anti-submarine efforts, and Bulkhead was really the man responsible for this major contribution. He insisted on getting good people and, once trained, he would never let them go. It wasn't until many years later that I realized his methods were necessary.

The second job for the PC 451 was to hunt and kill U-boats. There were plenty of them up and down the east coast and they were sinking ships in large numbers. We were sent out for this

9. PC 451

second job only when the U-boats did excessive damage – which happened quite often in 1942 and 1943.

On one of these "hunt and kill" assignments, we were off the northwest coast of Cuba. It was about midnight and we were steaming last in a column of three ships headed by the destroyer Noah.

Suddenly without any warning our column was attacked by one of our own Army bombers. The pilot reported sighting an enemy aircraft carrier (in the darkness) and dropped his bombs on our column of three ships.

Luckily his aim was as bad as his recognition skills, and only the Noah suffered minor damage. Apparently the ship's side was stove (pushed) in a little.

Of course, we were furious. But it is just another example of the terrible communications that existed among the different major commands in that area. Had his aim been better it would have been a repeat of the destroyer Sturtevant disaster.

One bright sunny afternoon, a funny, yet almost-lethal incident occurred. The battery at Fort Taylor, whose guns overlook the main channel entrance to Key West Harbor, fired a shot across our bow as we were heading back to port. Our signalman had not provided the correct answer to their routine challenge. They had ordered us to stop, but stopping in a narrow channel invites grounding dangers, so we kept going – even after they fired the warning shot.

Yes, we made a mistake. But we had exchanged replies to their challenges daily for months. We had a very distinctive design and there was no question that they knew us. It was probably the only time Fort Taylor fired a gun during the entire war.

Meanwhile, vicious U-boat activity off the east coast and in the Gulf of Mexico sparked more serious events.

We were ordered to assist a large Esso (Exxon) tanker off the coast of North Carolina that had been torpedoed by a U-boat. When we arrived, the huge abandoned tanker was still underway slowly, but ablaze from stem to stern. The water all around the tanker was on fire, fueled by oil spilling from the damaged ship. We spent half the day searching the water for survivors, steaming as close to the burning inferno as we could. We found no sign of life and departed after we got word that some salvage tugs were on their way.

We learned later that the fire was extinguished and the ship towed into port. High in the crow's nest of the tanker they found the burned ashes of the man who had been the lookout.

On another day, in response to a distress call we sighted a large tanker that had deliberately beached itself to keep from sinking, after being repeatedly shelled by a surfaced U-boat. When we arrived the U-boat was gone. Since the stern part of the tanker was in deep water, and safe for us to approach, we went alongside it. I then led a party of four armed men to climb aboard and search the ship.

It was spooky. We found no one aboard. Everything was in good shape. Nothing had burned. Apparently the ship had been abandoned just before lunch since the table in the messing quarters was fully set. However, we found no food in the oven.

In spite of our proximity to many sinkings, along with our convoy work, and patrols, we never sank any U-boats. I'd like to think we prevented many sinkings but that was not satisfying enough for us.

On our patrols in the Gulf we had a great deal of latitude on where to search. Early one morning, while it was still dark, our search brought us close to the Cuban harbor of Havana.

I think my captain was getting bored with our failure to find any U-boats. He decided to do something different. Without permission or notifying anyone, we entered the harbor at Havana and slowly steamed all around it. We were not challenged by anyone as we made a tourist type cruise of the harbor.

While that broke the monotony of unsuccessful patrols, it also made us realize how defenseless the ships in the harbor were. It would have been just as easy for a surfaced U-boat to make the same incursion and do a helluva lot of damage.

In spite of the war there were some people who never felt threatened no matter how close they were to death.

9. PC 451

One sunny afternoon, midway between Cuba and Key West, we saw a small dark object on the horizon. Thinking it might be a surfaced U-boat we headed for it at high speed. It turned out to be a small boat that was in the process of sinking. We came alongside close and looked into the boat. It was loaded with potatoes the occupants were carrying to Key West to sell.

There were two people in the boat: an older man and a big teenage boy. We got them both aboard just as their boat sank. As soon as he was aboard, the older man went after the teenage boy as though he wanted to kill him. When we finally separated them and kept them apart, we learned their story.

They had started out from a small port east of Havana loaded with the potatoes. The older man owned the boat and the boy was working for him. Not too long before we saw them, the boat started to take on water and the older man worked a hand pump as best he could. When he became exhausted he asked the boy to do the pumping. The boy refused unless he was paid in advance. Apparently the owner didn't have the money and the boy refused to do any pumping. He simply did not trust the older man.

Even as the boat took on more water the boy just sat in the stern while the older man apparently busted his gut in a hopeless effort to save his boat.

They were very lucky we happened to see them or they both would have been lost. There was no one else near them and they had no radio.

Once on our ship, the older man couldn't contain himself and swore that he would kill the bored-looking teenager. We had to lock them in separate rooms until we returned to Key West, and turned them both over to police.

We doubted that they could have saved the boat even if the boy helped with the pumping. The water was coming in too fast and the pump just couldn't get rid of it fast enough.

Figure 144: **USS R-12 (SS-89).** Shown underway, April 1942, when she operated primarily from Guantanamo Bay and Key West. The stern wave (behind her), the calm sea surface ahead of her, and the aft-looking officer on top of her conning tower all suggest that she is backing away, probably from a pier.

Chapter 10

We Lose the R-12

But the worst tragedy, by far, in my Key West tour on the 451 occurred on June 12, 1943. That was the day we lost one of our own submarines, the USS R-12. Forty-two men lost their lives.

Our ship and the submarine chaser SC 449 had been making practice runs on the R-12 as part of the scheduled training program for that day. It was late afternoon when the R-12 surfaced after our final exercise. Normally one of us would have escorted the sub back into port to make sure that some errant Army Air Force pilot didn't attack it as a U-boat. This time, however, the skipper of the R-12 released us and told us to go on home, and that he was going to conduct some drills on the way in.

We were faster than the 449 and were just tying up at the pier in Key West when we were ordered back out. Something was wrong with the R-12. I believe she missed a required radio report and was not responsive to radio inquiries.

The 449, which was several miles behind us, also got the orders to turn around. She arrived at the scene of the R-12 sinking before we did and picked up five survivors. The skipper of the 449 sent us a message that the captain of the R-12, who was among the survivors, said, "There will be no more survivors."

The 449 was ordered to return to Key West with the survivors while we remained out there to continue searching. We would ping and then stop and listen, hoping that there might be some

10. We Lose the R-12

communication from the R-12.

It wasn't long before we were joined by about thirteen more ships. We were formed in line abreast about 2000 yards apart to search back and forth over the area where we knew the submarine went down. It was just ten to twenty miles southeast of the main channel sea buoy in about 600 feet of water.

The entire task unit of 14 ships would steam slowly line abreast, pinging and hoping for an echo that would be the R-12. Of course, we acquired many echoes but none of them turned out to be the sub.

The sad and eerie part of the search was when we all stopped, shut off all the machinery we could do without, and just sat there for twenty or thirty minutes at a time. We would all listen with our sonar gear hoping the sub was still intact and trying to communicate with us.

That was when we discovered there were all types of sounds, most of them from within our own ships, that we simply had never heard because we had never stopped and just listened.

At first we swore that we could hear something like a hammer hitting a metallic bulkhead. But then we would find some activity or piece of machinery in our own ships making that noise. Gradually, we eliminated the self-inflicted noises so we could just lie there – listening and hoping.

Our ship had the most advanced sonar gear of all the ships in the search force. We could angle our sonar search beam to go straight down. We acquired many contacts that way but we couldn't very well identify what they were. We guessed that they were the remnants of old shipwrecks – but no R-12.

After about seven days and nights of back and forth searching, pinging, and then stopping and listening, the decision was made to install a long cable between two ships and have the catenary (the bottom of the cable) drag on the bottom. The objective was to locate the exact position of the R-12.

We were assigned to be one of the ships that would have one end of the cable while a large fleet tug would have the other end. It took us some time to rig the cable but we finally got going.

We could proceed only at a very slow speed because when the cable snagged on something on the bottom, we had to stop and maneuver to clear it.

We did manage, after a day or two, to drag the cable along a large expanse of the bottom. At different intervals debris would float to the surface, be picked up, and examined. It was very discouraging, sad, and in – our hearts – almost hopeless work, since we knew that in 600 feet of water there was no hope at all of any life in the sunken submarine, even if we found it.

I don't recall how many days we had been dragging, perhaps four, when some debris floated to the surface. Word came to us that it was a piece of clothing with the name of a sailor on it who was a member of the R-12 crew. Also, we heard there was a piece of wood, perhaps deck planking, that had the R-12 name on it. Since we did not pick up the debris we had no way of confirming the finds.

On the fourteenth day of the search, it was called off and we all returned to our duties. For many years during the war, and even after the war, the R-12 was never mentioned. But for those of us who continued our training runs in that same area, we couldn't help thinking about it almost every day. Only in 2011 did a research team locate the wreckage of the R-12 on the sea floor.

The PC 451 was a hard working school ship that had a big hand in training a large number of officers and enlisted men in the art of searching for, detecting, and attacking an enemy submarine.

On a typical day we would get underway about 6:30 in the morning and return about 6:00 p.m. We would usually take three or four prospective commanding officers to sea and teach them how to use their sonar teams to attack an enemy submarine. At the same time, we would teach the enlisted operators of the sonar equipment how to get the best results from their equipment.

There really wasn't much talk. We threw them right into a realistic scenario where one of our own subs was attacking us.

10. We Lose the R-12

They never knew when or where they would get a contact, and they got only one or two chances.

Our submarines, on the other hand, were also training their people – to find and attack surface targets. It was a very realistic two-way war game. We treated our subs like the enemy. But instead of dropping depth charges, we would simultaneously drop overboard a hand grenade and a dye marker (to color the water).

When the sub we were attacking heard the hand grenade explosion, he would release a large bubble of air. We could then measure the distance from the dye marker to the air bubble to determine whether the attack would have been lethal.

Often our own attack team, consisting of the captain, myself, and Bowman, would make the first run of the day to demonstrate how an attack team should operate.

We got quite good and gained a great deal of confidence that I believe rubbed off on our students. We also were the first ship to get new advanced anti-submarine equipment, which we would then check out at sea and evaluate for the Navy Department.

For example, we evaluated ahead-thrown weapons called "Mousetraps," consisting of four rockets on a rail welded to our foc'stle deck at a 45 degree angle. We tested these for quite a while but they really didn't work well. The idea was to launch the mousetraps instead of, or in addition to, dropping depth charges. We suggested that they use two rails, one on top of the other, to double the number of explosives launched. We thought that improved the chances of a hit somewhat, but the scientists didn't agree. I think some smaller ships (like PC boats) were outfitted with the single rail.

The most advanced ahead-thrown weapon was called the Hedgehog. Borrowed from the British, it gained widespread fleet acceptance and proved to be a most effective weapon for the larger destroyer escorts (DEs). We didn't see or test it in Key West. But I discuss it later during my tour on the USS Willis.

We were also the first ship to test and use the range recorder, a device that was connected to the sonar equipment. It presented the actual ranges to the target on heat sensitive paper, rather than as a difficult-to-read flash of bright light on the sonar operator's console. It was a big step ahead since it took some of the pressure off the sonar operator, who also had to read and report the compass bearing of the target, analyze and report the quality of the returning echo, plus control his immediate search arc with the console hand-wheel. We learned to use it quite well and I helped write the detailed instructions for its operational use in the fleet.

My experience on the PC 451 provided me with a sense of confidence in anti-submarine warfare that helped balance my fear and respect for the U-boats. It also placed me in a very small group of officers who are convinced that a well trained and equipped destroyer-type ship is more than a match for the best attack submarines.

One morning, when I was walking on the naval base, one of the Waves who worked in Bulkhead's office happened by.

"Good morning and congratulations, sir," she said.

"Good morning and thanks," I responded. "What did I do?"

"Oh, you haven't heard yet. You will be relieving Lieutenant Kellogg as captain of the 451. The orders came into the office yeterday."

"Wow," I thought to myself. "Well thank you very much for the good news. We haven't received the message yet on the ship."

She smiled as I turned around and headed rapidly back to the ship.

My skipper was very happy to hear the news since he was anxious to get command of a bigger ship. He immediately left the ship and headed for Bulkhead's office to get the message and see about his next job.

I was still patting myself on the back when he returned about a half hour later. He was glum.

"Your orders have been cancelled," he said. "You aren't going anywhere – and neither am I."

I was surprised and he was very angry.

"Bulkhead won't let me go," he said. "He doesn't care how qualified you or anyone else is. He won't accept change. Says

149

10. WE LOSE THE R-12

our work is too critical to be making changes."

And that was it. I was disappointed, but my skipper was really pissed off.

We were kept busy and didn't talk much about it for the next month. Then, surprisingly, I again received orders to take command of the 451. This time the orders came directly to the ship.

Bulkhead's office also received a copy of the orders, but in less than an hour he called and told us to ignore them. They would be cancelled.

And he was right! We received cancellation orders that same day.

It appeared that some people in the Navy Department tried to overrule Bulkhead and they failed.

This time I got angry.

I wrote a letter through the chain of command, requesting immediate transfer to a destroyer escort. I knew they needed officers for the large numbers of those ships that were being built – and I was right.

In about a week I had orders to the USS Willis (DE 395). She was a new ship, about to be placed in commission at the Brown Shipyard in Houston, Texas. My skipper, still angry at Bulkhead, was considering doing the same thing. I don't know if he did write a letter, but I learned that he too was detached shortly after I left.

Figure 152: **Tranquility at sea.** Although it is never completely routine for one ship to go alongside another, in good weather it can be a hypnotically calming experience to watch (and simultaneously hear) a close-by ship steadily knife through the water. Here, crew members of the aircraft carrier USS Bogue relax as the destroyer escort USS Willis steams alongside and refuels. The black fueling hose is visible at left.

Chapter 11

The Big League

I got my feet wet on the two PC boats, but it was my tour on the USS Willis (DE 395) that made a blue-water, sea-going sailor out of me. Until that time, my duty on the PC boats was confined to the Gulf of Mexico or within a couple of hundred miles of the U.S. Atlantic seaboard. I was never far from the U.S. mainland.

However, my tour on the Willis, which lasted from November 1943 to June 1946, covered the entire Atlantic Ocean and a large part of the vast Pacific Ocean. No doubt about it: going from a PC boat to a destroyer escort was like going from the minor leagues to the major leagues.

The USS Willis was commissioned on December 10, 1943, one day before my 24th birthday. I would become the executive officer (second in command) in November 1944 and commander in August 1945, shortly after the surrender of Japan.

My first job on the Willis was as the gunnery officer. On the PC boats the exec handled those duties, so I did know a little about depth charges, machine guns, and 3"/50 caliber deck guns. However, I didn't just walk aboard the Willis directly from the PC 451. Not by a long shot.

I was sent to a three week school for gunnery officers at the Washington, D.C. Navy Yard. It was an intense course, and I learned a great deal about my new job. For example, we spent a lot of time on fire control (the aiming and shooting of our guns).

11. The Big League

I got checked out on the handling and shooting of our three torpedoes (or so I thought) and the operation of that new ahead-thrown weapon, the "hedgehog." It was an excellent school and I felt well prepared for my new job.

On our first day as a commissioned ship, we got underway from the Brown Shipyard in Houston, Texas.

What a difference from my experience on the PC 476! The Willis was well organized, everyone knew his job, and the ship moved away from the pier smartly. I really had very little to do except enjoy the scenery and the excitement of the occasion.

An enthusiastic crowd of friends, relatives and shipyard workers gave us a royal sendoff. The shipyard rang its bells and blew its whistles. The crowd cheered and waved as we returned their stirring salute and steamed off to war.

But just out of sight of the shipyard, at the first turn in the very narrow channel, our steering gear went out. I was on the fan-tail at the time and suddenly felt the main engines back full as the ship shuddered a little. I quickly looked forward, expecting the ship to follow the left bend in the channel. Instead, I saw our bow angle upwards and gently insert itself into a thick grove of trees as we rode up on the shore.

The backing engines continued for a short while. But when we didn't move they were stopped. We were aground!

The ship was strangely quiet. I ran forward to the bow, which was indeed high and dry amidst a large cluster of tree branches and leaves. Luckily we had not collided with any of the trees. I looked over the side and saw mostly sand and grass below.

For the second time in my short career, on a brand new ship, I was aground. Luckily, however, our stern and propellers remained in deep water and, as we found out later, our underwater sonar dome was not damaged.

And for the second time in my career there was no follow-up inquiry, or investigation of the grounding. The war-time Navy has its benefits!

The skipper was a nice, quiet guy named George Atterbury, Lieutenant Commander, United States Naval Reserve (USNR). I think most of his seagoing experience prior to the Willis was operating large yachts out of Philadelphia. When I ran to the bridge to see if I could help by moving ammunition out of the forward magazines, he was so gloomy he couldn't respond. We also had a pilot aboard and he was standing nearby, just as gloomy. The exec grabbed me by the arm and quietly told me to wait and see if it was needed.

In less than an hour, a following tugboat had pulled us back into the channel. But the grounding wasn't the end of our troubles on that first day.

After we cleared the Houston Ship Channel, we were told to anchor in Galveston Harbor. Anchoring is a straightforward evolution. You steam to the navigational coordinates of the assigned anchorage, stop the engines, back the engines to stop forward momentum, stop the engines, and let go the anchor. Simple.

Normally, after the command "let go the anchor" you hear the chain rumble up and out of the chain locker as it is pulled by the heavy anchor falling into the water. Then, before it gets a lot of speed, the falling anchor hits bottom and digs in as the chain rumbling stops. The chain remaining on the ship is then secured and the ship is anchored.

However, that didn't happen when we "let go" our anchor. Much to our surprise, the heavy links of the anchor chain kept rumbling faster and faster until it sounded like a freight train was coming out of the chain locker.

The anchor did not hit bottom as we expected. It kept falling faster and faster, and the chain rumbled out of the chain locker (a storage compartment below the foc'stle) faster and faster as the weight of the chain was added to that of the anchor. There was no stopping it. All the men on the foc'stle ran aft.

In a few minutes the chain was pulled clear out of the ship. The metal hasp that held the "bitter end" to the bulkhead (wall) in the chain locker parted – as designed – and that too went into the water.

Eventually the anchor and its entire chain hit bottom, leav-

11. THE BIG LEAGUE

ing the end of the anchor chain, that should have been holding the ship, sitting in a heap on top of the anchor at the bottom of Galveston Bay.

That's when we discovered that we were in very deep water – too deep to anchor. I never did learn why the wrong anchorage was selected. I think we were told to anchor at discretion, and we mistakenly selected the wrong location.

In any event, the captain, exec (who was the navigator), and the quartermaster (who was responsible for accuracy of the charts) kept the details to themselves.

It was quite embarrassing, since the next day a diver had to go to the bottom (I never learned the depth) and attach a line on the chain so we could haul it back in.

After a few days in Galveston loading supplies, we were ordered to Bermuda for shakedown.[1]

Our luck was still with us when we almost made a serious mistake on our first night out of Galveston Harbor. It was a coal black night and our radarman reported a surface contact. This could mean a U-boat on the surface nearby, so we went to general quarters. We approached the target with our guns pointing at it and sent a challenge by blinker light. The challenge was not answered correctly so Captain Atterbury came a little closer and ordered us to turn a searchlight on the target.

None of us seemed to have any confidence in our challenge system. For it to work effectively we had to have confidence that everyone was receiving the correct challenge and reply codes in a timely manner.

We simply did not have that confidence. So risky as it was, we were not surprised when Captain Atterbury went in closer to investigate.

We got the surprise of our lives when we found ourselves looking at a huge merchant ship with a gun twice as large as ours

---

[1] "Shakedown" means we would repeatedly run realistic drills – including shooting and dropping depth charges – that test all the equipment and require everyone to demonstrate operational knowledge of battle station requirements.

pointing right at us. We quickly doused our searchlight and sped away.

Four weeks of shakedown at Bermuda was day and night work for everyone. But it was good for us. We came through with an outstanding grade in all departments, and a lot of confidence in our ability to go to war against the U-boats.

And that's just what happened.

We reported to Commander Destroyers Atlantic Fleet for our permanent assignment. He in turn ordered us, and four other new destroyer escorts, to replace four veteran destroyers in a Task Unit commanded by the captain of the USS Bogue (CVE 9).[2]

The Bogue had been converted into an escort carrier from a large merchant ship hull. She and her four destroyers, one of six hunter-killer groups in the Atlantic, had already destroyed seven U-boats, so we knew we were in the big leagues.

There is no doubt the Bogue captain was sorry to see his experienced destroyers replaced by five new inexperienced and smaller-gunned destroyer escorts. However, while we were slower and not nearly as powerful as the larger destroyers, we had much longer legs (could steam at least three times longer without refueling), and greater maneuverability.

We joined up along with the Haverfield (DE 393), Swenning (DE 394), Janssen (DE 396) and Wilhoite (DE 397). From time to time, other destroyer escorts or destroyers would operate with us. But the five DE's remained the main supporting screen for the Bogue for the remainder of the Atlantic war.

We were lucky to be assigned to work with the captain of the Bogue even though we caught a lot of hell from him. He was the commander of Hunter-Killer Task Unit 21.11 and his ship was a prime target for any enemy submarine. Our job was to protect him. We did this by staying in front of him day and night, good weather and bad, no matter what course he was on.

---

[2]The abbreviation CVE 9 is interpreted as follows: C is for carrier. V is for aviation. E is for escort. The 9 indicates the ninth vessel of that type. So, overall, it indicates that the Bogue is the ninth escort carrier constructed. The DE letters, of course, are an abbreviation for destroyer escort.

11. The Big League

Our squadron commander, who was in our squadron flagship, the USS Haverfield (DE 393), assigned each DE a station in front of the carrier. These stations were carefully designed and located relative to the carrier so that any water the carrier went through, no matter his maneuvers, would have been searched by our sonar gear. Essentially, this assured the captain of the carrier that his ship, with its precious torpedo- and fighter-planes, was always in waters free of any U-boat threat.

To launch a torpedo at the carrier, a U-boat had to to first get by a DE, or, as happened to another task unit, take out one of the DEs to get to the carrier.

It was no picnic maintaining that screen in front of the carrier. For the first three months we literally stumbled around, while the carrier skipper demanded around the clock assurance that his anti-submarine screen was one hundred percent effective.

And he wasn't shy about expressing those demands.

Figure 160: **Aircraft on the USS Bogue flight deck.** The three-man TBM Avenger was one of the key types of search and attack planes on the Bogue. "TB" stands for torpedo bomber, and "M" for General Motors, the builder. (Earlier models, built by Grumman, were designated "TBF.") Future-President George H.W. Bush flew an Avenger in the Pacific, until he was shot down, in 1944.

Chapter 12

Fox is at the Dip!

The Task Unit commander, who was also the captain of the Bogue, had simple tactical operating instructions. When he decided to launch or land aircraft, he would run the Fox flag (F) halfway to the top of the yardarm (the signal mast). Halfway up is referred to as the dip.

Then, exactly four minutes after Fox was at the dip, he would two-block Fox (hoist it to the top of the yardarm), start the carrier's turn to a new course into the wind, and increase speed to 17 knots. When his turn was completed and he was headed into the wind, he'd start launching or retrieving aircraft.

Sometimes he would launch aircraft as soon as he completed his turn. At other times, especially when there was little or no wind, he would maneuver right or left for four or five minutes until he found the wind velocity he needed.

He made some effort to let his escorts know what he was doing by running up informative flag hoists. At night he used shielded signal light guns that he could point right at us.

But just as often we received no information from him. Nevertheless, we were expected to maintain a tight screen in front of him.

In the beginning we were all nervous. For example, everyone topside had been told that a slim moving periscope protruding a foot or so above the waves and made a small silvery wake – so

12. Fox is at the Dip!

keep a sharp lookout!

Still, one quiet afternoon, it was a surprise when my starboard lookout started shouting frantically "Stob! Stob! Stob! Starboard beam, close in!" as he pointed down in the water broad on our starboard beam. I thought he had seen a periscope and was so excited that he had mixed up his words. I was about to push the general alarm when the quartermaster yelled, "What in the hell is a stob?"

I ran over to the sponson (a round metal bucket-like extension of the bridge that extends over the side of the ship to provide a clear view ahead) where the lookout was standing, and I saw it right away. It was a piece of wood floating upright, about a foot out of the water. "It's a broom handle, a broom handle," yelled the quartermaster who had his binoculars on it.

"Thank God," I said to myself as I watched it bobbing up and down as we steamed past it.

The lookout was from the South. I complimented him on his sharp eyes, then asked him, "What is a stob?" He didn't answer – but the quartermaster did. "It's a floating broom handle, sir!" he said with a wide grin.

From then on, whenever a lookout or anyone yelled "stob" (which did happen) we all knew what it was.

Nervousness wasn't confined to just our ship. It seemed that all the escorts were a little shaky. It took some time to get used to the Bogue's unexpected course changes as he hunted for the needed wind velocity across his flight deck.

It didn't take long before we surprised even ourselves with our ability to stay with him whether he communicated his actions or not. But there were hard knocks along the way, and early on he didn't always have a good screen in front of him during these maneuvers.

With his top speed of 17 knots he needed a pretty good wind velocity to launch and land aircraft. That wasn't a problem in the North Atlantic where it is almost always windy. But when we operated in the Central and South Atlantic he would often have to try a number of different courses to get enough wind over his deck.

The escorts were expected to start their maneuvers to their new station when they saw Fox at the dip. And we were expected to be on station when he two-blocked Fox for air operations.

That may sound simple, but it sure as hell wasn't. The top speed of the DEs was about 21 knots, just four more than the carrier's.[1] So when he put the "Fox" flag at the dip, we all had to move in a coordinated way, without delay.

One DE would head for a position a thousand yards astern of the carrier to act as "plane guard." His job was to rescue any pilots who went into the water.

The two DEs who were away from the direction of the turn had to speed up and overtake the Bogue to get in position. These two almost never got into position before he started to launch or retrieve aircraft.

The two DEs who were on the side toward which the turn was made could slow down a bit and usually get to their new station on time.

The Bogue almost never told us what the new course would be. We had to analyze the wind direction as best we could and use that as the anticipated new course. We were right about half the time. We learned later that the Bogue himself never knew what his final course would be for air operations. Many times he had to hunt for the right wind before he found what he wanted. So we just followed and did the best that we could.

At first it seemed that none of the escorts ever got on station in the required time. And the carrier captain raised hell. All the escorts caught his sharp barbs in equal amounts. After the first three weeks at sea, with air operations about every three or four hours from sunrise to sunset, I was the only officer of the deck (OOD) on the Willis that he hadn't jumped on for some position

---

[1] There is record of a DE reaching 28.5 knots during a desperate sea battle. See: Hornfischer, page 255.

12. Fox is at the Dip!

or maneuvering infraction. But that changed one sunny afternoon.

Visibility was excellent. We could all see from the activity on his flight deck that he was getting ready to launch aircraft. So we got ready. The task unit's current course was 005 and speed 14 knots. (A course of 005 is just to the east of due north.) We had the number two screening position, which was about 3000 yards ahead of the Bogue, 22 degrees to his port (left side). We seldom zig-zagged.

I went out on the starboard wing of the bridge where I could see the movement of the white caps created by the waves. I moved the bearing circle on the bridge wing gyro-compass to parallel what I perceived to be the direction of the white caps (and therefore the wind). Stepping to the voice tube that connected the bridge with the combat information center (CIC) directly below us, I ordered, "CIC, looks like the wind is from 130. Use that as his new course and let me know our course and speed to our new position."

"Aye aye, sir," repeated the reassuring and confident voice of Levin, our best CIC watch-stander.

"Fox is at the dip," shouted the bridge signalman who had glued his binoculars to the Bogue's bridge. At the same time Levin shouted, "Come right to 090 and slow to five knots until he turns."

Levin's recommendation fit with my "seaman's estimate" and I ordered, "Right rudder, slow to five knots, new course 090."

Of course I was nervous. The carrier still had not indicated his new course. After we slowed and turned right, he steamed right-to-left across our bow and was soon putting distance between us. I was certain he would turn to the right when his four minute delay was up. But for some reason the four minutes turned into seven plus minutes, and when he two-blocked Fox and indicated his new course to be 180 it seemed that we were almost out of sight of the carrier. I knew then that I was in big trouble.

Levin didn't help. "Recommend new course 180 speed five

knots." he said. That made sense I thought, "He'll catch up with me." That was my biggest mistake. I came to course 180 while the carrier was slowly turning to the right moving still further away from me.

After completing his turn to 180 the carrier increased speed to 17 knots, quickly moved left to 160 and then 140, hunting for sufficient wind speed across his flight deck.

He two-blocked the Fox flag and started launching his aircraft. All the other escorts were in or near their assigned screening position. But on the carrier's port bow there was a big hole in the screen where we should have been.

If there had been a U-boat in the area he would have had a clean unmolested shot at the carrier.

Like a jerk, neither I nor anyone on the bridge had caught the carrier's change to the left. I stayed on 180 expecting him to eventually parallel my course – which he didn't.

We were so far from our assigned screening position I knew I would catch hell. "Ask the captain to come to the bridge," I said, knowing full well that the carrier skipper would ask if the captain was on the bridge.

When the captain arrived on the bridge we were proceeding at full speed to our correct screening position. That didn't matter to the carrier skipper. He blasted away on our radio with a sarcastic, "Happy new year, Dick. Please join our task unit. Is the captain on the bridge?" Dick was our call sign.

Glum and disappointed as he was, the captain picked up the radio transmitter and said, "Chief, we dropped the ball and kicked it around a bit. We have it now and will be on station in a few minutes. Dick out." ("Chief" was the task unit commander's voice radio name.)

That was the end of that particular faux pas. But not for me. Captain Atterbury didn't say a word. He turned and left the bridge. I felt like two cents and swore to myself that it would never happen again, and it didn't.

But it happened to other OODs, and it happened to the other escorts. I was the senior watch officer on my ship and I wasn't

12. Fox is at the Dip!

supposed to make any mistakes. I had let my captain down and we both knew it. While he didn't raise any hell with me, I knew it bothered him.

And, of course, it bothered me. Even though I had more time at sea than any of the other officers, I had known from my first day aboard the Willis that Captain Atterbury thought I was too young to be the third in command and too young to be his top watch officer, the one who ensures the others perform well and the one he leans on to assure the task unit commander that the Willis was an effective part of his screen. But he was a fair and relatively calm skipper who took the barbs from the Task Unit commander without passing them on to his subordinates.

In those early days I thought that the Bogue's methods were really the source of our problems. For example, just prior to, and during, flight operations the carrier always seemed to be unsure of the course required for flight operations. Nevertheless, he expected the escorts to predict the direction of the wind accurately enough to preclude wasted maneuvering in their efforts to maintain the screen ahead of the carrier. Other times the carrier would delay more than four minutes from Fox at the dip to start his turn. And not infrequently he simply did not indicate his new course for flight operations.

Even though we all knew that the U-boats could detect any radio or radar transmissions we made, he continually used them to monitor our positions and raise hell with us. But if an escort violated an order for radio or radar silence, there would be hell to pay. I guess he felt that the risk of being detected by a U-boat was a small price to pay for a screen with no holes.

Communicating at night was difficult. We sent our messages back and forth by means of a portable signal lamp in a shielded round tube that looked like a gun barrel. The signalman on the carrier would point it at the ship that was to get the message and simply transmit. There was no required acknowledgement. You got the message or you didn't.

At first we all missed some messages during night operations. But we soon adapted and it was very effective – except when the carrier dropped the ball.

Another problem that worried us all was the Task Unit commander's assumption that the Bogue was collision proof. No matter the Bogue's maneuvers, he insisted it was the escorts' responsibility to keep out of the carrier's way. That changed one moonless night, however, when he was stingy with letting us know his new course for air operations.

The escort in the screening position dead ahead of the Bogue repeated the same mistake I had made earlier. He made a bad guess on the wind direction, set an equally bad course to his new position, and, at 17 knots, came within a hundred feet of the Bogue. The latter had just two-blocked Fox, increased to full speed and started his turn in the direction of the escort. Luckily he was at the start of his turn and they passed abreast on opposite courses at a combined relative speed of about 34 knots.

That incident must have put a damper on the Bogue's tactical abandon. He became more consistent and timely in announcing his course changes. And, at the same time, all the escorts got much better at estimating the wind direction and anticipating the Bogue's movements.

We learned quickly that, at night, the flames from the planes' engines could be spotted as they were revved. So by watching the carrier carefully we got the jump on his coming maneuvers for flight operations.

Even with this advance knowledge, however, we still needed to know the instant he raised Fox to the dip. That was our signal to hustle to our new position. More than once at night we missed that message. And more than once we failed to learn from the carrier just what maneuver he was going to execute to go to his new course.

The more we operated the faster we learned. While we kept getting better and better at maintaining the screen, it was still hairy during course changes at night.

We all learned to watch the carrier like hawks and stick with him like glue – both night and day. But that didn't mean we were

12. Fox is at the Dip!

always on station and his anti-submarine screen was always well disciplined and tight. It wasn't.

And when it wasn't he sure let us know.

✪ ✪ ✪ ✪ ✪ ✪ ✪ ✪ ✪ ✪ ✪ ✪ ✪

Figure 170: **Making the approach for refueling.** *Top:* A destroyer escort (left) is about to rendezvous with USS Bogue to take on fuel. Although the sea is calm, the DE has raised large spray on its starboard bow. *Bottom:* Refueling in progress. View is looking aft from the bridge of the Willis, with another screening DE in the background.

Chapter 13

Aircraft Carrier Operations

It took about three weeks of operating in waters that seemed infested with U-boats to appreciate the Task Unit commander's methods. As we got better, he got better at observing his own radio silence.

I said "U-boat infested waters" as though we had seen them. We hadn't. But almost every night we received distress calls from ships that had been torpedoed. So we knew they were there. At first I wondered why we didn't go to the aid of those ships. We plotted some of them and they weren't too far away. Later I learned that the Bogue was constantly receiving intelligence that we didn't, informing him that other ships were available for those rescue missions.

Launching and retrieving aircraft in the miserably rough North Atlantic was not a routine operation, but the Bogue fliers made it appear so. Day after day, night after night, in heavy weather with the carrier platform bouncing up and down, he would launch and retrieve planes.

The carrier skipper referred to his planes as his "Bluebirds." When he did talk about them, those of us listening on the intership voice radio could almost feel his affection for them. Watching them take off, and, especially when landing in rough weather, one couldn't help but admire the bravery and skill we saw over and over again. It wasn't long before we all shared that affection

13. AIRCRAFT CARRIER OPERATIONS

Figure 172: **USS Bogue.** Shown underway, heading into the wind, to land aircraft. This photograph was taken as we maneuvered into our "plane guard" (rescue) position.

and referred to them as our Bluebirds.

There was no better place in the world to see and feel the skill of those pilots than in the "plane guard" or "tailback" station. This was the station 1000 yards behind the carrier during flight operations. Our job in that station was to pick up any pilots who didn't make it.

Watching the planes come aboard from that close-in position gave us a real solid feel for the risks that carrier aviators live with. No matter how often we were assigned as "plane guard," almost the entire crew would stop what they were doing and watch. I would estimate that about half of all carrier landings were done while the carrier was pitching up and down to some degree, or were night landings.

There's no alternate landing site for carrier aircraft and they have to come aboard no matter the weather or the size of the seas. We were continually amazed at the way the landing signal officer and the pilots worked together.

Of course they had some problems. One particularly rough afternoon, the last plane scheduled to come aboard, a fighter plane, was waved off twice. Very seldom had we seen a pilot take two wave-offs. We knew immediately that he was in trouble when the landing signal officer discarded his wands and used the radio to talk the pilot down to a safe landing.

The pilot's call name was "Billy." And make no mistake, Billy was having problems. He was waved off eleven more times before he finally settled on the bouncing deck of the carrier almost out of fuel. It was a record that remained throughout the war. But Billy never flew off the Bogue again.

In another incident, when we were in the plane guard position, a torpedo search plane (TBM) could not lower his landing gear. After some time flying around, trying to loosen it or crank it down by hand, he was getting low on fuel and was told to make a water landing beside us.

That's just what he did. He set it down beautifully about a hundred yards on our starboard beam, and he and his two crewmates climbed out on the wing. We had a boat there in minutes and none of them even got their feet wet.

Of course they were grateful to us and we were really happy to have helped them. Because of the bad weather we didn't get a chance to high-line them to the Bogue for a few days. They got a taste of destroyer escort riding and stayed seasick every minute they were on our ship.

After that, every time we went alongside the Bogue for food, fuel or ammunition, our three friends were always there to wave at us and send us 5 gallons of ice cream.

All the incidents didn't end so happily. The Bogue planes each had search sectors. They would fly out for several hundred miles searching for U-boats. They depended on coded radio signals from the carrier to help them navigate a safe return to the carrier.

On the morning of August 15, 1944, we all heard this transmission: "Chief, this is Dixie, give me a steer." It was a weak radio transmission, but we could all hear it. "Dixie, Dixie, this is Chief. This is Chief," and he gave him a course. But Dixie never heard him. Dixie kept asking for a steer and Chief kept transmitting it but there was no communication.

13. Aircraft Carrier Operations

"Turn on your radars," ordered Chief to all the escorts. "Search for Dixie. Let me know if you pick him up."

But none of us did, Dixie's radio transmissions grew weaker and weaker and suddenly the radio was silent.

Most ships piped their radio and sonar activities through their ship-wide internal communications systems so all hands could hear what was going on. Dixie's sudden deathly silence hit the whole task unit. In days to come, the memory of Dixie's plea for a steer never left us.

But the business of war doesn't have time for "What should we have done better?" Dixie was gone. The flights had to go on.

In his book *The Atlantic Battle Won*, Samuel Elliot Morison writes on page 325 that Lieutenant (jg) Wayne A. Dixon had made contact on U-802 before he disappeared. It was only after reading that page that I learned the full name behind the weak radio voice that haunts me to this day.[1]

---

[1] The next day, U-802 was almost in position to torpedo the Bogue. Luckily, our formation was zig-zagging and the Bogue moved out of range. Three days later, one of the Bogue planes caught, and with newly installed special searchlights, illuminated and attacked the U-802 on the surface at night. However, the sub escaped. See Morison, pages 325-326, and Y'Blood, pages 240-241.

✪ ✪ ✪ ✪ ✪ ✪ ✪ ✪ ✪ ✪ ✪ ✪ ✪

Figure 176: **Avengers from USS Bogue.** *Top:* A flight of three Avengers passes over us. *Bottom:* Close-up of the top Avenger. The top arrow points to rockets carried under its wing. The bottom arrow shows the landing gear tire tucked under the wing as well. At the rear, the tailhook is also visible.

Chapter 14

Battle Stations

01:15:00, 14 September 1944 – OPERATING IN THE NORTH ATLANTIC WITH THE USS BOGUE (CVE 9) HUNTER-KILLER GROUP

It is three months until my 25th birthday. I am standing the Officer of the Deck (OOD) watch. In that capacity I am the direct representative of the captain. I am fully responsible for the safety of the ship as well as for implementing its mission and carrying out the captain's night orders.

Each night when underway, before turning in, the captain personally sits down and writes out the orders that the OOD for the mid watch (0001 to 0400) and the morning watch (0400 to 0800) must read, initial, and carry out. I will stop standing these OOD watches in a few days.

On this particular morning, we, like the other escorts, do not know where we are going. Only our Task Unit commander and his staff receive the intelligence information that dictates where we search.

All we know is that the mission of this particular carrier demands that it go where the U-boats are. Almost all aircraft carriers go out of their way to avoid enemy submarines. Not, however, the hunter-killer carriers in the Atlantic. They were a new breed of carrier, with new tactics.

14. Battle Stations

So, while we didn't know where we were going, we did know that, wherever we went, we would be sharing that part of the ocean with some deadly U-boats.

As OOD of the Willis, I am concentrating on maintaining our portion of a tight anti-submarine screen in front of the Bogue. Our assigned position is 30 degrees on his port bow, distance about 3000 yards. The Task Unit speed is 14 knots.

There are five of us DEs in a semi-circle ahead of the carrier. Each has a position as we do. The idea is to always be in position, since the screen is designed to search all the water ahead of the carrier with under-water sonar,

If we stay in position and do our job, the chances of a U-boat getting a clear shot at the carrier are poor.

Nevertheless, we know that is exactly what they will try. The carrier is the ultimate prize for a U-boat. An aggressive U-boat captain who finds himself in a good position will always try to torpedo the carrier. And while the odds are against him, it can be done.

Sonar conditions in the North Atlantic are variable, ranging from good to poor, but mostly poor. Contributing to the varied sonar conditions are water salinity, temperature gradients, disturbed water, high speed (14 knots is about right for good searching), and bad weather. Factors contributing to poor screen effectiveness include failure to maintain accurate screening position, a sleepy or lax sonar operator, a hesitant OOD when the Task Unit is maneuvering to launch or recover planes, and inadequate communications about timing and execution of course changes.

Given these variables, a U-boat can slip into position for a shot at the carrier. That is something we all worry about all the time, day and night.

On each DE, the OOD is a key player. During his four-hour watch it is his job to make sure that everyone on watch, topside, in combat information system spaces, and in the engine room, is alert, and that the ship's sonar screening capability is fully optimized to protect the carrier.

When hunting submarines day and night for months at a time, in all kinds of weather, it is easy to get bored, frustrated and inattentive. And that includes the OOD.

However, really good OODs are always on their toes and everyone on their watch remains alert. Continuous pots of black coffee for everyone, even in seasick type weather, help a lot.

I listened carefully to our underwater sonar as it searched the seas ahead – back and forth from starboard beam to port beam.

Pulsating from our ship-wide loudspeakers, the steady, rhythmic pinging of the sonar machine is almost a part of our breathing. Transmitted throughout the ship, except in compartments where the off duty people are sleeping, it is a normal, welcome, reassuring sound that helps neutralize the constant fear of an unseen torpedo.

But, what is a ping?

A ping is the sound we hear from a large, cone shaped device – called the sonar dome – that extends about six feet under the bottom of our ship. At regular intervals the sonar dome blasts a tremendous amount of sound energy that travels ahead about 2500 yards. The direction of the sound blast is controlled by a small steering wheel. The latter is in the hands of the sonar operator, who is sitting at a console in the sonar shack, just in front of the open bridge where I am standing my watch.

Why 2500 yards?

That distance (the range) depends upon the power of the sonar blast, on the water variables mentioned earlier (salinity, temperature, calmness, homogeneity), and on the speed of our ship. In homogeneous water devoid of temperature gradients and rough water, sonar will reach out further. For example, the average reach of our sonar in the Pacific Ocean was about 8000 yards, versus the 2500 yards (and sometimes less) typical for the Atlantic Ocean.

If there are no targets found within range of the outgoing sonar blast, the ping that emanates from our bridge sonar machine just fades away and we hear nothing more until the next ping.

14. BATTLE STATIONS

On the other hand, if the blasted sound waves hit a target – for example a U-boat, a whale, a school of fish, a half submerged log, or even a severely disturbed clump of water (called a "knuckle") caused by another ship's maneuvers – the sound waves will reflect off that target. They will return directly to a receiver in the sound dome as an echo and appear as a bright spot on the compass rose in the console used by the sonar operator.

The echo and bright spot indicate to the operator the direction and distance (range) in yards of a contact of some type that caused the echo. Any echo (or contact) is identified as a probable submarine until it is evaluated by the operator.

How does the operator evaluate the echo caused by a contact?

This is a highly subjective skill. A really good operator is one who has listened to many different types of contacts and learned to differentiate among the many different types of echoes that he hears. For example, an echo returning from contact with a submarine in undisturbed homogeneous water will be nice and clear. But for the most part echoes are not nice and clear. Most of the operator training is focused on teaching him how to evaluate the quality of an echo.

This is a life or death responsibility. Failure to correctly evaluate an actual submarine contact quickly enough can lead to the loss of the ship or the ships being protected – as you will see. On the other hand, evaluating all contacts as submarines leads to a waste and shortage of depth charges, a lot of dead fish, and nervous and sleep-deprived crews.

The sonar operator is not the only key player, however. An inexperienced OOD might just decide to make an emergency attack and drop a depth charge or two if he disagrees with the evaluation of the sonar operator.

Attacks can range from such an emergency action by a single ship to multi ship search and destroy operations that last for several days.

I believe that, at one time or another, every DE or destroyer OOD who stood a watch in the Atlantic in WWII initiated an attack on a contact that turned out not to be a U-boat. We even had single depth charge attack procedures for use in doubtful situations at night. By just pressing one button we could launch a single depth charge whose explosion would not only awaken our crew, but – we hoped – stop an aggressive U-boat captain.

The carrier captain used to raise hell when we launched these doubtful attacks at night because it awakened his pilots, interrupting the sleep they needed to conduct their patrols. But he was smart enough not to order us to stop. Our group survived the war and no one knows whether or not our use of these quick but doubtful attacks prevented U-boats from getting into position.

A U-boat captain always changed his behavior when he heard a nearby depth charge explosion. We believed it would make him much less aggressive, and post-war interviews with surviving U-boat skippers supported that belief. But even if it didn't make the U-boats less aggressive, dropping a depth charge is a tremendous morale booster for the ship dropping the charges.

More to the point, I personally initiated more than one attack and never regretted a single one, although none of them resulted in a U-boat kill.

Skilled sonar operators can sometimes discern whether such a contact is from a whale, a school of fish, or a U-boat. But operators with those skills were rare. Knowing these sonar contact evaluation difficulties makes it quite understandable why the U.S. Navy slaughtered tremendous numbers of fish during World War II.

For example, at 0115 on the morning of September 14, 1944, I was the OOD. The windy North Atlantic made sure everyone topside was cold, wet, and on his toes.[1]

Steaming at fourteen knots, with no lights, no radar, no communications, and not zig-zagging, our ship, the Willis, was in position two of the Bogue's five ship anti-submarine screen.[2]

---

[1]This date may not be correct, but the overall contact procedures and subsequent attack maneuvers are accurate.

[2]The five screening positions were: (#1) dead ahead of the carrier,

14. Battle Stations

Even though it was dark, we could see fairly well when we worked at it. It wasn't the type of visibility you have in the daylight. It was the type where, what you see registers somewhat of a picture in your mind.

Darkness at sea has different shades or intensities, especially on a night with some moon. If you spend enough time looking through your binoculars you acquire somewhat of a picture of what you see. And as long as that picture remains pretty much the same, things are O.K.

But any changes to that picture, even small ones, grab your attention right away. For example, it was not unusual to suddenly see a phosphorous streak much like the streak an incoming torpedo would make heading for your ship. No matter how many of these streaks you see, you can never be sure it's just a porpoise heading toward you – which is the usual explanation.

The point here is that we did derive some comfort in our ability to see this way at night. But there were always doubts. Could we see a periscope at night? Probably not, if it didn't leave any type of wake. Bit if it did leave a little white wake, I felt we had a chance to see it.

With binoculars pressed to my face, I searched ahead on both bows just as did our two lookouts. Spotting a periscope wouldn't be easy in these choppy waters. But who knows what we might see.

Three thousand yards behind us, on our starboard quarter, also not zig-zagging, was the Bogue. With a crew of about 950 officers and enlisted men and about 21 aircraft, it was safely in the center of our anti-submarine screen. However, I would have felt better if we were all zig-zagging. Course changes at various intervals make a more difficult target for the U-boats.

Suddenly we all heard it! A sharp echo had returned from an outgoing ping!

"Bridge – sonar." The loud voice coming through the voice

(#2) 30° on the carrier's port bow, (#3) 30° on the carrier's starboard bow, (#4) 60° on the carrier's port bow, (#5) 60° on the carrier's starboard bow.

tube had a tinge of urgency that split the black night like a bright searchlight.

"Bridge aye, go ahead sonar," answered my Junior Officer of the Deck (JOOD) speaking into the voice tube.

"Contact – two seven five, dead ahead, range eighteen hundred yards, possible submarine, sir."

"Roger, two seven five, eighteen hundred yards dead ahead," responded the JOOD.

I was not surprised. I had been listening to the pinging of the sonar machine on the bridge loudspeaker. So had many others: loudspeakers relayed the sounds throughout the ship, except in the sleeping compartments.

"Call the captain, and tell Chief (the Bogue)," I ordered[3] as I reached over and pushed a small red button just in front of me on the bulkhead that separated the bridge from the sonar shack.

"Gong, gong, gong, gong," the peculiar and distinct battle stations alarm erupted in all the loudspeakers throughout the ship. "Steady on 275. Standby for an urgent attack," I ordered as Captain Atterbury walked onto the bridge wearing night adaptation glasses.

"Anything else besides the contact, George?" he asked

"Yes sir. I have ordered an urgent attack. Our course is 275, speed 14, contact is at 275 about 1600 yards. Looks good sir. We've notified Chief and we're headed in."

"O.K., I relieve you, George" said the captain as he took off the glasses.

"Captain has the conn," I announced.

"Captain has the conn," shouted the quartermaster.

---

[3]This authorized the CIC people to break radar and radio silence, which they promptly did.

✪ ✪ ✪ ✪ ✪ ✪ ✪ ✪ ✪ ✪ ✪ ✪ ✪ ✪

Figure 184: **Hedgehogs.** *Top:* The hedgehog mount on the Willis, showing the protruding "spigots" that aim the projectiles. *Bottom:* Rocket-like projectiles, containing propellant and explosive, positioned on the spigots, await firing from a British warship. A propeller-driven arming device protrudes from each projectile. The operator stands behind a blast shield.

Chapter 15

Attack!

The battle stations alarm had galvanized the entire ship into action. As the gunnery officer, I remained on the bridge, but stepped away from the captain so the reports coming to me would not interfere with his thinking.

Back at the depth charge racks, linked to the bridge with headphones, Tim Maloney, wet and cold, but suddenly no longer sleepy, quickly moved a few steps to the starboard side of the after deck house, reached up and carefully removed 24 fulminate of mercury detonators from a small steel box attached to the bulkhead. He gingerly, but quickly, handed 6 of them to each of three other men, who were standing watch with him. Then, oblivious of the roll of the ship and the spray whipping them, each of the four quickly went to the depth charges for which he was responsible and carefully but rapidly inserted the little red detonators in all 24 depth charges.

With the detonators inserted and the depth charges now armed, each man carefully turned a small pointer to the 100 or 150 foot depth setting preassigned for urgent attacks.

"Pattern Urgent, armed and ready," reported Maloney to my bridge talker (the sailor wearing headphones who relayed my orders).

Then the four of them stood by the port and starboard depth charge rack release levers. Each rack held eight 300 pound depth

15. Attack!

charges. Each charge contained about 200 pounds of the explosive "Torpex." With their hands on the large levers they waited for the "drop" order from my talker.

They knew that the port and starboard K-guns would be fired remotely from the bridge.

On the focs'tle, Takis Adams, the hedgehog mount-captain, also wearing headphones connecting him to the bridge, shouted loudly above the whistling of the wind to his three fellow watchstanders, "Arm the hedgehogs, arm the hedgehogs."

The hedgehogs were a battery of 24 ahead-thrown (about 282 yards) projectiles each of which weighed 65 pounds. They landed in a 195 by 168 foot eliptical pattern and sank at a rate of 22 feet per second.

Using a small wheel secured to the blast shield behind the spigots holding the projectiles, Takis matched his wheel pointer to an arrow that was synchronized with the bridge sonar stack. And thus, when he matched his pointer with the arrow, his projectiles were pointing at the unseen sonar target.

Ignoring the slippery deck and cold, biting, spray, his three shipmates quickly straddled the hedgehog mount. Despite the darkness, they deftly removed the covers that protected the small propeller arming devices protruding from the top of each of the 24 projectiles.

Designed to detonate only if they hit a target, the hedgehogs were the preferred first weapon, since an explosion removed all doubt about whether the target was a submarine. Also, if the target was missed, there was no explosion to disturb the water.

Depth charges were different. They were set to explode at a preset depth, and when they did explode they created a distinct, hard water disturbance we called a knuckle that remained for some time after the explosion.

Any explosion underwater always caused a knuckle. And when our searching sonar gear detected it, the returning echo from the knuckle was quite similar to that from a real submarine. In fact, a skilled sonar operator rarely could discern the difference between an echo from a knuckle and one from a submarine. This

Figure 187: **Hedgehog pattern.** Two hedgehog patterns have been fired from this destroyer (USS Sarsfield) and have landed in the water ahead of it. Hedgehogs were still in use long after World War II ended. This photograph is from 1950.

characteristic of the knuckle was not lost on the more clever U-boat captains, who sometimes would release a powerful blast of air to create a knuckle or two to confuse their pursuers.

So, the fewer the explosions, the fewer the knuckles, and the better our chances of tracking the submarine. That's why we preferred the hedgehogs.

On the three inch fifty gun mount, just ahead of the hedgehogs, two sailors climbed into the point-and-train seats of the gun. Quietly but quickly, without any orders, they trained the barrel to the right to point at the invisible moving target identified by the sonar. This identification was transmitted verbally to the pointer and trainer by my talker on the bridge who got it straight from the sonar shack. A third man opened the gun barrel breech, then the ammunition locker, and placed his hand on the end of an armor piercing shell for quick removal.

The same "get ready to shoot" steps were performed by the gun crews at the two other three inch fifty caliber gun mounts.

Mike Turner, a torpedoman second class, wearing headphones and standing watch on the torpedo tubes, climbed on the tube mount and got in the torpedo control seat. He unlocked the fore and aft stowage position of the torpedo tubes, trained the tubes to follow the target as reported by my bridge talker. Then he

15. Attack!

waited.

In the combat information center (CIC), the position of the contact was accurately plotted on a chart. A message containing location plus estimated course and speed of the target was sent immediately to the Task Unit commander.

In the engine room, all generators and pumps were brought on-line to insure instant availability of all engineering resources, and especially the ability to respond immediately to all propulsion bells received from the bridge, as well as requirements generated by damage control center.

At the forward, mid-ship, and aft damage control stations, all water-tight doors were closed and all emergency repair equipment was made ready for use.

For the operator of the high frequency detection finding (HFDF) equipment, in his special small compartment back aft just above the K-guns, it didn't mean much. He was already searching all three hundred and sixty degrees of the compass for short high frequency transmission bursts. The latter were used by the U-boats to send messages back to their operations control center in France or Germany. Whenever he detected a transmission he was authorized to break radio silence and report it immediately to Chief.

In less than thirty seconds, without showing any lights or any confusion, I reported, "All gun stations manned and ready, sir. Pattern Urgent is set on the depth charges."

"Thanks, George," said the captain as he kept his eye on the gyro repeater on the bridge. It showed the direction from which the sonar operator was obtaining the echoes from the target.

On the Bogue, the OOD's first orders would have been, "Hard right rudder, new course one-zero-zero. Call the captain."

He didn't have to issue any orders to the remaining four screening destroyer escorts. His CIC (combat information center) duty officer had already ordered an emergency turn to the right, new course one zero zero. Before the carrier was halfway through its turn the captain was on the bridge.

"Which DE is it this time?"

"Station two sir, the Willis. Shall I sound general quarter?"

The captain didn't answer for a few seconds.

Back on the Willis, CIC reported, "All escorts acknowledge emergency right turn, sir, to new course one zero zero and we can see them moving out."

"Thanks," acknowledged Captain Atterbury.

I did not have to brief the captain on what was going on. I knew he had been listening to the loudspeaker which was always on in his sea cabin. As his battle stations phone talker was taking over from the watch stander, the captain walked over to the open door of the sonar shack, stuck his head in and asked, "Sy, how does it look?"

Sy was the sonar officer. He stood just behind the sonar operator who was sitting at the large four-foot high sonar console we called "the stack." Besides looking like the video display you would see in an arcade ashore, the stack, combined with a gyrocompass repeater, was connected to the sonar transmitter that extended beneath the ship.

At regular minute or two intervals the sonar transmitter would emit a blast of sound energy in the direction controlled by the stack operator. We would hear that blast as a loud ping and see a bright pinpoint of light at the zero range on the stack dial. Any object in the way of that sonar beam, such as a U-boat or large fish, would return an echo whose range and bearing was immediately visible on the stack dial.

It would have been nice if all we heard and saw was the outgoing ping and just one echo, but it didn't work that way.

At the outgoing ping, the stack operator would see multiple, but much dimmer, flashes of light caused by the outgoing blast. Similarly, many returning echoes of varying intensity (loud static) would show up on the display. So, simply watching the lights on the display for information about a possible U-boat target could be very misleading.

The most valuable information from the sonar beam, therefore, was the quality of the echo. A good sharp echo well above

15. Attack!

the background static would always get our attention and be a good candidate for an attack.

A good operator and sonar officer had to make their decisions and recommendations based on a quick analysis of different quality sounds they heard within the reverberations of the returning echoes – not an easy or straightforward task under the pressure of a possible incoming torpedo. Because the range readings from the console were so poor, a device called the range recorder was developed. Connected to the stack, it would mark the zero range of the outgoing ping on downward scrolling heat sensitive paper. Then it would mark the range of returning echoes to the right of the outgoing ping. A good echo would helpfully show up darker on the heat sensitive paper. Poor echoes appeared diffused.

A calibrated clear plastic attachment that I had helped design when at Key West, automatically measured the distance between the marks on the heat sensitive paper and converted their separation to a reasonably accurate range. Also, by examining the changing position of more than one of these incoming echoes on the downward scrolling heat sensitive paper, we could obtain the range rate of the target. That is, the speed of the target in relation to our own.

If that speed was higher than our own, we know that the target was coming toward us. If less than ours, he was probably going away from us. This type of information could also be obtained by the operator's analysis of the echo. An echo from a target coming toward us had an increasing pitch called "up doppler" (like the whistle of an approaching train). When going away, the pitch became lower, called "down doppler" (like the whistle of a receding train). All our operators could report doppler.

The captain needs all of this information. He is conning the ship with the goal of positioning it where our hedgehogs or depth charges have the best chance for a kill.

At the same time, the men grouped around a large display table in our combat information system (CIC) spaces maintained a running plot. It included all the information from sonar, the range recorder, radar, intelligence, the other ships, and the bridge. From time to time the CIC officer would make recommendations to both the captain and the sonar officer on where to search.

Sy, a junior grade lieutenant, was a sharp and confident officer. And Harris, the sonar operator, was one of the Willis' most reliable operators. So there was little discussion with them about their reports or recommendations.

"It looks pretty good, captain," said Sy.

Far from being a rookie in anti-submarine warfare, Sy's words reinforced my own analysis of what he was hearing on the sonar stack.

"Inform Chief we are attacking," ordered the captain.

CIC responded, "Aye, aye, captain. Chief (the Bogue captain) has already ordered an emergency turn to one zero zero and told the Swenning to join us."

"I knew that's what he would do," I thought to myself. "We have the screening position ahead and to the left of the Bogue's base course, while the Swenning has the position dead ahead of the base course. Although our contact is in an ideal direction from the carrier, he is too far to fire torpedoes at our carrier. But if he gets by us, his chances against the carrier are good. The Swenning is the logical ship to help us make sure he doesn't get through.

"If it is a U-boat, its captain knows by now that we have contact, and that we are coming after him. I'm sure he won't be going after the carrier while we are heading right for him, but you never can tell.

"The risk of a torpedo being shot at us isn't that high as long as we keep him ahead of us. Yes, he can and might, in desperation, fire a 'down the throat' torpedo spread at us, and then go after the carrier. But U-boat skippers know that such shots are tough, and are effective only with inexperienced destroyer escorts. The Willis is not in that category."

When an attacking ship is heading directly for a submarine, he presents a very narrow target. He is a "bow on" moving tar-

15. Attack!

get, which is an exceptionally small target when compared with a shot at the surface ship's beam (side). A submarine shooting a torpedo spread at a "bow on" target is making a "down the throat" shot. I never heard of a U-boat trying such a shot. However, some U. S. submarines did it successfully in the Pacific.

I didn't have to tell our lookouts to be sharp and alert for torpedo tracks. The JOOD was already telling them. They knew that a torpedo launched at night usually creates a visible phosphorous streak in the water heading right for you. Playful porpoises often scared the hell out of us with such streaks.

Less than a minute after the general quarters alarm had been sounded, the executive officer reported, "All stations manned and ready, captain."

"Thanks, John," replied the captain. "We're going in. Be sure to tell the Swenning what to do."

"Contact bearing two eight zero," reported Harris.

"Contact moving right two nine zero, sixteen hundred yards, down doppler."

"Come right to course two nine zero," ordered the captain.

"Right to two nine zero," repeated the helmsman.

"Steady two nine zero," he reported.

"Bridge this is CIC. The target appears to be on course 290 at about four knots."

"Contact bearing three zero zero moving right, range fourteen hundred yards."

"Recommend course three zero zero." It was the exec's voice from CIC. "It looks like he is starting a tight turn to the right."

"Steer course three zero zero," ordered the captain.

"Three zero zero," responded the helmsman.

"Contact bearing three one zero, range twelve hundred yards, no doppler. Range rate is dropping," reported Sy.

"Steer course three two zero," ordered the captain.

"Three two zero," responded the helmsman.

"Hedgehogs are tracking the target," reported CIC.

"Standby hedgehogs," ordered the captain.

"Hedgehogs ready, sir."

"Contact bearing three two zero range eight hundred yards, slight up doppler, still moving right."

Harris's sonar reports started to come faster along with an increase in the excitement in his voice.

"Steer three four zero," ordered the captain.

"Three four zero, sir," responded the helmsman.

"Tell the exec to give the orders to hedgehogs."

"The exec acknowledges your order."

"Contact bearing three three zero range six hundred yards, up doppler, still moving right."

"CIC recommends course three five zero."

"Steer three five zero," ordered the captain.

"Three five zero, sir," responded the helmsman.

"Standby hedgehogs," ordered the exec from CIC.

"Shifting to short scale on the sonar. Last bearing three five zero range five hundred yards." This decreased the interval between sonar transmissions, so we could get more frequent updates about the target's position.

"Fire hedgehogs," ordered the exec.

We all heard the sharp pistol-like shots as one after another hedgehog was fired from its spigot. "All hedgehogs clear and on the way" came the report, but it was too dark to see them fly out over the water and come down in their large elliptical pattern, hopefully to sink straight down and to hit the submarine.

"Depth charges standby," ordered the captain.

"Depth charges ready, sir," I reported as I stood to the right of the captain with my hand on the remote K-gun button.

"Range two hundred yards, bearing three six zero, sharp up doppler, losing contact due to short range."

"Steer zero one zero," ordered the captain.

"Zero one zero, sir."

"Range rate seventeen knots, looks like he's turning in to us. Stand by to drop depth charges," said Sy as he hunched over the range recorder, squinting in the dim blue light so he could see the heat sensitive marks about to be swallowed into the outgoing ping.

15. Attack!

The captain nodded to me, indicating I should drop the charges on Sy's orders.

"From the Swenning, captain, she has acquired the target," said the exec whose team in CIC had coached the Swenning onto the contact.

"Roll one," said Sy. I repeated the order to the men back aft and pressed the K-gun switch to launch a depth charge on each side. Four depth charges entered the water,

"Depth charges report, roll one," said the phone talker.

After waiting 10 seconds I ordered, "Roll two," and pressed another set of remote buttons to launch a port and starboard K-gun.

"Depth charges report roll two," said the bridge talker.

The same firing procedure was repeated two more times, at ten second intervals.

"Twenty-four depth charges launched. Starting to reload," relayed the bridge talker.

The depth charge explosions filled the night air, one after the other. The men back aft could see the explosions, but not too clearly. The JOOD and I were the only ones looking back there with binoculars. In the blackness, we could see some of the white geysers made by the explosions.

I kept looking even after the water subsided, hoping to see a broaching U-boat. But no.

"Hedgehogs reloaded and ready."

Since it was so dark, we couldn't see behind us to determine if our depth charge attack had damaged him. Nor, after the explosions subsided, did we hear any noise on the sonar that indicated a damaged submarine.

The reports flowed in quietly, but disappointingly. Hedgehogs explode only if they hit the target. There had been no hedgehog explosion. The depth charges had been set to explode at a specific depth. But even five depth charge attacks are only about 30% successful at damaging a submarine (if the contact is indeed a submarine). Depth charge attacks were, however, very successful in reassuring us, and probably even more successful in scaring the hell out of the U-boat crews.

"Steady as you go zero one zero," ordered the captain.

"Steady on zero one zero."

"Sonar, search from the starboard quarter forward," ordered the exec from CIC.

"Contact regained, one five five, six hundred yards," reported Harris.

"Not a good contact," reported Sy.

"Captain, I have cleared the Swenning to make an attack, she is going in," reported the exec from CIC.

"Your regained contact is the same one that the Swenning is attacking," reported the exec.

The Swenning's attack was no more effective than ours. But it was a good enough contact to attack, even if Sy thought it doubtful.

By now, the explosions and the sharp turns of our ship had created an immense amount of turbulence and many knuckles in the water, causing the sonar beam to return echoes much like that of a submarine. However, we couldn't afford to ignore the contact we had.

Did we feel the explosions?

You bet we did. At 14 knots we moved away quickly from the explosions and they didn't impact the ship much. However, we felt them.

With no luck after four hours of combined searching, Chief ordered Swenning to rejoin the Task Unit while we were to continue the search. Of course we were disappointed. I reviewed in my mind what might have gone wrong. From the track we had, it should have been a kill – but it wasn't. All I could say to myself was that we attacked a large school of fish, or the U-boat skipper out-maneuvered us and got away, or he was at a depth well below the reach of our depth charges.

Despite our extensive training and experience, it was far from straightforward to detect, attack and sink a U-boat. I had no doubt about the quality of our contact or whether we should have attacked. My biggest concern was that this particular U-

15. Attack!

boat, if it had been one, could have survived to possibly torpedo other ships and kill people. This, which was occurring much too frequently, often filled our radio receivers with emergency distress calls pleading for assistance.

While nobody kept track of the number of unsuccessful attacks made by all the Bogue's escorts, the Task Unit commander did complain to his captains. Not only were our attacks causing his pilots to lose sleep, he was running low on the stock of depth charges he was carrying for us.

In October 1944, I was ordered to relieve Lieutenant John Badman as executive officer of the Willis. John was a top notch officer. We all liked him and we all hated to see him go, including myself, even though I was going to take over his job.

The order came to us by radio when we were at sea. John was transferred to the carrier for a flight to the U.S. I don't think my skipper was too pleased. I suspect he would have preferred someone more mature. In any event there wasn't much he could do to change it because we were at sea and all of my records showed I was fully qualified for the job. Had we been in port, however, I had the feeling that he would have called the Navy department and tried to influence the selection of his new exec.

I had been the exec just a short time when, during a particularly bad storm, I was awakened at midnight by the boatswain's mate of the watch.

"Sir," he said, "the OOD requests permission to change the junior officer of the deck watch bill."

I wasn't sure I heard him right. "Change the watch bill? Why? What's wrong with it?"

"He says that Ensign Deers is too sick to stand his scheduled watch."

"You mean seasick?"

"Yes sir."

"Who says so?" I was getting angry. I had never experienced such a request or even heard of one. Ensign Deers was one of our newer officers. A big, six-foot-two, former second-string All-

American football player from a major college, he had every reason to be seasick. The ship was rolling and pitching and even the boatswain's mate of the watch had to hang on to something as he talked to me.

"He called the bridge and reported himself too sick to stand the watch," said the boatswain's mate.

"He has to stand his watch," I said angrily. "Get four big sailors and tell him that you have orders to carry him to the bridge. Let me know when he is up there."

"Aye aye, sir," said the boatswain's mate. I could tell from his response that he agreed with me.

Fifteen minutes later I received a call from the OOD. "Mr. Deers has just assumed his watch, sir." I learned later that, when he heard the boatswain's mate repeat the orders, Deers climbed out of his bunk and struggled to the bridge with no help.

That should have been the end of that incident, but it wasn't.

Three days later, after the seas had calmed, I was walking on the midships boat deck and Ensign Deers was coming the other way. As we passed, he grabbed me by the shirt and pushed me against the smoke stack.

"I've got a good mind to throw you overboard," he said angrily.

I was surprised and tried to push him away. "What do you think I'll be doing while you're trying that?"

At that instant two sailors happened to walk towards us. He let go and continued on his way.

I didn't pursue him or even mention it again. I knew it was a major infraction of discipline and could have been quite rough on him. But something told me to forget it and I did.

He turned out to be a fine officer and I never saw or heard of him being seasick again. Strangely enough, we became good friends.

Figure 198: **USS Janssen (DE 396) picks up survivors of the U-575.** A group of men hang on to life rafts to the right of the Janssen. A line has been lowered to a man in the water on the left. Ships and planes from the Bogue hunter-killer group, in concert with others, had sunk the 575 minutes before. See Figure 68 for a closer view. March 13, 1944.

Chapter 16

Three Kills

Our entire days were devoted to searching for enemy submarines in all kinds of weather.

Sometimes, when there was no wind, the carrier would go at his top speed of about seventeen knots and generate just enough wind across his flight deck to launch planes. We'd see them taking off, dip below the carrier flight deck, then fight for altitude. They always made it, but it was nerve wracking to watch.

In bad weather, the launches seemed easier as the heavy winds swept across the small flight deck. But we could see that the launches had to be timed to match the upswing of the carrier as it rode over the large waves. We shuddered to think what might happen if the launch occurred after he rode over a large wave and his flight deck was slanting down into the sea. But again he was good – although not perfect enough to prevent some tense moments.

The really heart-stopping ones occurred after he started night flying.

We had been flying only during the daylight hours, when suddenly the decision was made to send search planes up at night. As would be expected, all our night steaming was done with completely darkened ship. The latter was no big deal once we got used to it. But flying at night introduced problems for both the carrier as well as for the escorts.

16. Three Kills

I remember the first time we did it. Chief executed the night launches just as we did the daylight launches. Speed and course information were transmitted to us via signal light guns. Since we were all in radar silence (because we knew the enemy could detect it), we had to maneuver in the dark to our new screening positions without accurate knowledge of our distances to the carrier or to the other maneuvering escorts. Radar would have been a big help at night, but we were never dependent on it. Believe it or not, we all managed to see well enough to perform some really intricate maneuvers.

The blue flames from the aircraft engines, warming up for takeoff on the carrier, were like beacons in the darkness, helping keep us out of his way. Of course, they would also be beacons to any U-boat on the surface, or one looking through his periscope.

Getting to our new stations in the dark, with complete radio and radar silence, using only the directional signal guns, was hairy the first time! But it worked out fine.

The real problems came when the planes returned from their four-hour patrol and had to land in complete darkness. We were assigned as the plane guard for the first night recovery. We took station 1000 yards astern of the carrier and, at his instructions, turned on our yardarm lights. These were three red lights located on the horizontal yardarm at the near top of our mast. The idea, of course, was to give the pilot a horizon as he made his approach to the blacked-out carrier.

At our plane guard station, the planes wobbled right over us and then settled nicely on the carrier's deck. We could clearly see the landing signal officer's lighted paddles guiding the pilot down. It was extremely stirring, impressive, and heart stopping all at the same time. But after the first pilot landed, they held up the other landings until several lights bordering both sides of the flight deck were turned on. Apparently the first pilot to land suggested it, to give the incoming pilot a clearer view of the flight deck landing area.

Unfortunately, these new lights, even though shielded to only glow upwards, also increased the carrier's risk of being seen by a

U-boat. Clearly, Chief thought the additional lights for the pilots were worth the risks he was taking. We all thought so, too.

We knew that Chief had sent his best pilots out on that first test of night flying. As we did more of it, all the other pilots had their turn, and it wasn't always that easy. It took specially skilled pilots to operate off the Bogue and, believe me, our pilots were really good.

There's no doubt that the hunter-killer groups like the Bogue's – there were six such groups – did a great deal to turn the Battle of the Atlantic around. And in the early days of the war, one didn't have to be at sea to witness the carnage caused by U-boats.

The east coast of the United States and the Caribbean were happy hunting grounds for the U-boats. They sank merchant ships in full view of people ashore in coastal areas. The U-boats surfaced whenever and wherever they pleased to chase and overtake slow merchant ships on the surface. In some instances, they didn't waste torpedoes on their targets, using only their deck gun.

During the 24-month period from May 1943 to May 1945, in just the North Atlantic and Caribbean areas alone, the U-boats sank 73 ships.[1] It will be hard to forget the desperate messages requesting help that filled our radio room.

But gradually that all changed. A collection of land based long range Navy, Coast Guard, Army, Canadian, and British patrol planes, plus the aircraft from the six hunter-killer groups, established a near umbrella of air coverage over most of the Atlantic and Caribbean.

From late 1943 onwards, this combination of air coverage and hundreds of anti-submarine surface ships steadily turned the Atlantic war. For one thing, it forced the U-boats to change their tactics, remaining submerged as they looked for their targets. That drained their batteries and made them partially blind, by forcing them to rely on their sonar to hear targets – a change

---

[1] Morison, page 365.

16. THREE KILLS

they never did accomplish successfully. They found themselves being the hunted – instead of the hunter.

For example, on March 13, 1944, a British Vicker Wellington bomber, two U.S. Flying Fortresses, and a torpedo plane from the Bogue, along with the destroyer USS Hobson, the Canadian frigate Prince Rupert, and our flagship DE (the USS Haverfield), all contributed to the sinking of U-575.

Sinking a U-boat was not a small deal. In her 28-month operational lifetime the U-575 completed nine war patrols and was destroyed in the middle of her tenth. During those 28 months, she spent a total of 463 days at sea, 15% of it underwater. She torpedoed and sunk nine ships, and damaged three. Allied aircraft and ships dropped a total of 188 depth charges on her. She, in turn, had fired a total of 45 torpedoes, registering 19 hits and 26 misses (10 of which were misfires). On four of her patrols she didn't fire a single torpedo. And only two of her patrols were depth charge free.

On March 11, 1944, her last and fateful patrol, she torpedoed and sunk HMS Asphodel, a British corvette, northwest of Cape Finisterre (the upper left corner of Spain), then escaped from an 18 hour pursuit. However, her luck ran out two days later when the ships and aircraft mentioned above found and destroyed her, killing 18 men, with 37 surviving.[2]

The point in providing a few operational details about the U-575 is to help the reader appreciate that behind each bland U-boat number there is almost always a battle hardened history of combat effectiveness – a history usually far out of proportion to the cost of the U-boat itself. And even though I still have trouble saying it, I can't help but express admiration for the guts and perseverance of this most formidable enemy. Indeed, the U-boat and its crew was truly a remarkably effective weapon.

Two months later, in the evening of May 13, 1944, northwest of the Cape Verde Islands off Africa's coast, the escorts had been ordered to refuel from the Bogue and all had finished except the

---

[2]Wynn, pages 50-52.

Robinson and Haverfield. A few minutes later, Robinson had finished and was pulling away as Haverfield was coming alongside the carrier. Then all hell broke loose! Robinson, by now 1500 yards ahead on the carrier's port bow, without any warning to the rest of us, let go with a full depth charge and hedgehog pattern.

Of course Haverfield and the carrier parted company in a hurry. Belching black smoke, the carrier turned away from the explosions in frantic haste to separate herself from whatever it was that Robinson was attacking. "It's a submarine!" reported Robinson as he continued attacking. One DE and several planes stayed with Robinson as the Bogue moved away at flank speed.

There were good indications that Robinson had attacked a submarine, but we weren't sure that he had sunk it. Almost all the escorts, at one time or another, had made such attacks with no positive kill evidence, such as survivors or debris. But this was the first time it was that close to the Bogue – the contact range had been only 800 yards!

We learned after the war that Robinson had sunk the Japanese submarine RO 501, which had been the U-1224. The Germans turned it over to the Japanese on February 28, 1944. After being trained on the operation of the U-boat, the RO 501 left Hamburg, Germany for Japan on April 4, 1944.

In its short life the RO 501 didn't sink any enemy ships, but it sure had an opportunity! Not mentioned in the literature on this incident, is the fact that the RO 501 had gained good position from which to launch a torpedo. She was about 2300 yards on the Bogue's port bow while the Bogue was in its most vulnerable formation – steaming a steady course at twelve knots while refueling her escorts. She was a perfect target for a torpedo from the RO 501.

We will never know why the RO 501 didn't fire a torpedo at the Bogue or at an even closer target – the Robinson. She was certainly capable of such action. It would be hard to deny that the Robinson's quick, no nonsense, response to her sonar contact, without a lot of time-consuming analysis, saved the Bogue

16. Three Kills

from the fate suffered by the Block Island.

The Robinson was good. It is rare for a single ship to sink a submarine all by himself. But he was also very lucky! To get sonar contact at 800 yards and not be the recipient of a torpedo is damn good luck. A submarine that close to a DE couldn't miss him. There were no survivors from RO 501, so we will never know if the submarine was going after the carrier or if he just happened to be at the wrong place at the wrong time. Nevertheless, to kill a submarine with one attack, as the Robinson did, is something of which they can be very, very proud.[3]

About two weeks later, Robinson again provided us with some more excitement. Four planes returning at midnight from search missions were in their landing circle awaiting word from the carrier to land. However, the sea was flat as glass and there was little or no wind. The carrier kept changing course at his best speed in an effort to find enough wind over his deck to bring the aircraft down. It was a black night and all the escorts had to remain on their toes in an effort to stay with the carrier as he repeatedly changed course in his hunt for enough wind.

Robinson was having trouble maintaining station and soon was hopelessly out of position, five or six miles behind the formation all by himself. The four circling planes were finally told to come on in. Three landed safely, but suddenly our radar couldn't see any more planes in the air. The fourth plane had disappeared completely.

We realized immediately that the fourth plane was in the water somewhere, but before the carrier even started a search, we were surprised by a voice radio message from Robinson. He reported that the plane had gone into the water near him and that he had rescued the pilot.

It was a great relief and Robinson got a pat on the back from all of us.

There was no let up in our work. A few weeks later, on June 24, 1944, after some excellent intelligence, a Bogue search plane

---
[3] Ibid page 236

got a radar contact and then saw a submerging submarine. He dropped an acoustic torpedo, which apparently hit and damaged the submarine (an acoustic torpedo homes in on the cavitation noise created by a ship's propellers).

His excited radio report back to the Bogue, which we all heard was, "We got the sonofabitch!"

The pilot, Lieutenant Commander Jesse Taylor, then dropped a sonobuoy[4] – a cylinder-shaped device that, when it hits the water, releases and suspends a microphone at about 40 feet below the surface. Powered with a saltwater-activated battery, it picks up underwater sounds and transmits them to the aircraft. By dropping multiple sonobuoys, each with a different preset frequency, the underwater noise source can be tracked. Taylor's sonobuoy recorded an explosion that confirmed a "kill." We learned later it was the Japanese submarine I-52.

However, sonobuoys dropped at the scene shortly afterwards by another Bogue aircraft, piloted by Lieutenant (junior grade) "Flash" Gordon, indicated that the submarine had not sunk and was still underway. More attacks were ordered. Decades later, re-analysis showed that Gordon's recordings contained sounds from the propellers of a U-boat 20 miles away (probably the U-530) that had reached the sonobuoys through a ducting phenomena that could transmit underwater sounds enormous distances.[5] So Taylor had gotten the sub.

Sonobuoys were a new capability. For a while we all thought they would be quite useful for both aircraft and the DEs. During another search for a U-boat wolf pack, the task unit commander thought enough of them to have 60 dropped in a line to establish an underwater acoustic fence. It was not successful. The Bogue also distributed some to the DEs, including the Willis. The one time we tried to use them to detect what we thought was a U-boat, they were more of a bother than help, and we never tried to use them again.

---

[4]Morison, page 299.
[5]Unreferenced account in Wikipedia: Japanese_submarine_I-52_(1943)

16. Three Kills

By a strange coincidence, about 40 years later my boss at the U.S. General Accounting Office, Walter Anderson, told me he had been an electronics maintenance officer on the Bogue during the last few months of the war, and had been asked to look into the poor performance of the sonobuoys. After some rigorous tests he concluded that the performance problems were caused by erroneous or deliberately improper tuning, and he recommended an investigation. With the end of the war with Germany there was no follow-up, but Walter never forgot the mysterious incident. In a 2004 article he wondered in print whether it was error or sabotage.[6]

All of us, including the Bogue, steamed to the scene of the sinking to search for survivors. At the time we on the Willis had no idea that it wasn't a U-boat kill. All we knew was what we heard and saw, namely, that our planes had detected and sunk a submarine.

When we saw the debris we knew immediately there was something different about this particular submarine. A large area of the sea was full of oil and bales of raw rubber. It was all over the place. We didn't see any bodies or survivors, but some of the other ships reported pieces of flesh in the debris.

All the ships picked up some rubber, as did we. It was obvious to us that the submarine had been some kind of a cargo vessel, but we knew nothing else at the time. We learned later that another enemy submarine, the U-530, had just transferred several German technicians to the I-52. But luckily for the U-530, we did not detect them and they got away.

It was also lucky for us that U-530 didn't take a shot at one of us when we stopped to pick up debris from the I-52.

I learned the I-52's identity shortly after the war with Germany ended. Some 66 years later, I learned further that the I-52 was one of the largest submarines in the world and the largest submarine sunk in World War II. It was headed for German-occupied Lorient, France, and was loaded with raw rubber, met-

---

[6]Anderson.

Figure 207: **Rubber from Japanese submarine I-52.** The bales are displayed on the deck of the USS Bogue. Photo courtesy of Captain Jerry Mason, USN (Ret.).

als, and $25,000,000 in gold from Japan. The gold was to be exchanged for radioactive uranium that would be used in a radiological bomb the Japanese were planning to build and use against San Francisco and the Panama Canal. It has been claimed that this indication of Japanese plans helped convince President Truman to use the atomic bomb on Hiroshima and Nagasaki.[7]

Strangely, even though we were cautioned to keep our mouths shut about our experiences, I was surprised about four weeks later – when we had returned to the U.S. – to see some of those same rubber bundles displayed prominently in the window of a major New York department store.

[7] Billings.

16. THREE KILLS

Salvage specialists located and filmed the wreckage of the I-52 on the Atlantic sea-bottom in the 1990s. Its gold, now worth more than $80 million, has not yet been raised. Recovering something from the bottom of the ocean in 17,000 feet of water probably doesn't seem like much of an accomplishment to this generation of Americans, but for someone like myself, anything or anyone diving to that depth under the control of humans is nothing short of miraculous![8]

---

[8]Billings.

Figure 210: **Survivors of USS Block Island.** On our way out of Casablanca harbor a few days later after it was torpedoed and sunk, we saw the survivors from the USS Block Island mustering on the dock.

Chapter 17

We Lose a Carrier

When, after about eight months of operations, the Bogue received a new commanding officer, our operations got even hairier.

The Bogue's new skipper, who also functioned as the Task Unit commander, was a former Naval Academy football player. And believe it or not, he tossed out all our old maneuvering signals based on standard Navy guidelines. He substituted football plays. If this sounds wild, it was! We were probably the only operating task unit in the history of the U.S. Navy to implement this particular football oriented maneuvering system.

For example, when the carrier had to turn more than 45 degrees to the right of his base course he executed a "right end run," An "off tackle to the right" meant a change of course between 10 and 45 degrees to the right. A "statue of liberty play to the right" meant a course change greater than 90 degrees to the right. Plays to the left used the same degree course changes as to the right.

For all these maneuvers, we had to figure out the new base course for ourselves, until he hoisted flags indicating the new base course. It really wasn't so bad if we could figure out the wind direction, since that usually was pretty close to the base course for air operations. But even though we got pretty good at estimating wind direction, all of us made substantial mistakes.

At first we thought our new Task Unit commander was a little

17. We Lose a Carrier

nuts. But we soon got used to it and it turned out O.K. The nice part about his system was that the Task Unit staff stopped getting on our backs about being in the correct screening position all the time. The new commander, Captain Aurelius Vosseller, expected us to do our best to screen him all the time, no matter the maneuvers, but he didn't spend any time raising hell with us.

We all adapted, and it wasn't long before the simplicity in his system actually made our maneuvers relatively stress free. It wasn't all about maneuvers, though. He launched search planes in all types of weather, and the hard working pilots searched for, found, and helped destroy enemy submarines.

But it also worked the other way. The U-boats searching for carrier targets finally did find one.

On the morning of May 27, 1944, about 400 miles southwest of Casablanca, our Task Unit was relieved by the carrier Block Island hunter-killer group. We had been at sea searching and chasing contacts for about thirty days and now it was time to replenish our supplies, fuel and ammunition.

On the morning of May 29, just two days later, we were entering Casablanca Harbor. The sight before us was rare indeed. Close aboard on our left, keeled over and lying on its side was the huge French battleship Jean Barte. She, and a number of other units of the French Navy, had been pulverized and sunk at their piers by aircraft from the USS Ranger and guns from the U.S. battleship Massachusetts during the North African landings.

As we steamed past these battered ships we received word that the USS Block Island and one of her escorts had been torpedoed. The Block Island sank with a loss of thirteen lives; 951 men were saved by the escorts.

Well before his ship was sunk, the Block Island captain knew there was a U-boat in the area. At 0050 on the 28th of May, one of his planes, 64 miles away, had evaluated a radar contact as a U-boat. At 0615 the USS Ahrens, one of two DEs ordered to the scene, gained contact. She attacked unsuccessfully with 24 hedgehogs, before losing the U-boat.

At 0252 the next day, a plane 78 miles from the carrier got a radar contact, dropped a flare, and briefly sighted a U-boat. Unfortunately, flying problems caused by the flare and the weather prevented an attack. The sub submerged and disappeared.

The Block Island group continued the search. Later that day, at 1725, the carrier launched six fighter planes. At 1955, the carrier changed course into the wind at speed 15 knots, preparatory to landing the 6 fighter planes and launching two search planes. All four escorts were in screening positions. The Ahrens, on the port bow, was reported a little out of position.

Eighteen minutes later, at 2013, before he could land or launch any planes, two torpedoes exploded three seconds apart against the Block Island's port side. At 2016 a third torpedo hit the Block Island, sealing its fate. The U-549 had slipped through the DE protective screen and gained ideal position to torpedo the carrier.

The Ahrens started rescue operations for the Block Island crew who, at her captain's orders, had been told to abandon the sinking ship and swim to the Ahrens which had stopped about 500 yards away.

While stopped, the Ahrens picked up a sonar contact and guided the USS Elmore to it. At 2022 the Elmore sighted a periscope and started an attack, but the U-549 captain was aggressive and fired a torpedo at the USS Barr, hitting its stern at 2033. Four men were killed, with 14 injured and 12 missing, but she stayed afloat and was later towed to safety. At 2038 the Elmore dodged a torpedo. At 2113 the Elmore attacked again and sank the U-549.

In just 60 minutes the Block Island was sunk, the Barr disabled, the U-549 destroyed, and six fighter planes were left in the air with no hope of landing anywhere except in the water.

What happened? How did the U-549 get in such a favorable position to sink a carrier, disable an escort, and take a shot at another escort before being destroyed?

We can never be sure of the answer to those questions without knowing the track and actions of the U-549. All four escorts were highly qualified veterans who apparently had the complete

17. We Lose a Carrier

confidence of the carrier skipper. A key question is, why did the two screening ships on the port side of the carrier (the Ahrens and the USS Paine) fail to detect the U-549 before he got into a favorable shooting position?

The Ahrens was reported as being "slightly" out of position in the carrier skipper's after action report. In my experience, being "slightly" out of position could not have contributed to the carrier's sinking. An escort would have to be 800 or 900 yards out of position for it to be a factor.

I could not find the exact time that the Ahrens gained sonar contact on the U-549, but, as mentioned above, it apparently occurred when she stopped and was picking up survivors from the Block Island. When stopped, she was an excellent target, but fortunately the U-boat did not shoot at her.

The Ahrens then coached the Elmore onto the target. Fortunately the Elmore made a quick attack with hedgehogs and eventually destroyed the U-549, killing all 57 aboard.

My research indicated that a key factor contributing to the U-549's successful attacks was the aggressiveness of the two top leaders, the U-boat captain and the carrier captain. Instead of maintaining a safe distance between the U-boat and his carrier, Captain Hughes led his group to where he thought the U-boat might be.

The Block Island group had been tracking and pressing the U-549 since relieving us (the Bogue group). In the process they did extensive maneuvering, which unknowingly could have placed the carrier in the U-549's periscope cross hairs.

Captain Detlev Krankenhagen of the U-549 had to know that he had little chance of surviving an attack on a well disciplined professional hunter killer group. Nevertheless, he pressed home the attack.[1,2]

In Casablanca, our flagship, the Haverfield (DE 393), and the Wilhoite (DE 397) were ordered to the scene to help find the

---

[1] uboatarchive.net
[2] Roscoe.

planes and tow the Barr. We heard later that only two of the six aircraft crews were rescued.

A few days later, as our hunter-killer group steamed out of Casablanca harbor, we saw the Block Island crew being mustered on a large dock nearby. It was a sad, sad, sobering sight.

The Block Island sinking was a shock to all of us. It reinforced the critical role that the destroyer escorts had in protecting their carrier. It raised questions in my mind about the optimum number of escorts for a carrier.

The number of escorts plus the expected sonar range are key factors in establishing the distance between escorts and therefore the quality of the screen. The Bogue group always had five escorts. When she was sunk, the Block Island had four escorts. Also, for reasons mentioned earlier (water conditions, etc.), actual sonar ranges in the Atlantic were always much less than expected. Fewer escorts plus shorter sonar ranges could easily leave unmonitored gaps through which a U-boat could slip.

Because there are so many unknown variables, we cannot confidently determine how the U-549 managed to get into that ideal firing position. And matters will remain so, because the really thorough investigations and analyses required to uncover the answers were simply not undertaken. The magnitude of such an investigative analysis is large enough to discourage such efforts.

But I think a more accurate assessment is that no single command has the responsibility, motivation, or authority to pursue and develop answers to such questions. The Navy would be taking a large step ahead if, for such incidents, it established an investigative and analysis capability similar to that in the Federal Aviation Agency (FAA) that covers aviation accidents.

It was these damn variables and the seriousness of our responsibility that resulted in many attacks against sonar contacts. It was nerve wracking for the people on the carriers to be subject to so many false alarms – but we never really knew, for certain, which ones were false.

In the final analysis, however, we blunted the U-boat attacks

17. We Lose a Carrier

and helped make U-boat duty the most dangerous of any military service on both sides. The German submarine service suffered losses of 70%.

Yes, we lost pilots and aircraft. But for the kind of weather they flew in, and with radar and radio silence, we lost remarkably few.

Some of these losses were the result of accidents. In February 1945, we were operating with the Bogue in Casco Bay outside of Portland, Maine. It was cold winter weather and the Bogue was training fighter pilots for carrier landings.

One plane made a poor approach. His plane slid off the flight deck into the water as the Bogue went right by him. The pilot was uninjured and got out of his plane but he got very wet and the freezing water soon made him so weak he couldn't help himself. A DE steamed up close aboard but discovered that the heavy ice prevented them from putting their boat in the water. The same was true for a second DE that arrived. All of us were covered with ice and it was impossible to lower our boats. (See Figure 217.)

A young officer on the second DE who had run out to the foc'stle in his shirtsleeves to see what was going on, tied a light heaving line around his waist and jumped down into the water alongside the now unconscious pilot. He grabbed him in his arms and hung on. The sailors on deck with the other end of the thin line knew it wouldn't hold both men if they tried to pull up. So they gingerly pulled them aft alongside the ship toward the mid-ships gangway, where they could reach down and grab them. However, before they could move them that far, the young rescuer also lost consciousness and the pilot slipped from his grasp and disappeared.

The sailors on deck managed to pull the rescuer alongside and one jumped in the water to help bring him aboard. The rescuer was brought to sick bay in pretty bad shape but later recovered. The pilot, however, was lost.

We watched helplessly from a distance of about three thousand yards, unable to launch our boat in time because our boat

Figure 217: **Icing topside.** Icing of topside structures in the North Atlantic could be so severe, as shown here, that systems, such as boat-lowering mechanisms, were inoperable.

davits were covered with ice. It was all over in just a few minutes and all we could do was feel a strong pang of sorrow and guilt.

One result on our ship was the development of a skilled rescue swimming team that could go into the water in any kind of weather.

On a happier note, we were able to help when one of the Bogue's search planes became lost. Like Dixie begging for a steer, his voice grew fainter and fainter and, like Dixie, no one had him on radar. It didn't look good.

We, however, were one of three ships in the task unit who now had specialized radio receivers, called high frequency detection finders (HFDF), that we used to locate U-boat transmissions. All three of the ships got a bearing on the lost plane's transmissions. The other two bearings were different from ours, and the task unit commander was having trouble deciding which

17. We Lose a Carrier

Figure 218: **More ice in the North Atlantic.** The ice is pretty, but can be destabilizing.

one to use. A good reliable bearing was, of course, critical to giving the lost pilot a steer, and time was running short.

The bearings from the two other ships were in close agreement, but ours was not. The HFDF equipment was known to have a reliability problem that sometimes resulted in grossly inaccurate bearings.

The carrier captain got on the radio and asked if our operator had confidence in his bearing. Apparently the other two did not.

I ran back to the HFDF shack and talked to the 18 year old operator. It took me only few minutes to see that he was confident of his bearing, although he was a little scared and didn't come right out and say so. I ran back to the bridge, and at the captain's instruction, told the carrier skipper that we were confident in our operator's bearing.

The carrier skipper immediately told his CIC officer to use it. It was used. The pilot got a good steer and returned just as his fuel was about to run out. Of course, we were all happy and proud of our operator who was later awarded a medal for his work in saving that pilot.

With the technology of today, or with the improved air search radars of 1946, search planes wouldn't have to worry about getting lost. However, the Bogue and its planes didn't have such equipment. I understood that they had a radio transmitter on the Bogue and specialized receivers on the planes.

By and large the system worked well. Our planes could and did go out several hundred miles in all kinds of weather while the Bogue maneuvered on various courses and speeds. But sometimes the equipment simply didn't work correctly, as in Dixie's case.

A hot run in a torpedo tube is another incident worth recalling. It occurred in the afternoon one cold windy day in the North Atlantic when I was still the gunnery officer. I was on the bridge when the torpedo tube watch reported smoke coming from one of the torpedo tubes. I immediately ran back there and, sure enough, there was a steady wisp of smoke coming out the after end of one of the tubes.

Our torpedoes were loaded in a single torpedo mount consisting of three side-by-side tubes welded together. Smoke was coming out of the number two, the center tube. I placed my hand on the tube and it was hot! I quickly withdrew it or I would have had a severe burn. I could also hear the torpedo propellers whirring. The torpedo thought it was in the water heading for a target.

Dyrda, my chief gunners mate, showed up and quickly rigged a hose. He started spraying water on the top of the tube. We reported it to the bridge and the captain wanted to know if there was a danger of an explosion if the heat reached the warhead at the head of the torpedo.

My answer was that I didn't know.

The captain reported it to the task unit commander on the Bogue, who asked the same question, "Is there any danger of an

17. We Lose a Carrier

explosion?" The captain's reply was the same: he didn't know, but we were attempting to cool it with water.

We were ordered to leave the formation until the crisis was resolved. As we pulled out of the screen the DE on our port side replaced us.

I got a little worried that there might be an explosion. Otherwise, why would the task unit commander reduce the effectiveness of his anti-submarine protection by ordering us out of the screen? He had a lot of smart guys on the carrier, and perhaps they knew something about hot runs that I didn't. The captain must have come to the same conclusion because he came on the ship's loudspeaker and announced that we had a serious hot run going on in the torpedo tubes. He then ordered that all hands not on watch should either go as far forward or as far aft as they could to clear the midships area where the torpedo was smoking.

I requested permission to fire the torpedo in a direction away from the task unit. After a few minutes the captain said no. But Dyrda pointed out that, because of the heat, the torpedo was now probably fused to the tube itself and there was no way we could fire it out of the tube even if we tried.

I could see that he was right. He and I remained beside the smoking torpedo wetting it down with salt water from a garden size hose.

I don't know how long the hot run continued. It seemed forever as we stood there helplessly spraying a thin stream of salt water all over the tube. Suddenly I stopped hearing the whirling propellers, and a few minutes later the smoke stopped. We kept spraying the tube for at least another half hour until it became cool to the touch. The crisis was under control and we soon rejoined the screen in front of the carrier.

One thing, of course, was certain. Our entire torpedo battery of three torpedoes was not ready for use. Although we believed that the other two could be fired, we weren't sure that they could be fired safely. Anyway, that's what we reported to the task unit commander after we returned to our screening station.

He never did ask us what caused the hot run and, despite a lot of theories, I never found out what caused it. I had been to gunnery school before joining the Willis, and there was no mention of hot runs. In retrospect, it is clear that very little was known about that subject in the U.S. Navy in general, and among destroyer escorts in particular.

While the hot run didn't reflect well on the quality of our overall readiness, the U-boats had their problems too. In his memoirs as first officer of the U-156, Paul Just relates a really boneheaded but tragic experience. It seems that the gun crew of the U-156 forgot to remove the plug from the gun muzzle before a firing. This caused the shell to burst in the muzzle killing one man and causing another to lose his leg.[3]

On June 29, 1944, about a month after the loss of the Block Island, our task group entered Port Royal Bay, Bermuda.

I was the officer of the deck as we entered port. They have a particularly difficult channel there, and I was really on my toes. Even so, I couldn't help but notice what I made out to be a submarine, anchored well away from the channel. We had U.S. submarines there for training, so seeing a submarine was not unusual.

I wondered why this one was so far out in the bay. There was no nearby activity, so I took a good look at it. The more I examined it, the more puzzled I became. I had never seen an actual U-boat, only pictures of them. And this one sure looked like one of the U-boat pictures I had seen.

I mentioned my suspicions to the others on the bridge and got several laughs in return. Eventually, I, too, thought it was laughable. It was crazy – a surfaced U-boat anchored in Bermuda's Port Royal Bay!

So I shut up and dismissed it from my mind as we continued in.

---

[3] Reference: Just.

17. We Lose a Carrier

We departed Bermuda a few days later. Once again, I saw the strange vessel, sitting by itself – but said nothing. We returned to hunting submarines and I never gave my "U-boat sighting" another thought. That is, until after the war ended and the nation learned that the U-505 had been captured on June 4 by the hunter killer group of the aircraft carrier Guadalcanal, commanded by Captain Daniel Gallery, USN.

It was the U-505 I had seen anchored in Port Royal Bay. The extraordinary value of the communications encryption equipment and other materials that had been recovered with her would have vanished if the Germans had known we had her. Thus, the sub had been towed and parked in Bermuda by the Guadalcanal group as part of a successful effort to keep the secret.

The capture of that boat was such a fantastic accomplishment that it merits a few more words here.

Events began when one of the Guadalcanal's screening ships, the USS Chatelain (DE 149), got a sonar contact 800 yards on its starboard bow. With the help of two fighter planes from the Guadalcanal, the location of the U-boat was pinpointed and the Chatelain dropped 12 depth charges which bracketed the U-boat. When the charges exploded the U-boat lost power, its rudder was jammed to the right, and water spray from damaged machinery made the engineers think the hull had been pierced. The captain, Oberlieutnant Harald Lange, believed his ship was fatally wounded and brought her to the surface. As the ships and aircraft attacked, he ordered his men to scuttle the ship and abandon it.

With the exception of one German sailor who was killed, Captain Lange's entire crew was rescued. Three of them, including Lange, were wounded.

The U-boat's wounds proved to be nonfatal. She remained underway at about 7 knots, steaming in a tight circle, after she had been abandoned.

A team from another escort, the USS Pillsbury (DE 133), boarded the U-boat, fully expecting it to sink from exploding demolition charges typically used to scuttle a vessel. Fortunately, for them, however, Lange's crew did not carry out his orders to set demolition charges, although they did open critical valves to let sea water pour in.

The Pillsbury boarding party, later augmented by a group from the Guadalcanal, managed to find and close key valves that were letting the sea water in, and so saved the boat. Subsequently, 14 demolition charges were found and destroyed.

It was an incredible feat.

I could appreciate first-hand their amazing accomplishment since I was the leader for a similar boarding team on the Willis – a team which I thought was just a paper capability, since we had absolutely nothing to practice with, no information about possible demolition sites or key valves, and no one who had ever been in a submarine – except for the one visit I had in a U.S. submarine.

Their actions in saving the U-505 and capturing materials that were immediately put to effective intelligence use were almost miraculous!

The boarding team was subsequently honored and its leader, Lieutenant (junior grade) Albert David, was awarded the Congressional Medal of Honor.

Captain Gallery, who had planned and commanded the mission, was initially less fortunate. Although Gallery had acted with approval, the Navy's top admiral, Ernest King, was livid when he heard of the capture, and demanded Gallery be court-martialed. King knew that, if the Germans learned of the capture, they would immediately change their cryptographic systems and start new ones from scratch, erasing years of successes and extremely valuable gains the Allies had already made in reading German classified communications. And it would make useless even the cryptographic equipment captured with the U-505. That is exactly what happened in 1943, when guerillas broke into the Japanese embassy in Portugal. The Japanese then changed their entire cryptographic system, thereby destroying the considerable gains the U.S. had made in reading Japanese communications – gains the U.S. never again achieved.

17. WE LOSE A CARRIER

In the U-505 case, great pressure was put on everyone to not reveal any information about the capture. Every sailor in the Task Group was required to sign an oath of secrecy. The prisoners from the U-505 were sent to an isolated prison camp and, contrary to the rules of the Geneva Convention, were barred from letting their families know they were still alive until after the war ended.[4]

Eventually, however, Captain Gallery was awarded the Distinguished Service Medal. Today, the U-505, which once was one of the most important secrets of World War II, is on public display at the Chicago Museum of Science and Industry. It remains the only enemy warship that the U.S. Navy has boarded, captured intact, and towed home since the War of 1812.[5]

---

[4] Keith, page 270.

[5] Gallery, a Chicago native, arranged for the U-boat to be displayed there. The Museum of Science and Industry is housed in the former Palace of Fine Arts which had been abandoned and left to deteriorate after the 1893 World's Columbian Exposition. I know because, as a 12 year old (1931), my 5:00 am to 7:30 am newspaper route ended a block away at 57th and Lake Park Ave. Together with other paper boys we would sneak in and tour the huge abandoned building. It was a spooky place with large statues lying in a water-filled basement.

Figure 226: **High line during refueling.** The "high line" is a method to move people, supplies, or mail between two ships at sea. The ships steam side-by-side, about 50 feet apart, and rig a strong cable between them. The arrow shows a bag of movies and ice cream being transferred from the Bogue to the Willis as First Lieutenant Roy Thompson watches (upper right). Pharmacist Mate Jorgenson is at lower right. When a person is transferred, he or she sits in a specially designed chair, the "breeches buoy," hanging from a wheel that rolls on top of the cable. Once in the chair, sailors on the receiving ship pull the chair, and its passenger, over. High-lining is often done during refuelings.

Chapter 18

We Lose the USS F. C. Davis

In our type of operations it was rare for just one plane or one DE to sink a U-boat all by itself. For the most part, it was a string of cumulative individual events, sometimes over days, in which both aircraft and DEs participated. Then a hedgehog barrage or a depth charge attack by one plane or one ship was usually the final blow – the coup de grace – that sealed the U-boat's fate.

For example, on August 20, 1944, a torpedo plane from the Bogue detected a U-boat. It was attacked and damaged before it could submerge. Part of the damage was an oil leak that created a track on the surface. Other planes followed the track, continued the attacks, and sank the U-boat which turned out to be the U-1229. My ship was one of the DEs ordered to the scene to assist and/or pick up survivors.

However, to our dismay the U-1229 was destroyed before we got there. We did see survivors and bodies from the U-1229, and stopped to pick up three bodies whose clothing we removed to search for intelligence. Then the naked bodies were returned to the sea.

It is not a good idea to stop completely in an area where a U-boat has been sunk. It was common knowledge that they often hunted in groups known as "Wolf-packs," so we worried there might be another boat nearby.

In picking up the bodies from the U-1229, we remained stopped

18. WE LOSE THE USS F. C. DAVIS

for just a few minutes. To our horror, when we rang up ahead one-third on the engine order telegraph to get underway again, nothing happened. A phone call to the engine room revealed that there was not enough air in the air banks to restart our diesel engines. "Give us five minutes and we'll be ready," they said.

Looking down from the bridge, as we sat there with no propulsion power, I watched, for four very long minutes, as the bodies of the three naked, dead young men, now directly below me, bumped gently against the side of our ship. It was a bright sunny day and the dark blue sea was as flat as glass. The contrast between the exceptional whiteness of their skin and the dark blue water was startling and disturbing.

"It must be miserable in those submarines," I thought to myself as I realized how long they must have been without sunlight. In just those four minutes before our engineers got enough air pressure to start the engines, that sight seared itself forever into my mind. Thankfully, they were face down and I didn't have to look at their faces.

I often wondered what life was like in the U-boats. I knew they were a lot worse off than we were. But submarine sailors are a different species. The U.S. submariners I knew actually preferred submarine duty.

At one time, I too, thought I might like submarine duty, until I made a dive in one of the R-boats at Key West. It was cramped, noisy, stuffy, and it leaked. Of course the leaks were routine to the submariners but I thought otherwise. I felt like I was in a steel coffin and that cured me of any desire for the submarine service.

When I was on the Nitro, I was convinced that sooner or later we would get a torpedo. During the day, at sea, we always carried a life jacket with us and most kept our shoe laces untied (so if we ended up in the water we could quickly kick off our shoes and swim).

After about two weeks of waiting for it to happen, I suddenly realized that my fear and apprehension were making it worse for me. Realistically, if the Nitro had ever been torpedoed our life jackets would have been useless.

I forced myself to accept a fatalistic view of my circumstances and went back to conducting myself as I had before the war started. Except, I was much more alert and tense when I stood watches.

On the Willis, whenever we dropped depth charges – which was quite frequently – I didn't spend any time thinking about the guys in the U-boats. I worried about their torpedoes.

It wasn't until long after the war ended and the U-boat captains started writing books that I understood and appreciated how really miserable life was in the U-boats. Not only does all this information put my experiences into perspective, and answer many of the questions I have lived with, it gives me a deeper and more profound appreciation for the complex, unanswerable questions which still make mortal enemies of people who don't really know each other.

Especially startling to me is seeing formerly top secret reports now spread all over the Internet. One example is the questioning of the survivors of the U-1229. When the U-1229 sank, one of the other DEs picked up several survivors, among them a German spy named Oskar Mantel. The U-boat was going to put him ashore at some lonely U.S. beach.

Oskar had spent a lot of time in America and spoke perfect American English. He also had $10,000 in U.S. money on him when he was picked up. At first, Oskar was reticent and would not respond to questions. The DE captain sent for an interpreter who tried to speak to the prisoner. Instead the interpreter, a sailor named Tailor, and the prisoner got into an argument.

"He won't speak to me because I am Jewish," Tailor told the captain.

Without thinking, the captain asked the prisoner, "Is that right?"

Then, in perfect English, Oskar said, "That's right. No member of the master race will soil himself by having contact with a pig such as this one. If you have any questions I will be glad to answer them to you."

Later, when the DE was transferring the prisoners to the Bogue by high line (see Figure 226), the weather was a little rough. An

18. WE LOSE THE USS F. C. DAVIS

alert officer on the DE noticed that Oskar was frightened at the prospect of the high line transfer. The process can be scary if you are not accustomed to it. The rumor was, that by threatening to give him slower, even wet rides between the ships, they got him to talk freely.

Even more bizarre, some years after the war ended, Oskar sued the U.S. Government, asking for return of the $10,000 that he claimed was his property. He did not succeed.

Some of the newly available information helps answer questions that all of us in the Bogue group had during the war.

For example, on April 16, 1945 a force commanded by the Bogue, consisting of 22 destroyer escorts and two carriers (Bogue and USS Core), formed a barrier sweep line off the east coast of the United States. Code named "Operation Teardrop," the DEs were stationed about five miles apart, producing a sweep barrier line about 100 miles long.[1] My ship was approximately in the center of the sweep line.

This technique was effective. We relieved a similarly sized group that had just destroyed three U-boats: U-518, U-880, and U-1235.

We knew something was up as our group of 20 DEs steamed back and forth, but we had no idea, at the time, what it was. All we did knew was: stay in formation, steam in line abreast, and search. The Bogue anchored one end of the sweep line, while the USS Core anchored the other end. Of course, their planes were always in the air searching.

Years later we learned there were intelligence reports that German commanders had ordered six U-boats to operate off the U.S. east coast. British and American code-breakers issued these reports after reading messages the Germans had encrypted with their "Enigma" machines – messages the Germans thought were unbreakable.

Although the mission of these six U-boats had not been intercepted, Oskar Mantel, the captured spy, said submarines were

---

[1] Morison, pages 347, 350.

going to strike east coast cities using flying bombs like those already launched on London. Two other captured spies corroborated this. Very large explosions that occurred as U-1235 and U-880 went down increased concerns they had some type of special weapon aboard.[2]

Thus, the objective for Operation Teardrop was "to bar off the entire Eastern seaboard of Canada and the United States to a phalanx of snorkel boats."[3] (Snorkel U-boats were equipped with a 26 foot long steel cylinder which permitted them to run their diesels submerged, charging batteries if needed.)

On April 23, a Bogue search plane discovered the U-546 on the surface, about 70 miles from the Bogue and not far from the sweep line. But the sub dove and escaped. DEs sent to the scene could not locate the U-boat.[4]

The next morning the U-546 torpedoed and sank the USS Frederick C. Davis, one of the DEs in the sweep line. Only 66 of the 192 crew survived.

Because I thought this an exceptionally heavy loss of lives with so many ships nearby, I tried to learn more. It was difficult to reconstruct what actually happened that morning of April 24, but my analysis, summarized below, may throw new light on the events.

Here is the timeline:

08:29 – Frederick C. Davis acquires a sharp clear sonar contact 2000 yards on her starboard bow. Davis tracks the contact down its starboard side and loses it aft in the noise from its Foxer gear (a noise maker protection against acoustic torpedoes). She then reverses course to the right in an effort to regain contact.

08:34 – Davis regains sonar contact on her port side and starts to attack. At the same time Herr Kapitan Leutnant Paul Just, captain of the U-546, is tracking the Davis through his periscope. He sees the range between his U-boat and the Davis closing –

---

[2]Morison, page 349.
[3]Morison, page 345.
[4]Morison, pages 351-353.

18. We Lose the USS F. C. Davis

800 meters – 700 meters – 400 meters. He knows he must kill the Davis or be killed!

08:35 – At 400 meters (432 yards), a can't miss range, Kapitan Just fires one torpedo, hitting Davis amidships on the port side (note: Kapitan Just's manuscript says he fired at 08:40).[5] The torpedo explosion splits the Davis in two and she sinks in five minutes. The U-546 submerges to 120 feet and tries to escape from the remaining DEs.

The high death rate on the Davis was caused by a number of factors.[6] First: the terrible explosion from the torpedo killed a large number – for example, all the officers and stewards at breakfast in the wardroom, and most men on the bridge, including the captain who was cut in two by a wire shroud when the mast snapped off.

Second: two of the Davis' depth charges (which were damaged and could not be set on safe) exploded when she sank, injuring many of the men in the water.

Third: some of the men who assembled on the after section had been sleeping and did not have life jackets.

Fourth: one of the rescue ships was forced to temporarily stop rescue efforts when she detected the U-boat nearby.

And fifth: the frigid waters of the North Atlantic helped increase the toll.

What could the Davis have done to prevent itself from being hit? That's a very tough question to answer with certainty, given the myriad variables involved. I can speculate, however.

Our anti-submarine school in Key West, and others, trained sonar operators to report a new contact as "possible submarine," then go through a quick evaluation procedure before classifying it as a positive submarine justifying an attack.

Although it is unclear how much time the Davis took to evaluate and classify the contact, she did take the time to track the contact down her starboard side, lose it, reverse course, and re-

---

[5]Just.
[6]Morison, pages 351-353

acquire the contact before starting her attack – when she was hit. Those are precious minutes.

My personal policy was to attack upon first receipt of a good returning sonar echo. In this instance it would have been upon receipt of the initial sharp, clear contact at the 2000 yard range.

However, I am aware that my personal policy was considered a trigger happy, shoot first and ask questions later procedure. It was also known as "evaluation by depth charge."

But for me it was comforting. I had listened to underwater sonar contacts with our own submarines at the Key West sonar school almost daily for a year. Even though we taught the evaluation procedure I had no confidence in it, except when I knew the sonar operator and trusted him. Even then, I was convinced that we should attack doubtful classifications.

As officer of the deck on the Willis I followed that policy on at least three occasions when we acquired contacts.

The downside of my particular policy was that everyone in the task unit went to battle stations, the pilots on the carrier lost sleep, we used a lot of ammunition, and many fish were killed.

Nevertheless, my experience tells me that the Davis outcome might have been different, had the Davis attacked immediately upon first acquiring the sonar contact at 2000 yards instead of waiting for six minutes.

I cannot help but wonder, also, about the U-546. What was it like in that cramped, hot, oxygen-limited U-boat trying to escape from battle-tested professional U-boat killers?

"Five destroyers against one U-boat. Hell awaits us," Captain Just wrote in his manuscript. And he was right!

For twelve hours the search by multiple DEs was unrelenting. They would go away and raise the hopes of the embattled Germans. But they always came back. There was attack after attack. The depth charges damaged the U-boat, but he hung on.

"The boat is a mess. Whatever that is not bolted or nailed on, lays smashed on the floor, total darkness," he wrote. "Everywhere gurgling, hissing water sounds. Hastily, the biggest leaks are covered as well as possible," he continued.

18. WE LOSE THE USS F. C. DAVIS

Figure 234: **Survivors of the U-546.** A life raft carrying survivors from German submarine U-546 floats near U.S. Navy destroyer escorts, which are dangerously stopped in the water. The Willis, nearby, bore the same camouflage paint scheme.

The boat took on 8 tons of water through the leaks and sank to 590 feet (maximum safe depth is 656 feet). Water was everywhere in his boat and his crew fought to prevent further sinking. Just had to decide what to do, and he did: "... the devastation of the boat is unbelievable. – Surface. ... All men abandon ship."[7]

It was a sunny day, relatively calm sea with good visibility as, from about five miles away, we watched the U-546 surface within a ring of destroyer escorts. They all were shooting at her even as aircraft attacked. In a short time she was gone. There were 33 survivors, including Kapitan Just. (See Figure 234.) The sweep line was reformed and we continued our search with no more contacts.

Kapitan Just stated that, when rescued, he and his crew were treated fairly and with dignity aboard the DE that picked him up. However, he was transferred to the carrier and flown to Newfoundland where he was interrogated and, as he claims, tortured in an effort to obtain information.[8]

---

[7]Just.
[8]Just.

As mentioned earlier, our massive sweep had been prompted by fears that specially-equipped U-boats would attack New York and other major east coast cities with "buzz bombs" similar to the V-1. This, however, was news to the U-boat kapitan and, despite torture, there was nothing he could reveal. The torture was stopped when the captain of the DE that had picked him up learned about it and forced a cessation. Ultimately, the two captains became close friends after the war ended, even spending vacations together.

It turns out that there was no German plan to attack New York or other cities. But, for a period, it was a major concern of our military high command.

As a group, the Bogue and her escorts were credited with the highest number of kills (13) among all the American units in the Atlantic. The destroyer escorts, including the Willis, who were with the Bogue for six of those kills, were all awarded the Presidential Unit Citation for combat operations in the Atlantic.

When the war ended in the Atlantic, we couldn't believe it. It was so unreal that we didn't relax any of our war time steaming readiness.

It was on May 8, 1945, my brother Gus's birthday, that we received the message that Germany had surrendered. That was followed by copies of messages that the German high command transmitted to their U-boats. All U-boat captains were ordered to remain on the surface, fly a large black flag, and try to make contact with, and surrender to, the closest Allied ship.

We were elated at first, convinced that we would see the hated U-boats on the surface flying the large black flags, hopefully surrendering to us.

But no. Our hunter-killer group remained on war time alert for a good four days after the surrender, while other ships, mostly the Coast Guard, contacted the surfaced U-boats and accepted their surrender.

The U-boats did not all surface and surrender quickly. They took their time. Fortunately, the ships that were receiving the surrenders were considerate enough to let us all know what was

18. We Lose the USS F. C. Davis

going on. But our group steamed about, ready to continue the war at a minute's notice.

I have to agree it was a good precaution. One of the U-boats that did not surrender was the U-530. He was on patrol off Long Island and made unsuccessful attacks on convoys after the war ended. He then sailed south to Argentina, arriving there on July 9. A month later a second U-boat, U-977 joined him. Unfortunately for them, their crews were interned in Argentina and their ships turned over to the United States.

The skipper of the U-234 had a different problem. His ship was en route to Japan when the war ended and he was ordered by the German high command to surrender his ship.

He discussed with his crew the option of continuing to Japan since they were still allies and he apparently had cargo of value to the Japanese. He also had as passengers two senior Japanese naval officers. The latter tried to convince the captain that they would be well received and not made prisoners as would happen if they surrendered to the U.S.

It was not a simple decision. The U.S. had announced that U-boats failing to surrender would be considered pirate ships, and would be destroyed on contact. Hearing a radio broadcast that said Germans in Japan were being rounded up, and surmising that he and his crew would not be welcome in Japan, the U-boat skipper informed his two passengers that he was going to surrender to the Americans.

Both his passengers, who had a great deal of classified knowledge, decided to commit suicide rather than face the interrogations of the Americans. They chose a slow process for the suicide attempt and could have been revived had the U-boat captain so desired. However, he let the process continue until they died.

His surrender was significant since the cargo, which included radioactive materials intended for Japan, was of great intelligence value.[9]

---

[9]Morison, page 360.

About four days after the war ended, we were released and steamed into New York. By then the celebrations were done, and all we had to look forward to was the refitting of our ship for the different war in the Pacific.

It took about a month to add to our armament. And during that period, of course, we all took a welcomed leave to visit our homes and families.

Figure 238: **USS Franklin burning and listing.** Two bombs dropped from a Japanese airplane on March 19, 1945 caused massive secondary explosions of the Franklin's own ordnance and aviation fuel, crippling her. 724 men were killed and 365 wounded. This picture was taken hours after the attack by PHC Albert Bullock from the light cruiser USS Santa Fe, which went alongside to help the stricken carrier. The Franklin was the most heavily damaged carrier to survive the war. As my ship, the Willis, was departing New York City for the Pacific about two and a half months later (early June 1945), we saw the Franklin as she sailed up the Hudson River for repairs in the Brooklyn Navy Yard. We passed close aboard on opposite courses and got a close frightening look at the horrible damage she suffered.

Chapter 19

Guam

When I got back to the ship after my leave I was amazed at the changes. The Brooklyn Navy Yard people were really fast and thorough.

Our torpedo tubes were gone and we had a brand new 40 mm automatic anti-aircraft quad-gun mount. It consisted of four gun barrels that could really pour out the ammunition. It was very comforting to see them since they were very effective against enemy planes. And we knew we would need them when we got to the Pacific war.

We also had several more 20 mm guns installed. I was disappointed that they didn't do something about our 3"/50 main battery guns. We had three of these guns, but, just as on the Nitro, each one was controlled and aimed locally. This was far different from the bigger, faster destroyers, that had a centralized director, with its own fire control radar, that controlled all three of its bigger 5"/38 caliber guns.

For good shooting we were dependent on two men: the pointer (who manually controlled gun movement in the vertical plane) and the trainer (horizontal plane). If they were really good and worked together, we had a chance against enemy aircraft. (Figure 240, Figure 241.) But our gun crews never did enough shooting to have confidence in their skills. Hell, we had trouble hitting sleeves towed by aircraft in our gunnery practices. We knew we

19. GUAM

Figure 240: **Crew for a 3"/50 gun.** From a 1944 Navy training document, this photo shows the people needed to fire a 3"/50 gun like the ones we had on the Willis. The pointer and trainer aimed the gun. The shellman caught the hot casing ejected from the gun after the shell was fired. (Note his thermal gloves.) The gun captain was usually one of our more experienced sailors. The bridge would give him target information, but he was in charge of the gun.

One of our hot shellmen was a tough, rugged kid from New Jersey. Always, just before the gun went off, he would pull up his gloves like he was getting ready to catch the ejecting shell. Invariably, however, he was still pulling on his gloves as the shell whizzed past him. I never saw him stop or catch one. We finally changed him for a tall 19 year old kid from the south. He would put his gloved hand on the breech and keep it there when the gun went off. He would catch the shell as it came out of the breech (they're big), hold it up with one hand, then drop it to the deck. We called that "riding the breech" and he became a very popular sailor because he was the only one who ever did it. It was something of a spectacle, but he didn't seem to think there was any other way to do it. We never saw him miss one.

Figure 241: **Gun 1 on USS Willis.** This 3"/50 gun is almost identical to the one shown in Figure 240, but a bit cramped. The seat for the pointer is visible just right of center. The sailor on the left has put cotton in his ears to block sound – good in theory, but not very effective.

would have a tough time against attacking enemy aircraft.

Boosting our morale somewhat was the new proximity-fuzed shells for our three inch fifty guns. Those shells were designed to burst when they came near, and sensed, a target. That meant our gun crews didn't have to actually hit the target. All they had to do was come close, and hopefully shrapnel would do the rest.

But at that point we were just speculating, since we had never gone into combat against attacking aircraft, as was common in the Pacific. We didn't need any one to tell us how rough the air war was out there. On our trip south to the Panama Canal and into the Pacific, we would see one smashed ship after another limping to an east coast shipyard.

It started on the day of our departure from New York. While

19. Guam

still in the Hudson River, we sighted a huge aircraft carrier coming toward us. It was the USS Franklin. It had been severely damaged in action in the southwest Pacific and was in the final leg of a long trip back for repairs in the Brooklyn Navy yard. At first we had difficulty recognizing it as a carrier because it was visibly deformed. The flight deck didn't look right. It was completely clear of planes, and it was rippled over some of its surface. Normally, the entire ship's complement lines the edges of the flight deck when a carrier enters port, but only a handful of sailors were standing on the Franklin's.

As we passed close aboard (about 50 yards) on opposite courses, we got a much closer look, even as we rendered honors, which they promptly returned.

Even though she was underway under her own power, she was in really bad shape. The below deck damage from midships to the stern made it look like some very powerful force had tried to pull the flight deck right off the ship. It seemed as though a giant can opener had cut her open.

It was a hard sight to forget, and certainly an eye opener, letting us know the type of war we were heading for. Our close aboard look at the Franklin sobered all of us.

But that wasn't all we saw while steaming toward the Panama Canal. It seemed that every day we saw at least two or three kamikaze-battered ships. Most of them were destroyers, each with metal sticking out all over. The guns were twisted and pointing in every direction, gun tubs stove in, boats smashed, radars and other equipment missing.

Worse, all these ships were limping to the east coast because the west coast shipyards were completely full of other ships damaged by kamikazes, each, like the Franklin, with its own harrowing story.

The euphoria we had over Germany's surrender started fading the moment we saw the Franklin. It disappeared entirely as we witnessed the depressing procession of damaged ships. It was a very gloomy trip, but certainly helped motivate our antiaircraft gun crews as they worked with their new guns.

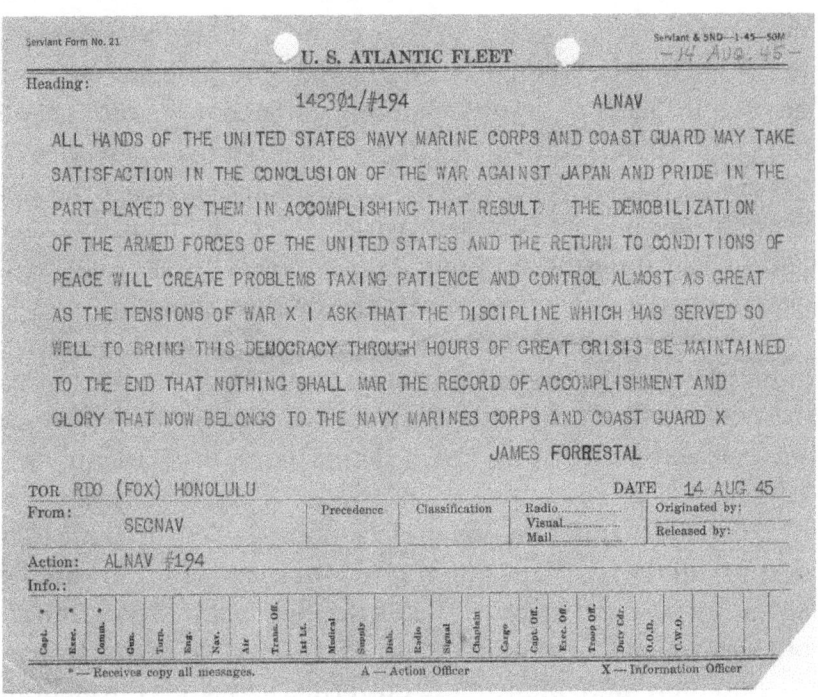

Figure 243: **Victory over the Japanese.** This congratulatory "ALNAV" message from the Secretary of the Navy to all members of the Navy, Marines, and Coast Guard, after the surrender of Japan, concludes with a plea to retain self-control.

We stopped only for fuel in the Canal Zone, refueled again in San Diego and then kept going to Pearl Harbor.

As luck would have it, we were just securing to a buoy in the Pearl Harbor anchorage on August 15, 1945, when the Commander in Chief Pacific sent the message "Japan has surrendered. Repeat, Japan has surrendered!"

We couldn't believe it at first. We had no idea it was that close to ending. Of course we had news of the atom bomb drop, but we didn't grasp the significance of the bomb until the war actually ended.

The flash end-of-war radio message was accompanied by a

19. Guam

mass volley of guns going off all over the harbor, and especially in the anchorage where we still had men on the buoy securing our chain. The celebratory shooting got so bad we ordered all our people inside the ship for protection from flying shells.

In just minutes the message announcing Japan's surrender was followed by an urgent message from the Commander in Chief Pacific Fleet ordering all commanding officers in Pearl Harbor to get control of their ships and stop the random shooting.

I quickly made sure no one on our ship fired a single shot, although several men had almost started.

We knew how fortunate we were! Ironically, our concern now was celebratory shooting, not the lethal barrages of December 7, 1941.

And what a difference from December 7, 1941! Of all the battleships hit that day, only the USS Arizona was still sitting on the bottom, with most of her crew still trapped inside. The vast harbor was now full of huge, ready-to-shoot, combat-tested ships.

And there were many more powerful Navy ships throughout the southwest Pacific. Veteran carrier, battleship, submarine, and amphibious task forces, with their supporting ships, made us feel that the vast Pacific was now an American Ocean. It's a really good feeling to be part of a "no nonsense" fleet that is so visibly strong. And it's a feeling that stays with you for a very long time!

When things finally settled down in the harbor, we started liberty for the crew. I went ashore with several officers, and we immediately ran into a bedlam of celebrations. We finally made our way to Honolulu and it seemed the whole city had emptied into the streets.

We tried to find a restroom but couldn't get near the bars. Hoping to find one in a nearby mini-high-rise office building, we entered the building on the main floor. To our surprise, there was no one there. The reception area was empty, and there were no guards – just the three of us. The elevators were still operable. So after finding a nice restroom on the third floor, we decided to explore the building.

There were many desks piled with papers and some private offices with their doors open. But there were no people anywhere. We sat down at the telephones and were about to start using them to call back home. But good sense returned and we left the building. I believe it was the offices of a large insurance company.

We rejoined the crowds in the street and just walked around trying to find a bar that wasn't packed. Giving up, we decided to return to the naval base and check out the officers' club. That turned out to be a good idea. It wasn't as packed as the city, and we spent the remainder of the day there before returning to the ship.

The end of the war did not change our orders. About five days later, the Willis and our sister DE's, Swenning and Janssen, departed for Saipan.

We had become so used to steaming "darkened ship" at night we hesitated at first before turning on our lights. It was a strange, vulnerable feeling to look around and see the lights of other ships. But it didn't take us long to adjust to the joys of being underway in peacetime.

The trip to Saipan was pleasant and we spent a lot of time wondering what we would do when we got there. But old habits are hard to change and we still spent a lot of time in gun loading drills.

In Saipan we were assigned to escort the USS Wharton, a troop ship, to Eniwetok Atoll. Then we escorted another troop ship, USS Lycoming, back to Saipan. Our next trip was to Guam, where we arrived on September 13, 1945.

Compared to the harbors on the east coast of the U.S., Guam's Apra harbor was a dinky little place. It had one long pier and a fairly large anchorage. (See Figure 246.) We soon found, however, that it was an important Pacific Fleet submarine base. There was a squadron of submarines based there, plus the USS Sperry. The Sperry was a large submarine tender that also housed the Senior Officer Present Afloat (SOPA), to whom we reported for operational and administrative control.

19. Guam

Figure 246: **Guam's harbor.** The anchorage is full of warships.

We were immediately assigned to work with the submarines, and told to maintain complete operational war readiness. I had the impression they weren't quite sure everything was under complete control in the southwest Pacific.

We spent a lot of time at sea acting as targets for the submarines. They would make war-like runs on us and fire their torpedoes. Of course, the torpedoes were set to run beneath us and their warheads were filled with water. At the end of every run the torpedo would bob to the surface and we would chase it down, retrieve it, and return it to the Sperry, which remained nearby.

We got pretty good at retrieving the torpedoes. It's not a difficult task but we had to sharpen some old skills and create new ones.

The torpedo would run a mile or two after it passed beneath us. We would turn and follow it at fifteen knots to make sure we didn't lose it. Getting as close to it as possible, we would quickly lower our boat. The sailors in the boat would go alongside the torpedo, which at the end of its run would bob up and down vertically. Securing a line through a ring on the nose of the torpedo, they would bring it alongside their boat and tow it to the Sperry.

Even though they were friendly runs it was, nevertheless, a

Figure 247: **American torpedo.** Crewmembers of the USS Willis recover a torpedo fired at her by an American submarine during an exercise in 1945. German U-boats fired similar torpedoes with great success – early in World War II (see Figure 20).

troubling experience to see torpedoes pass beneath us. Our submariners were very good shots and there were no misses.

We didn't try to prevent the attacks. We just steamed along at about fourteen knots and acted as targets. Apparently, it was badly needed training for the submarines, and we were happy to participate.

Even though we spent a good amount of time at sea with the submarines, we really didn't get to know the submarine officers very well. Our closest contact to them was the operations officer on the submarine tender. He gave us all our orders and handled all our requests.

Since the war had ended, people wanted to go home. Each of our ships was directed to draw up a schedule for those enlisted

19. Guam

men and officers who qualified for discharge from the Navy. One of the first on the list was Lieutenant Commander Joe Gunn, my captain.

I also had enough points to go home, but oddly I never considered it. I began to realize that the Willis was, indeed, my home. I knew I wanted to return to the states aboard the Willis.

Gunn had relieved George Atterbury in December 1944. At the time I was disappointed, since I had hoped that I would fleet up to command the ship when Atterbury left.

However, I wasn't surprised when that didn't happen. I was Atterbury's exec and he knew I was doing a good job running the ship. While we got along fine I also knew that he considered me not serious enough to be a commanding officer. My fitness reports under him were pretty good, but in one that I saw he indicated that I lacked maturity.

I knew he considered me too young for command of a DE. I probably could have changed that view by altering my relations with my subordinate officers. That relationship was more of a collegial nature than that of their senior officer. For example, I ran a three month long wrestling tournament among the officers. It was an ongoing tournament which we conducted on the large black leather wardroom couch. And even though I wasn't the biggest officer I was tied for first place. I knew Atterbury didn't like the idea of the tournament, but he never told me to stop it.

Gunn was an experienced DE captain when he took over and we all liked him immediately. A short time after he assumed command he got sick. We were in New London, Connecticut at the time, working with our own submarines. It turned out that he had the mumps! The medical doctor at the submarine base said that he had to be isolated for ten days.

I was asked if I could handle the ship if Gunn was confined to his cabin. The alternative was to transfer Gunn ashore and assign a new skipper. I said yes, and Gunn strongly recommended that I be the acting captain.

This was my first experience as a commanding officer. It

was a thrill to control the ship without anyone looking over my shoulder, and cleanly backing it away from the pier in New London the first time gave me a confidence in ship handling that kept growing.

So for the next ten days I was indeed the captain as we operated the ship with the Bogue group. I can still remember Gunn sticking his head out of the porthole in his cabin and looking up at the bridge where I ran the ship. He was a very calm and laid back officer who talked to me from his port hole but never issued any orders or even gave me any tips.

He was pronounced well after nine days and I went back to being the exec. He was an ideal commanding officer, much more sociable than his predecessor, and the ship continued to do well.

Captain Gunn was anxious to go back home to his family, and we put his name at the head of the list. It was returned promptly with full approval, and Gunn was among the first to leave. He could do that because months earlier, well before the end of the war, he had written in my routine fitness report that I was fully qualified to command a destroyer escort, and he strongly recommended that I be so ordered – and that's what happened: I received orders to relieve him.

My pay and rank remained the same when I assumed command. However, it turned out that my date of rank as a lieutenant commander preceded the dates of the skippers of the two other DEs that were with us. As a result I immediately became the acting division commander of the three ships.

This really didn't mean anything operationally because we knew each other so well that they needed no direction, but it meant that I was the conduit for all directives to the DEs from the local commander.

One of the questions on my ship was whether we could operate and fight the ship, if necessary, without replacements for the men who were being sent home. Fortunately I knew the crew quite well. It had been obvious to me for some time that we had quite good depth in all our departments. I assured the

19. GUAM

Figure 250: **Willis pier-side in Guam.** Moored outboard of the Willis (DE 395) in December 1945 are the other two ships of Escort Division 51: USS Cockrill (DE 398) and USS Swenning. The starred flag on the bow of the Willis is the "Navy jack." Navy ships fly it only when moored or anchored.

Navy Department that, although we could use replacements for the men going home, we were equipped to operate effectively without them – and we were.

Our time in Guam, except for operating with the submarines, was boring. Because the submarine squadron commander never had a division of destroyer-type ships to plan for, there really were no plans to use us, except to make sure we were ready if needed.

The little time we spent ashore with members of the submarine force was another factor. The submarine force spent much time at Camp Dealey when they weren't actually on their ships. Camp Dealey was a very large berthing and recreational site used exclusively by submariners. For some strange reason, the officers and enlisted men of the DEs were neither invited nor encouraged to use those ample facilities.

Instead, we surface officers populated a large officers' club known as the "Democrats' Club," which had no membership requirements.

Our enlisted men had no similar club, but I assigned one of my officers to organize and implement recreational activities for them. These activities included extensive tours of the bombed out areas. Perhaps seventy percent of the island had been pulverized by bombs at one time or another. So there was a lot to see, even if it was rather gruesome.

Also, there were about 100,000 battle tested U.S. Army soldiers and U.S. Marines on the island. Apparently Guam was to be a staging point for the invasion of Japan and these men were to be part of that force – as were our ships.

As for the enemy, there was a large number of them, too. You couldn't drive anywhere on the island without seeing a clump of several hundred Japanese prisoners guarded by American soldiers or Marines. Of course, we kept well clear of them. More ominously, a large number of Japanese soldiers who refused to surrender were roaming the more remote parts of the island. We needed no one to tell us to stay away from those areas.

The Democrats' Club was just a large building full of chairs

19. GUAM

Figure 252: **Japanese prisoners of war on Guam.** Guarded by a U.S. Marine, 1945.

---

and tables with a large bar where whiskey was a nickel a glass. It was within walking distance of the waterfront, and the officers of all ships were welcome there, including, of course, the numerous merchant ships that came in.

The only entertainment, aside from the drinking, was a never-ending crap game alongside the club. It seemed to go on all day, and only folded when it got too dark to see the numbers on the dice.

The afternoon of December 31, 1945, four of my officers and I had been shooting craps until it got too dark to see. We went inside and sat at a table with officers from the other DE's, and were enjoying the whiskey. It was about 9 pm when we were all startled by a female voice, not too far from where we were sitting. Startled is the correct word because in 1945, except for several Red Cross ladies, nowhere in Guam were there any American women.

Of course, the young lady behind the voice got our attention. She was sitting with three officers of a small Swedish refrigerated ship that was delivering fresh fruit and produce to Guam. It was a conspicuous white ship and we had all noticed it before we came ashore.

After some discussion, my chief engineer bet me a drink that I could not become acquainted with the girl. I suddenly had an idea as to how I might win the bet, and accepted.

With their eyes on me, I went over to the booth holding the three Swedish officers and the young lady. I introduced myself as the captain of one of the DEs. I knew they saw my ship because we were directly ahead of them on the pier.

They were very courteous. One was the captain and he introduced me to his other officers and the young lady, whom he identified as the ship's steward. He asked me to sit down and have a drink with them. Of course I accepted. Then I told him the purpose of my coming over was to see if there was any way we could purchase some of the fresh fruit and produce he was carrying. He knew that all our ships were low on such supplies but said regretfully he was not allowed to do that. His entire cargo had to be delivered to the naval supply depot. Perhaps I could contact them.

He insisted I remain for a few drinks and we exchanged sea stories until about 10 PM when he looked at his watch and stood up.

"Sorry, we have to leave now," he said. "It's a custom on our ships that we all share a late New Year's eve dinner aboard ship, so we must go now."

The other two officers stood up and he looked down at the young lady expecting, I guess, that she would stand up and join them to leave. But instead, she suddenly slammed her fist on the table, "Dammit, I'm an American and I'm going to spend New Year's eve with the Americans," she said.

"Fine, Elise," the captain replied quietly, and to my amazement the three of them left her sitting there with me. Up to then

19. Guam

I hadn't really addressed any words to her and now I was sitting there alone with her.

Of course, she had been drinking, and so had I. Nevertheless I got a little nervous. It was only a minute before my officers cheerfully joined us at the table. We agreed that perhaps it would be a good idea for all of us to drive out to the submarine officers' club at Camp Dealey, where we had just recently been authorized access.

At that time it was a base regulation that any one in the company of a female on that island had to wear sidearms. Fortunately I had mine with me so I piled Elise into my jeep and the other three officers took theirs and we headed out to Camp Dealey, which was on the coast about 20 miles away.

The guard at Camp Dealey was astonished to see us. Elise was a well built young lady. She was dressed in black but her turtleneck sweater was tight fitting and didn't leave too much to the imagination.

When we entered the club it was almost like a grand reception. The club was full of young officers from the submarines and from the DEs. As Elise walked in ahead of us, all the DE officers stood up, cheered, and clapped. They were soon joined, it seemed, by everyone in the club.

And that's the way the evening started and remained. Every time Elise got up to go to the ladies room, everyone stood up and cheered. No matter what kind of a movement she made she was the object of affectionate applause and cheering.

At midnight two of my officers grabbed me, pushed me under the table and held me there until the magic moment had passed. I was the only one in my group who did not receive a Happy New Year kiss from Elise.

Our celebration continued until about 3 AM, when the party started to fold up. The five of us got in our two jeeps and drove to the guard station at the end of Camp Dealey to take the road back to the pier.

However, the Marine guards made us get out of our jeeps and go behind a nearby brick and stone structure for protection against some shells that were being shot into Camp Dealey. The guards told us the shooters were either Japanese soldiers still on the loose, or some of our own people celebrating New Year's.

For some strange reason there were tracers among the shells they were shooting into the camp so we could see where the shots were going – which was far over our heads.

We sat there for about a half hour until the shooting died down and then stopped completely. We were told to drive without lights and not to stop until we were well on the road back to the waterfront.

I delivered Elise back to her ship and returned to mine. It was then I discovered that she had stolen my side arm (my revolver). I got back in my jeep, went to her ship and asked for the captain. When he came down I asked him to retrieve my gun from Elise. He left and returned a few minutes later with the gun and a wry smile about Elise's souvenir hunting.

That was the end of my acquaintance with Elise. Her ship departed the next evening.

During the New Year's eve celebration at the Camp Dealey club, we learned a great deal about this adventurous young woman. "What is a young American girl doing way out here in Guam during a war?" I asked her early in the evening.

She told us she was looking for her husband who was in the Army and was somewhere in the South Pacific. She had left four young children at home with her mother and, as she said, "shipped out in the Merchant Marine to look for him." It was a strange and entertaining story, especially the part where the previous ship she had been on was torpedoed. Oil-soaked and half dead, she was pulled from the water by surprised and startled rescuers.

That was just the first incident involving American girls that made the submarine officers wonder about destroyer escort sailors.

One afternoon about a month later, my first lieutenant, Rod Haney, knocked on my cabin door and asked if I wanted a date with an American nurse. "Sure," I said, knowing full well there weren't any American nurses on the island.

19. Guam

"The USS Comfort is entering the harbor, and if you give me your permission, I'll get a boat and go over and make arrangements for all our single officers." He was the only married officer on the ship. The other three had already earned enough points to go home.

"O.K." I said, "Just invite them over for dinner on the ship." And off he went.

We all saw the huge hospital ship come in and drop anchor. Several hours passed without word from my first lieutenant. I had forgotten all about his venture when he suddenly showed up.

"Captain, guess what? I couldn't arrange for four guests. The chief nurse wouldn't let any of them go ashore without her, and she said there were more than four girls that wanted to come ashore. They have come here directly from San Francisco and it's the first time in this war zone for a lot of them. So I invited 18 nurses and the chief nurse to visit our ship."

"Are you crazy? We can't feed 19 people. Besides, that's far too many crawling all over the ship."

"Oh no. We won't feed them. They just want to tour the topside and see the ships alongside the dock."

"No. Hell no," I said angrily. "There's no way we can show them the submarines."

"They don't want to go aboard. Just look at them from the dock."

"Do you realize that those sailors have been out here for two or three years and haven't seen an American woman in all that time. What do you expect them to do? Besides you know the regulations here about armed escorts for women."

"Captain, I've already called the provost marshall's office and received a waiver on the armed escort requirement. I also called the motor pool and they offered me a bus to take everyone to Camp Dealey for dinner and drinks. I called the manager at Camp Dealey and he said to come on out. He can feed as many as we want, just let him know the number. I told him there would be at least 24 on the bus and maybe a few more."

"No way," I said. "We can't handle all those people on this crowded dock."

"Captain, I spent a half hour convincing the chief nurse that this was a wonderful opportunity for the nurses and doctors, and they are getting ready to come ashore. I can't go back there and call it off." My first lieutenant was a very successful insurance salesman before he volunteered to became a Naval officer. He was one of my most enthusiastic, caring, and competent officers, whose judgment I trusted completely. But now I was getting very nervous.

Against my better judgment I went over every detail with him to make sure we were conforming to all the base regulations. Finally I said, "O.K. But get four or five officers to help you."

He was ecstatic. "By the way, captain, you are the escort for the chief nurse." And with that he was gone.

An hour later I heard a big ruckus on the dock and there they were: about 20 very pretty uniformed Navy nurses escorted by my first lieutnant, plus two senior medical doctors, walking down the dock toward our ship.

Just what I expected happened. The sailors from all three destroyer escorts, including mine, and the sailors from two nearby submarines began raising holy hell, waving, whistling, and shouting friendly remarks.

The girls, in turn, were also friendly, stopping to talk to some, and seemed genuinely thrilled with the reception.

I had no choice. They filed aboard the Willis and I met each one at the gangway. They were indeed all very pretty and I soon lost my anger. The chief nurse and the senior doctors were grateful that we had invited them over,

After a quick tour of the topside of my ship, they all left and went directly to the bus waiting for them on the dock. I was the last one on the bus as we headed for Camp Dealey.

I had to admit my first lieutenant had set it up very nicely, and by now I was pleased I had approved the whole thing.

The ride to Camp Dealey through roads lined with bomb damaged buildings and other reminders of the war was something

19. Guam

none of them had seen before, and somewhat quieted the group.

That changed after we arrived at Camp Dealey. There was much to eat and drink, and in a few hours they were all having a rollicking good time. It seemed that every submarine and destroyer escort officer somehow found his way to our party.

The festivities ended about 11:00 PM when the chief nurse announced it was time to leave. We bussed everyone back to the boat landing, saw them into their boats, and complimented ourselves, and especially my first lieutenant, on a splendid morale boosting job.

But that's not where it ended.

The next morning I was called to the office of the senior officer present afloat (my boss) where I was read the riot act. Fortunately, the officer doing that was a friend. He told me I came very close to getting in some serious trouble.

"There are 100,000 combat veterans on this island and most of them are living next door to Camp Dealey. Had they discovered that party, and tried to crash it, there was nothing anyone could have done. We don't need that kind of stupid activity on this island. Do you understand?"

He mentioned the complicity of the provost marshall, the motor pool, and the management at Camp Dealey who apparently all caught the same type of hell from him that I did.

He sent me off with a warning. "Watch your step, George. You lucked out this time!"

I didn't say anything to my first lieutenant as he read the thank you messages we got from the chief nurse and the nurses who came ashore.

It was an incident that brought me a great deal of notoriety that I would never live down all the time we were in Guam.

Figure 260: **USS Sperry hulking over three DEs.** DEs Willis, Swenning, and Janssen appear puny beside the enoumous mass of the submarine tender USS Sperry in Guam.

Chapter 20

U.S. Subs vs. U.S. DEs

Historians say there were 131 different, significant battles in the Pacific during WWII. Wikipedia lists seven major campaigns in the southwest Pacific theatre, which included over 29 battles. Just one of these 29, the New Guinea Campaign (1942-1945), included fourteen separate battles, with the famous Battle of the Coral Sea being just one.

The aircraft in these battles flew thousands of sorties over the endless Pacific waters. In spite of the well-organized and effective procedures for locating and rescuing downed aircraft in the southwest Pacific, many were lost, along with their crews.

I mention these historical facts to emphasize the extensive geographical scope of the air fighting and to suggest why, shortly after the war ended, an organized search of most of the islands in the southwest Pacific was made to locate any stranded Americans.

Our three DEs, the seven submarines, as well as the very large submarine tender USS Sperry, participated in a small part of this search. Our search was combined with three weeks of war game training operations that pitted Guam's seven veteran, war-tested U.S. Pacific Fleet submarines against the three hunter-killer destroyer escorts from the Atlantic. Our job was to protect the Sperry, much as we had protected the Bogue in the Atlantic.

It was to be a no holds barred war game. Knowing our gen-

20. U.S. Subs vs. U.S. DEs

eral route, the subs would treat us as an enemy convoy. They were to use all their war time tactics in an effort to "sink" the Sperry and the three DEs protecting her.

By "sink," the operation order said they could fire actual torpedoes to pass beneath their targets. As before, the torpedo warheads were filled with water, not explosives. The DE's were told that we could act as we did in war time and attack any subs we contacted. We were to drop hand grenades instead of depth charges.

We had often wondered among ourselves how such a contest would shape up. We were considered top-notch anti-submarine ships, and we had a track record against the U-boats that supported that reputation. On the other hand, the U.S. submarines also had a top-notch track record and reputation in the Pacific.

So, we welcomed the operation as sort of a "World Series" test between top professionals from the Atlantic and the Pacific.

In a pre-operation get-together at the officers' club at Camp Dealey, I had a lively discussion with one of the submarine captains about the relative merits of our particular skills. In particular, he touted the "down-the-throat-shot" that had been perfected by some of the Pacific fleet submarines.

We had read about the successes they had with that shot against Japanese destroyers, but none of us could see that tactic being successful against an experienced Atlantic Fleet DE.

Our discussion got so heated we ended up making a bet. If my ship was attacked successfully with a down-the-throat-shot, I would pay that sub skipper ten dollars. "Successful" meant that he had to fire a torpedo that passed beneath my ship. If he missed, he had to pay off.

We had a lot of respect for the Pacific Fleet submariners. I fully expected they would give us a hard time and probably succeed in "sinking" the Sperry. However, I also had a feeling that such respect was a one-way street. They really didn't know us.

All three DE captains were very confident that we had skills the U.S. submarines hadn't seen in the Pacific war. One reason for this confidence was the unusually long ranges we had been experiencing with our sonar equipment in the Guam area.

In the Atlantic we considered ourselves very lucky if we acquired an underwater contact as distant as 2000 yards. But working with the subs off Guam, we were getting excellent and consistent contacts at 8000 yard ranges. In short, we knew that the sonar conditions were very much in our favor.

The war game operation went off very smoothly from our perspective. However, I can't say the same for the submariners.

The operation consisted of a series of war games held before and after each island stop to check for survivors. I was the senior captain among the DE's and hence was the screen commander. But we were so accustomed to working together in a screen that I did very little in that role.

We had made arrangements with a searchlight-equipped plane to join us the first night of the exercise. We had worked extensively with such planes from the Bogue and knew what they could do. They are torpedo planes, but instead of carrying a torpedo they carry a large, powerful, blinding searchlight to illuminate targets.

On the first night of the operation, using our HFDF equipment and radar, we accurately located the positions of all seven "attacking" submarines. I promptly vectored the searchlight plane out to their positions.

The plane caught all seven of the submarines on the surface and blinded them with its powerful searchlight. It was embarrassing. They were all caught flat footed. I was directed not to use the searchlight plane any more, and told him to return to base. Even so, from that point everything went downhill for the submarines.

From an attack perspective, the remainder of the cruise was very frustrating for the submarines. The DEs prevented all of them from even getting near the Sperry. The 8000 yard ranges we were getting on sonar simply made it impossible for any of the submarines to mount an attack on any of our ships. The submarines' torpedoes had about a 6000 yard range, but their

20. U.S. Subs vs. U.S. DEs

most effective shooting range was closer to 1000 yards. With our distance advantage, we would break off and attack them first, or the entire convoy would just turn away from them.

During the entire three-week cruise the seven submarines made 254 attacks on the "convoy," and fired about 30 torpedoes. In every instance but one, the destroyer escorts detected the attackers and completely frustrated them. Had we been using depth charges they all would have been destroyed.

Near the end of the extensive war game cruise, my ship acquired an underwater contact at 8000 yards. As was our procedure, I headed for the contact at 15 knots.[1] After I had closed the distance between us, we saw the submarine fire a single torpedo.

It was an unusual shot. We saw the torpedo track immediately because we knew exactly where he was and the sea was flat. The torpedo started out heading ninety degrees to the right of the course I had set to run over the top of the submarine. That is, the torpedo was moving rapidly to my right and away from me. Then as we watched, it started to turn and come around a full 180 degrees, heading directly at me with just about the right amount of lead.

Had we not been watching and listening to the torpedo, and had I kept the course I had set to run over the submarine, I expect he would have registered a hit on me.

However, because we saw, and our sonar heard, the torpedo, I turned right with sufficient rudder to parallel the torpedo in the opposite direction, and we watched as it sped right by us. Then I changed course back to run over the submarine and dropped a hand grenade to signify our depth charge pattern.

Later I learned the submarine was the USS Blenny and it was her captain with whom I had made the bet. He never did pay off!

While his "down-the-throat" shot was easy for my DE to avoid, I did appreciate the kill potential of that type of attack, especially if made at night. Had I not been able to see the torpedo track,

---

[1] The top speed of the Willis was about 21 knots. At that speed, however, sonar conditions deteriorated, so our usual attack speed was about 15 knots.

there is a chance, a good chance, that a torpedo spread might have registered a hit.

On the whole, however, the dramatic maneuverability of my twin rudder DE and the absolutely ideal sonar conditions we found in the Pacific combined to place the odds well in my favor.

SOPA (senior officer present afloat) held a critique after the conclusion of our war game with these seven WWII combat-tested submarines. At this critique, the submarine skippers themselves made one thing abundantly clear by the comments they placed in the official record of the cruise: these seven U.S. Pacific Fleet submarines were no match for the three veteran Atlantic Fleet combat tested destroyer escorts.

Indeed, one of the submarine captains told me that if the Japanese had the anti-submarine capabilities demonstrated by the three DEs, the war in the Pacific would have been different.

As far as the search for survivors, we had no immediate finds. One of the submarines reported that, as they approached an island, they could see several people on the beach attempting to get their attention. The area military commander took their report for further investigation.

The war game marked the end of any real activity for us in Guam. For a change, we now started to have a great deal more time on our hands.

One of my young officers, let's call him Greg, claimed to be a research chemist with an interest in biology. He was an interesting "out of the box" type of guy and he talked me into letting him spend a lot of time roaming around the island so he could study different areas of Guam. He had become acquainted with some village elders and had access to village areas prohibited to the rest of us. This was no small feat since the villages were off limits to everyone, including ranking officers like myself.

Because we didn't see or meet the villagers, it was easy to forget that Guam had been captured by the Japanese early in WWII, and had survived under rough Japanese domination. So, except for the waterfront area, the logistics supply center, and the recre-

20. U.S. Subs vs. U.S. DEs

ational areas, we really did not see much of the island or the native Guamanians.

Greg was also on the committee that published our ship's newspaper and his "research" resulted in informative articles about the island and especially its inhabitants.

Through his connections with the village elders, Greg told me he could arrange a social dance for enlisted members of the crew. I was reluctant, at first, because of my earlier "social" experience and the cautions they had earned me.

However, the village elders themselves convinced me. At a meeting arranged by Greg, they explained that their young people had gone through about seven years of a war environment and that many didn't really know what a dance would be like. In fact, most of the youngsters didn't even know how to dance.

After setting really strict ground rules, I approved the event. It included a sumptuous buffet, soft drinks, dancing, and dance contests. We supplied all the food and drinks. This, too, was another first for the villagers.

A half-dozen village elders and I were the chaperones. My ground rules included strict control of all entrances and exits and absolutely no alcoholic drinks. I personally provided instructions to the guards at the doors and had my exec monitoring behavior.

About a hundred and fifty of my crew attended, and there was about an equal number of young people from the villages, most of them young ladies.

The villagers listened wide-eyed to the Navy band we had obtained for the occasion. Many of them received dancing lessons from members of my crew and the behavior of all hands was exemplary with one exception: we caught one of my sailors sneaking in a bottle of liquor.

I don't know if this was the first post-WWII dance for young people on Guam, but it sure looked like it. My sailors all wore their dress white uniforms. The young girls, and even the young men, who showed up wore their best clothes. Even though none of the clothes were by any means new, it was obvious that they had made a great deal of effort to dress up.

It turned out to be a wonderful affair. Some of the girls were exceptionally pretty and I could see that my sailors really enjoyed themselves. The village elders and their spouses couldn't thank me enough and I felt pretty good about the whole thing. I complimented Greg and thanked him for his hard and considerate work.

Greg kept busy in other ways. He was an accomplished electronic technician and skilled photographer. Somehow, in his tours around the island, he became very friendly with a group that was disposing of excess U.S. military equipment.

He got their permission to remove wing cameras from many of the planes that were being hauled out to sea and dumped in the ocean.

I didn't learn about his arrangement until one afternoon when I found a wing camera on my cabin desk. After I sent for him, he explained that he had removed over a dozen and handed them out to different members of the crew who had an interest in movies.

I had seen barge after barge loaded with planes being towed out of the harbor only to return empty some hours later. So I knew he was telling me the truth. I still have the camera.

This was the beginning of an interest in souvenirs for many in my crew. There was nothing illegal about it, and it did keep many of them busy in a constructive way.

Weapons, of course, were taboo. I knew that some of the sailors had obtained some, and I quickly put a stop to it.

I wasn't surprised when a group came to me and asked for permission to refurbish three boats that had been abandoned in the harbor as useless. I went with them and looked at the boats. They were a mess.

The first one, a dirty, green, wooden, Japanese suicide boat was about 25 feet long and 4 feet wide. It was full of water and sitting on the bottom at the water's edge. Stripped of anything useful, all that remained was the beat up leaky hull and a use-

20. U.S. Subs vs. U.S. DEs

less, inoperable, skeleton engine. I could see what it must have looked like in its better days. It was good-sized, streamlined, and had a large empty compartment in the bow that would be loaded with explosives. My engineers told me it was designed to only go forward at a high speed and crash into its target.

The second boat was a small 10-foot runabout. Its hull had several conspicuous holes and its engines had been torn apart.

The third one was a catamaran that had been built on two large aircraft pontoons. It appeared to be some type of recreational boat the Japanese sailors had assembled. And it, too, appeared to be nothing but junk. It had no engine at all.

All three were sitting on land at the water's edge, near the large dock where we were moored. I never asked the men how they got the boats there, but I knew it had to involve someone who had the necessary heavy equipment.

I readily gave them permission to go ahead. The only caveat I gave them was that if they ever did get the boats operational they would be used by all of the crew for recreational purposes.

I think it took less than four weeks before all three boats were zipping around the harbor. The showpiece that attracted widespread attention was the suicide boat. My sailors had fixed it up, and it was clearly the fastest boat in the area.

It was interesting to watch. It could go only forward. They would rev it up at high speed and it was literally flying. To slow it down or come to a stop they had to cut the engine and let the bow drop into the water.

The boats proved to be a huge morale booster. All the sailors watched and kept tabs on the engineers as they struggled to put the boats back into shape. Then the guys that did all the work had fun driving the others around.

Eventually, we found ourselves with literally nothing to do on Guam. I tried to obtain information about our planned use, only to learn there were no plans.

As the captain and senior officer of all the DEs, I guess it was my responsibility to see that the ships kept up their tactical skills. But with the entire U.S. Navy winding down, and no enemy even on the horizon, I just felt as though training for war made no sense. So I did nothing in that direction.

Instead, the major focus throughout the Navy was getting people home. This provided a glimmer of motivation for the old timers, who spent a lot of time counting and recounting the points needed to go home, but it was hard to avoid the general sense of boredom that descended on most of us.

At the same time, I was very curious about our planned use had Japan not surrendered. My efforts to learn those plans also drew a blank. We knew that Guam was a staging point for invading Japan, with over 100,000 battle-tested troops getting ready for something, but that was all we really knew.

Many years later, when I did learn the plan, I realized how really damn lucky we were that President Truman made the decision to drop the atom bombs.

Our three destroyer escorts were to have been in the forefront of a huge force – 4.5 million American servicemen – being assembled to support an amphibious invasion of the Japanese homeland. The 100,000 troops on Guam were a portion of the 1.5 million combat soldiers who would actually be invading Japan.

The overall invasion, code-named "Operation Downfall," was to be executed in two phases. The first, "Operation Olympic," called for 14 divisions to invade heavily fortified Kyushu early in the morning of November 1, 1945 (a division is 10,000 to 15,000 men). That was just ten weeks after we arrived in Pearl Harbor.

In the second phase, code-named "Operation Coronet," 22 divisions would assault the main island of Honshu and the Tokyo plain on March 1, 1946.[2]

The entire U.S. Navy in the Pacific was committed to Operation Downfall, as were the entire U.S. Marine Corps and the 7th, 8th, 20th, and far eastern U.S. Army Air Forces.

But what about the Japanese? Were they prepared to resist Operation Downfall?

---

[2]Davis.

20. U.S. Subs vs. U.S. DEs

Of course they were.

We had already seen the evidence. In July and August of 1945, less than two months before Japan surrendered, a relatively small number of kamikazes plus the remaining Japanese air force sank 32 of our ships and damaged 400 others, thereby clogging America's shipyards.

Although our strategy for the invasion anticipated such fierce resistance, captured Japanese documents and post-war interrogation of Japanese military leaders disclosed that our intelligence about the Japanese defenses was dangerously in error.

In just one example, it turns out that the Japanese had 12,725 more aircraft available than intelligence had estimated. That's just a simple number now, but visualize the damage that number of planes could do to a vulnerable landing force!

The Japanese defenders also had an elaborate, widespread scope of suicide operations. It included not only the kamikaze (suicide) planes, but over 1000 rockets manned by suicide pilots. They also planned to use human-steerable torpedoes, as well as human frogmen who could stay underwater for ten hours and attach to ships the mines they were carrying.

Most submarine torpedoes have a range of about 6000 yards. The Japanese had an inventory of "long lance" torpedoes with ranges up to 12,000 yards.

The Japanese also had an excellent homeland defense plan called "Ketsu-Go." There is no telling what might have happened had they ever put it in operation. Their intelligence had correctly identified where and when we would invade. This was critical because an important part of Ketsu-Go was killing the invasion troops before they set foot on Kyushu or Honshu. To do this, they planned to send a total of about 5,075 aircraft of different types, most of them suicide, to attack the 250 troop transport ships of our Kyushu invasion force.

Of course, we had very powerful forces. The naval units alone had well over 3000 combat ships of various sizes. So it would by no means have been a cake walk for the Japanese. There would certainly have been carnage on both sides, and we would have lost an inordinately large number of our troops at sea.

So when President Truman approved the bombing of Hiroshima and Nagasaki with atom bombs, he saved not only my life, but the lives of perhaps a million U.S. servicemen and probably the lives of 4 million Japanese. And it ended a war that otherwise would really have had no end, because our invasion would probably have created a horrifying stalemate – a quagmire to dwarf those of Viet Nam or Iraq.

Controvery over the decision to drop the atomic bombs has grown since the war. It is impossible for me to understand criticism of President Truman's decision to drop those two bombs. I simply don't see how any knowledgeable, responsible person could believe the criticism is justified. Once the atom bomb was operational, can you imagine the national reaction had his decision been otherwise! Even at that late stage of the war, American servicemen were taking 900 casualties a day.[3] Some have argued that the greater tragedy was the inability to use the atom bomb earlier in the war, when so many more deaths could have been prevented.[4]

Truth be known, I believe that even the Japanese themselves would agree that Mr. Truman's decision served their national interest.

---

[3] Sweeney, page 270.
[4] Gottfried.

Figure 272: **Crossing the line ceremonies aboard the Willis.** "The line" is the equator. This was an old fun tradition that today's Navy considers demeaning and has banned.

Chapter 21

Going Home

In early January 1946, we received orders to return to the U.S.

As the senior of the three destroyer escort captains, I was designated Task Unit commander with responsibility for getting them home. I had just turned 26. I ordered all ships to be ready to depart at 0800 on January 10.

Of course we were happy to be leaving Guam for home.

We got all our stuff together, hauled the three boats out of the water and secured them on our boat deck. Then at 0800 on the 10th, we waved goodbye to our friends as we steamed out of Apra harbor and set course for Pearl Harbor.

The weather was nice, sunny and the sea as calm as the long Pacific swells permit.

On the third day at sea I happened to walk back aft. I noticed a large line that lead over the stern and into the water. Normally, we discourage lines over the stern to avoid any risk of entangling them in our propellers.

"What's on the other end of that line?" I asked the sailor on watch.

"Oh, Mr. Greg is bleaching something."

Not surprised by Greg's bleaching efforts with salt water, I asked, "How big is it?"

He didn't know, so I asked him to pull it in so we could see.

21. GOING HOME

We were both surprised to discover a human skull, with some brown skin still attached to one side that Greg apparently was trying to remove.

I was shocked at what I saw. "Put that thing in a bucket and tell Mr. Greg I want to see him. Don't drag anything over the stern unless I O.K. it."

"Yes, sir," he responded as he started looking for a bucket.

About ten minutes later Greg knocked on my door.

"Where did you get that skull?" I asked as soon as he entered.

"One of the old native cemeteries was all bombed out. Bones, skulls, everything was scattered all over the place."

"Why did you pick up the skull?"

"Well, you saw it," he replied. "It's kind of small and I thought it would make a good ashtray. That's why I was trying to bleach it."

"How about the family it belonged to?"

"No one knew who it belonged to and they didn't mind when I picked it up."

"Who is 'they'?"

"One of the village elders I was walking around with."

"Get out of here and don't drag it over the stern."

For some strange reason, what he was doing then didn't seem as offensive as it does now that I am looking back on it. However, that wasn't the last I heard about the skull.

About a day after we left Pearl Harbor we hit some pretty bad weather. The after berthing area, where our junior officers bunked, flooded when the storm caused the toilets to back up.

One of our stewards walked back there at night to see how bad things were and was startled to see the skull swishing around the compartment. It scared the hell out of him. The exec had to order Greg to get it and stow it out of sight.

Our three ships arrived at San Diego for a five-day rest and recreation visit, and that's exactly what we did.

Two weeks later we were at the Pacific end of the Panama Canal. It was about noon, and there were only two pilots for the three ships. I told the head pilot to go ahead and take the other two ships through the canal – we would wait until the next day.

He sensed the disappointment in some of my crew and said, "Listen, you don't have to wait. Just follow me at about five hundred yards and we'll all go through together."

"Sounds good," I answered and away we went. The pilots wanted to get through the canal before dark and put on a little speed.

At first I kept pretty close to the ship ahead of me, the Swenning, which had the second pilot. But my caution got the better of me and I kept falling further and further behind until we could no longer see the Swenning. That didn't really bother me, since it was one-way traffic going in my direction, and all I had to do was remain in the center of the channel. Besides, I had the channel all to myself.

However, that changed in a way that really shook me up.

We were in a curvy section of the canal transit. All of a sudden, something I never expected to see was coming my way. It was a huge oil tanker smack dab in the middle of the channel, coming right toward us. I didn't have time to check the chart to see if there was any room on my right. And to tell the truth, we didn't know where we were on the chart. We had not been charting our position. No one does that on a Panama Canal transit. So neither the navigator nor any one else could check for me. I only knew the channel was narrow. But how narrow?

I knew something had gone wrong. Traffic in the canal was regulated. Two ships, going in opposite directions, were simply not supposed to be in that part of the canal. The Panama Canal does not have two way traffic except in the wide Gatun Lake. And we were not anywhere near the lake.

I was doing 12 knots and the tanker was heading toward me at about ten knots. I could tell he was moving at least that fast by the tremendous bow wave he was making as he continued to head right toward me.

Neither one of us blew any whistles. That was the last thing on my mind.

21. Going Home

I quickly decided to continue heading right for him and then at the last moment move out of his way to the right. He helped me make this decision by moving slightly to the right of the center of the channel where he had been.

It didn't all happen in seconds, but it happened very quickly.

About five ship's lengths before we would have collided, I ordered right twenty degrees rudder. My bow responded nicely to our large twin rudders and we started to move right even as we kept moving ahead. But of course my stern was dead ahead of him. Then I immediately ordered, "Shift your rudder," and silently prayed as my helmsman quickly spun his wheel to left twenty degrees rudder. That stopped the bow's swing to the right, and for an instant steadied our course as though we would head for the right bank. Then it quickly started swinging left, pulling my stern to the right and clear of the tanker's path as he steamed past almost close enough to touch.

To my great relief, we were clear of each other and the Willis was once again alone in the channel.

"Reverse your rudder and steady on new course" (I have forgotten the course heading now, but it was the channel course).

All this happened in a very few minutes and without any whistles or other noise. It went off so easily that I think my crew considered it a routine maneuver. It was not! The helmsman, a young quartermaster named Dan McHugh, who should have been nervous as hell, was not. Thank God! But that wasn't the only tough, critical steering challenge for McHugh as you will read later on.

In this book I really don't cover the heavy daily responsibilities of my different crew members in the detail warranted. An experienced, dedicated crew makes the really complicated critical tasks seem routine.

The Panama Canal channel incident is an excellent example of a critical task appearing routine. Any hesitation or failure to respond perfectly to the steering orders the helmsman was receiving could have easily resulted in a devastating collision. Yet the helmsman made it appear routine.

The same is true of crew performance in other parts of the ship, especially in the engine room where ship speed and the power supply throughout the ship is provided and controlled.

One of the more remarkable aspects of the way these responsible tasks were performed on the Willis (and probably on most well-run Navy ships) is a surprising absence of issued orders. Most people aboard ship know their jobs and their responsibilities, and they rarely require direct orders.

I'm probably the only man alive who actually played "chicken" with another ship in the Panama Canal! For some reason I was not as shook up then as I became after I realized how close to disaster we had come.

Normally, I would spend a lot of time studying our planned navigation track. I would even take notes, especially for confined waters like narrow channels, and keep them on a card in my pocket for quick reference. Since no one on a large ship like ours expects to pilot his own way through the canal, neither I nor my navigator had taken any of these precautions.

Also, as I found out later, there was a federal law at that time prohibiting any large ship from going through the Panama Canal without a registered, qualified, Panama Canal pilot. I was not registered as a pilot. But on that day I sure qualified, or I wouldn't be here writing this.

I violated that law. Not deliberately, but nevertheless most definitely. I doubt whether this is true of many other destroyer skippers.

A collision would have tied up the traffic in the canal for a substantial amount of time, and made me infamously famous.

We had one liberty stop on the Atlantic side of the canal. As at the beginning of the war, the venereal disease (VD) rate in Panama was very high. Almost all the ships that visited Panama wound up with six or seven of the crew getting VD of some sort. VD was a major problem for the Navy. On the Nitro we spent a lot of time warning the crew before they went ashore in Panama,

277

21. Going Home

but it never seemed to do any good. The Nitro never left there with a clean slate.

How was the VD detected?

On the Nitro, we held "short arm" inspections. These inspections, which are exactly what you think, would take place several days in a row starting a few days after leaving Panama. They were held by the doctor and his medical staff, but each division officer, as I was on the Nitro, had to be there to make sure everyone showed up,

VD was such a serious problem during the war that the Navy Department prepared an educational movie on the subject. The name of the movie was *DE 777*, and it was exceptionally graphic. In addition to showing the details of the different types of VD, it stressed the impact of the disease on morale and the operational readiness of the ship. It was a very gruesome, realistic, and depressingly vivid movie. But, I thought, it was also very effective in reducing the problem of VD among the ships' crews. Many ships would show the movie over and over again, especially before sending liberty parties ashore after long cruises at sea.

The development of sulfa drugs, and later penicillin, reduced the impact of this disease considerably and eliminated the need for "short arm" inspections.

On this occasion, I took special pains to warn my crew before they went ashore. "It's not worth it," I cautioned repeatedly, "to mess up your lives by acquiring a disease that can have a terrible impact on the rest of your lives." Since large numbers of them were scheduled for discharge as soon as we returned to the states, I had no way of knowing whether my warnings reached all of them. But, in dangerous Panama, most did return from liberty on time and sober – always an encouraging sign.

After my Task Unit got separated in the Canal Zone, I dissolved it and ordered each DE to proceed home independently.

Two days north of Panama, in pretty rough weather, at about 10 pm, I was standing on the bridge, shooting the breeze with my officer of the deck.

"Is the captain up here?" I recognized the voice of "Doc" Brooks, our chief pharmacists mate.

"Over here, Doc," I said.

He walked over. "I have a report on Stewart, sir. It's not good."

He had earlier reported to me that Stewart, an 18 year old seaman first class was ill and that it looked like appendicitis.

He said he was convinced that it was a serious case and that Stewart might need immediate surgery.

"Let's make sure," I said. "Write down all the indications that have convinced you he has it and we'll send a message to the Chief of Naval Operations (CNO). He'll get the medical people to look at it and give us a quick answer."

Well, we did get a quick answer. They agreed completely with Doc and said to pack Stewart in ice (to provide some relief), which Doc had already done. They further added that Stewart needed surgery as soon as possible.

I immediately responded with a message asking if there were any ships nearby that had hospital facilities. Again I got an immediate reply. "No ships your area. Proceed immediately to nearest port that has suitable facilities, keep us advised."

I had never faced this problem before. Here I am, hundreds of miles from the closest port, which is some Central American country I have never been in. The weather is getting worse, Stewart's condition is getting worse, and all I have is Doc, an excellent, solid, smart chief pharmacists mate, but not a surgeon.

Both Doc and I had recently read of a similar incident aboard a U.S. submarine on war patrol in the Pacific. In that incident the pharmacists mate, using primitive tools, had actually done the surgery. And the patient had survived.

"Doc, are you sure you can't do it?" I asked.

"Not only am I sure I can't do it. I am certain I won't do it," he responded firmly, without an explanation for his decision.

I didn't push him. "How long do you think we have before that appendix might burst?" I asked.

21. Going Home

"I really don't know," he answered. "At this point I don't think any one can tell. All we can do is keep him in ice and hope nothing happens."

We had a similar incident on the Willis during the war. A seaman first class became sick and, in the absence of advanced medical facilities (X-rays), subsequently died. Doc had been in the medical group at that time, but he wasn't in charge as he was now. We both remembered that incident and, without any spoken words, it bothered both of us.

I asked my radarmen to be alert to any contacts, hoping that we might run into a ship – any ship, any nation – that might have a medical doctor aboard. But there was nothing on the scope.

I called my navigator and we broke out the books that described the facilities in the countries closest to us. We finally settled on a country that had a very large American Fruit Company presence. Its description said that it included medical facilities. I asked the navigator for a course to that port and our estimated time of arrival if we were at full speed (20 knots).

He gave me the course, and I was about to order it when our radarman shouted "I've got a contact. Looks like a big one." The contact was ahead of us and we had been slowly overtaking it.

I increased speed to the maximum permitted by the growing bad weather and headed for the contact. Of course we didn't know who or what it was, so we were not surprised when we couldn't contact them by radio.

I asked my signalmen if they could contact that ship by light. It wasn't until they turned on our largest searchlight and angled it up to the sky in the direction of the contact that we got a response.

It turned out to be a large U.S. Navy cargo ship returning from the Pacific as we were. They had a hospital and a team of surgeons.

But, again, a communications snafu had occurred. Had they been using the same radio frequencies we used, and had the CNO's office (or someone) been aware of their location, we could have promptly and simply been placed in communication with each other. I was not surprised. At the war's end, many, many procedures unraveled as the Navy shrank at high speed. Ships were pretty much on their own.

But I couldn't believe my luck! I can't describe the relief that I felt. It was almost as though my prayer for that kind of assistance had been quickly answered.

The big ship slowed down to help close the distance between us. After about an hour we were just a few thousand yards from the big ship. I sent them a message.

"Can you put your boat in the water and pick up the patient?" He had much larger boats than I did. I thought surely he would say yes.

"No, unsafe to use my boats in this weather. Use your boat."

"Hell," I thought, "if he can't do it, how can he expect me to do it?" I walked over to the side of the ship where our boat was secured in davits (steel beams that hold the boat). Then I looked down at the black, very turbulent water and decided that using our boat was too risky.

I sent him a message. "Too risky for my small boat."

I was going to suggest that we wait for the weather to get better. But by now Doc had established radio contact with the doctors on the big ship and they insisted the patient be transferred without any delay.

"Come alongside. Transfer the patient by high line," ordered the big ship.

Had it been daylight, it would have been a no-brainer, even though the weather was bad and the ship was being pushed around by the wind and waves. I had gained a lot of experience going alongside in the daylight, but not at night, and not in such bad weather – and not transferring a sick and helpless patient in a stretcher.

My first lieutenant, Rod Haney, an imaginative, competent, enthusiastic man about eight years older than me, came to the bridge and we discussed how the transfer would be made. "He must have a short ride across," I said. "So be sure you can move him quickly once we get hooked up."

21. Going Home

He assured me he could do that. They had a nice strong steel stretcher they could use. His confidence was very reassuring to me. I then asked the exec to see what he could do about minimizing the lights on the ship so the men could do their job but still keep the lights from interfering with my visibility in bringing the ship alongside.

In no time he allowed one light on the bow and one light at the stern and shielded light on our boat deck from where the stretcher would start its journey across.

He then asked the big ship to turn off all their bright lights and shield the lights in the area where the stretcher was coming aboard. They promptly did as requested.

The setup was perfect for my visibility. I could see my bow and stern and I had a clear view of his entire port side from his small bow light to his stern light.

I then went down into sick bay with Lieutenant Haney (who was also the patient's division officer) and Doc to see and tell Stewart what we were going to do. He had never been transferred to another ship by high-line and I had never done it at night in bad weather. I guess I was somewhat scared and wanted some assurance from the one guy I should have been assuring.

When I went to see him they were about to remove him from his sick bay bunk, where he was packed in ice, and place him in the stretcher, along with some more ice.

He was surprisingly calm. A really red headed young man about my size, he talked to me as if he was just going for a ride on a very tame roller coaster. I asked him how he felt and he said O.K., but I could see he was the type of kid who would say O.K. no matter how he felt.

I explained what was going to happen; that we were going to come alongside the big ship, hook up as quickly as we could, and zip him across. "The crossing will be just a few seconds," I said. I told him that it would be very dark, he might get a little wet and he probably wouldn't be able to see much until he was actually on the other ship.

The most surprising thing happened when I finished and asked him if he had any questions. He simply shook his red head and said, "No. Thanks, captain." But the way he said it spoke volumes. He had complete confidence in me and the entire crew, and wasn't one iota as nervous as he had a right to be.

Never once did he ask, "Is there any danger of me falling into the water between the ships?" It would have been a legitimate question since the ship was far from being a stable platform.

Nor did he ask, "What will happen if I do fall in the water? Is there any ship in the tailback position to pick me up?"

I had thought about both of those questions and would have answered truthfully had he asked. But he didn't.

His complete and utter confidence that his shipmates, including me, would get it done rubbed off on me. And I was less nervous as I shook his hand and said "Good luck with the doctors." His smiling thank you sent me on the way to the bridge.

Once there, it took a few minutes for my eyes to adjust to the darkness again. I took another look at the small light on the other ship's bow, and then on my bow. I checked the small light on his stern and on my stern, and could see a soft glow of light leaking around the shields where they had Stewart in the stretcher. I wanted to make sure I saw everything I needed to see – and I did.

I watched my helmsman (it was Quartermaster Dan McHugh again) to see how hard he had to work to keep the ship on the courses I gave him. Although he worked hard and quick, he made it look easy and I could see he was in complete control.

I had a good feeling about how we were riding. "Pass the word. We are going alongside." I said. And I heard the bridge talker quietly repeat to the people on deck, "Going alongside."

The big ship had selected a course that put the wind and the heavy seas on his starboard bow. We were on the other side of him, in his lee.

I gave the steering and speed orders to move us in closer to the big ship. In an alongside maneuver the major concern is how

21. Going Home

much and how long the incoming ship deviates from the designated course as he closes the distance to the receiving ship.

The receiving ship always steers a steady course at a steady speed. The incoming ship (the Willis) has to steer a number of different courses and speeds to overtake and gradually move in close to the receiving ship. Then, when in the desired position for transfer, he matches the speed and course of the receiving ship.

No helmsman can keep a ship on a designated course all the time, even in good calm weather. There is always a little deviation to one side and then to the other. In rough weather, where the sea can literally pick the ship up and move it one way or the other, a good helmsman sees what is happening and always brings it quickly back to the designated course.

In bad weather, as we were experiencing, McHugh had to move the rudder back and forth repeatedly in varying amounts to stay as close as possible to the courses I called out to him. He worked hard and smoothly, minimizing deviations from the designated course no matter how the sea pushed the ship and tried to wrest control from him.

If I have to blow my own horn on this incident, I will. The next ten minutes were almost out of a textbook on really good seamanship. Both ships hooked up in just minutes, and before I knew it Stewart was on the big ship and we were unhooking.

I was so happy as we steamed away from the side of the big ship that I got on the loudspeaker and thanked my crew for such an outstanding job. I complimented the helmsman and all the deck force, as well as the engineers for their response to engine orders.

Shortly after the transfer we received word that, indeed, Stewart was in bad shape, but the surgery was successful and the patient was fine.

I passed the word on to CNO. I never mentioned that his people were not aware of the location of all their ships.

I did not see Stewart again until 2009 (63 years later), at a reunion of the Willis crew. Even though much older, he was easy to recognize with his still vivid red hair. He still considered his transfer at sea routine, and never doubted at any time that it would turn out O.K.

That deep, almost unlimited, confidence and complete trust that the officers and sailors have in their commanding officer and each other is something I never really thought about until my experience with Stewart. It is something I have never forgotten.

We stopped for a week at the Philadelphia shipyard to discharge a lot of our crew and pick up some replacements. The sailors who owned the boats we brought back were discharged there, and I offloaded the boats for them. I often wondered what happened to that very unique Japanese suicide boat.

I knew that our ship was scheduled for preservation and then assignment to Green Cove Springs, a small port in northern Florida. The Navy had contracted to build a dozen or so huge piers there to berth the WWII destroyer escort fleet of about 300 ships.

From Philadelphia we went to the shipyard at Charleston, South Carolina, for two months. There, all required maintenance was done to put us in good shape should the ship ever be needed in the future.

Figure 286: **Wilbur.** Posing with Boatswain's Mate 2nd Class Bolce, one of his best friends.

Chapter 22

Wilbur

It was in Charleston that I said goodbye to Wilbur, our ship's dog. One of his favorite sailors, who was getting a discharge, asked if he could take him home, and I approved.

I had been instrumental in acquiring Wilbur in 1943. I talked Captain Atterbury into letting us get a ship's dog and sent two sailors to the dog pound in Norfolk. They returned with a little, coal black puppy. He was short and stubby, with a personality that made all the sailors like him, even those who had to clean up after him.

Whatever his breed was, it turned out to be perfect for a seagoing life. He was quickly named Wilbur, which was the ship's voice radio call name at the time.

Wilbur was assigned a bottom bunk in the crew's compartment. It was low enough that he could crawl into it. During one of my evening tours of the ship, when I was the exec, I saw Wilbur sleeping on his back, his black paws out over the cover as though some one had tucked him in.

But he was seldom in his bunk. He ranged all over the ship, including the officer's wardroom where he often took a snooze on our leather couch.

He soon learned that there was a group on watch on the bridge around the clock and spent a lot of time there, just keeping them company.

22. Wilbur

One of the most amazing things about Wilbur was that he learned to climb the slanting vertical ladders that were all over the ship. If he hadn't learned, he would have been stuck down below in the crew's compartment all day. He was only about a foot and half long and the rungs on the ladders are a foot apart. He was smart enough to stay away from the vertical ladders and use only those that had a slant to them. He scrambled up those almost as fast as we did. I never tired of watching him go up and down the ladders, even though it soon became routine.

Often Wilbur seemed to disappear. But we soon discovered that was mostly at night, and meant he was topside somewhere on a weather deck. We simply couldn't see him when the ship was darkened at night, and that was all the time when we were underway.

You'd think that the sailors would complain about having to clean up after him. But they didn't, and he was usually smart enough to use the weather decks where a simple stream from a fire hose could do the job.

It was especially heartwarming to find him on the bridge during the mid-watch (midnight to 4 am). If the men on watch fed him, he would sometimes stand an entire four hour watch.

He had the run of the mess hall, but no one ever fed him there. He seemed to sense that the master-at-arms didn't want him there begging for food. If anything, he was overfed, and he grew into roly-poly proportions. But his increasing weight didn't seem to affect his ability to get up and down the ladders.

We never gave much thought to what life at sea would be like for a dog. Wilbur taught us one day after we had tied up at a pier in Newport, Rhode Island. It was in the middle of winter and there had been a heavy snowfall that covered the entire pier. Wilbur had never been ashore since we brought him aboard as an eager, strong, inquisitive pup about nine months earlier.

He was at the gangway, and sailors were leaving and coming aboard performing different errands. He was a good sailor, never got seasick, and in port never tried to go ashore.

However, this one afternoon, a bright, sunny, very cold, snowy day, he hopped on the gangway and trotted out to the pier. After he got off the gangway he was immediately engulfed in snow. That didn't bother him since he had seen snow before on the ship's topside.

We watched him turn left and walk through the snow toward the end of the pier. To our surprise when he got to the end he didn't stop as we expected. Instead, he walked right off the end of the pier. It was about a six foot drop but it wasn't into the water. He fell on a large thick sheet of ice and struggled there to get on his feet. But we could see that he was hurt.

A couple sailors scrambled down to the ice and retrieved him. Our pharmacist mate examined him and pronounced that he had suffered a broken leg.

They patched him up and made a small wooden splint for the broken leg and soon Wilbur was hobbling all over the ship. It took him a little time before he could again use the slanting ladders.

Wilbur never went ashore after that incident. He rode the ship halfway around the world, from the east coast to Guam and back, and was the only one not to go on leave or go ashore in all that time.

It was with genuine feelings of sadness that I said goodbye to Wilbur. We all hugged him there at the quarterdeck then watched as he walked hesitantly ashore at the end of something he had never experienced in his entire life – a leash.

While our experience with Wilbur was really wonderful, I can't say the same for our un-named cat. He just appeared aboard ship one day when we were underway, and was adopted by members of the crew. His personality was the opposite of Wilbur's. He was a loner with a small circle of friends who took care of him.

One night when we were at sea, our lifeguard sentry back aft heard a loud splash on the starboard side. As he was supposed to do, he threw over a lighted life ring and initiated a man-overboard alarm.

The OOD brought the ship around and headed for the lighted life ring, hoping that whoever fell in the water would be near it

22. Wilbur

or hanging onto it. As he slowed the ship to a stop not far from the life ring, two of our trained expert swimmers went into the water looking for whoever had fallen overboard.

They returned to the side of the ship and one of them handed up our wet and shivering cat. They had very luckily stumbled across him struggling to keep afloat not too far from the life ring.

All "man-overboard" alarms require that a complete muster be held of the entire crew to make sure no one is missing. When our muster was completed we realized that some one had probably thrown the cat overboard.

That was not the end of the incident.

A few days later the cat disappeared completely.

I had not really thought much about the cat's disappearance but, apparently, some of the sailors had.

About a week later, the master at arms came to me and said there was a fight down below and I was needed. Normally the master at arms can handle fights without coming to the exec.

When I went down in the compartment I saw two men facing each other about five feet apart. One had a large wrench in his hand and the other held a fairly large knife. Despite the master at arms' efforts, neither man would give up his weapon, and that's why he called me.

They both promptly obeyed my order to put down their weapons, and we hustled them off to our small brig.

The sailor with the wrench had accused the other guy of throwing the cat overboard. He had no real evidence, other than his knowledge that the guy hated the cat.

They were both disciplined, and that ended the "Cat Incident."

Ships are not encouraged to have pets aboard. But while the cat was the source of some trouble, Wilbur was the perfect ship's mascot.

No matter how many different ways it is written, the life of a captain aboard a seagoing ship is more lonely than it is exciting. In many ways, Wilbur was as close to me and as much a companion, as he was to the sailors in the crew. I started to miss him the moment he walked down the gangway.

On the lighter side, our stay in Charleston suddenly left me with a great deal of time on my hands. There were not many ships in the yard, and there was little or no social life at the officers' club, which was in the process of shutting down.

There was a small, nine hole golf course on the base within walking distance of the ship, so I started playing golf. It was fun, but the game was much too slow for me. I shot below 50 only once for the nine hole course. But that once (a 39) was good enough to win a tournament!

I had little or nothing to do in the evenings. During the war we could usually find some type of dance or social event sponsored by local groups, but not now.

It was next to impossible to meet girls, so I did a little research to find locations where I might meet some. That's when I enrolled in a night school that taught shorthand for aspiring secretaries.

I was the only man in a class of 24. Some of the 23 girls were really good looking. I thought I had hit gold until after the class ended on the first night. There was a mob of guys waiting outside. Every one of my classmates seemed to have a boy friend.

I stuck with the class for several weeks and did learn the rudiments of short hand. But I never got a date.

Figure 292: **USS Willis after the war.** She is 31 months old in this early 1946 picture, taken after returning from Guam and shortly before repainting, preservation, and final berthing in Green Cove Springs. The items hanging in front of the smoke stack are not laundry – they are probably signal flags being hung for drying. A signal flag is visible, flying on the main mast.

Chapter 23

Life Span

By the time our overhaul in the Charleston Navy Yard was finished, about seventy-five percent of my original crew had been discharged back into civilian life. For every ten men I discharged, I received about two or three replacements. So shipboard life, as I had known it, had just about disappeared.

With about one-third the number of my original crew, we got underway and brought our completely overhauled ship to the mouth of the St. Johns river in Florida. We picked up a pilot and continued on toward Green Cove Springs.

The St. Johns river is the longest river in Florida, with a length of about 300 miles, mostly in a north and south direction. After about an hour and a half, the river started to widen considerably and we saw about 70 or 80 DEs. They were nested in groups of about eight or ten with obvious room for many more (see Figure 294).

"They can't all be secured to buoys, and they can't be anchored out there like that," I said to the pilot.

"You're right," he replied. "They're secured to some heavy steel beams that are embedded in the bottom of the river, and that's where I'm taking you now."

"What about all those piers they were supposed to have?" I asked.

He didn't have to answer. I could see the construction ac-

23. Life Span

Figure 294: **Green Cove Springs before construction of piers.**

tivity over on our right. Only one of the 12 planned piers was finished and it was full of more DEs.

In about an hour we were nested alongside another DE and both our anchor chains were secured to the underwater beams.

It was a sad silent arrival. There was no one on any of the other ships in our nest, except for the few line handlers securing our lines. It reminded me of a graveyard.

I was unhappy with our berth. I had expected to go alongside a pier where we could leave and come aboard as we pleased. Now we had to put our boat in the water for that purpose.

I went ashore as soon as I could and found my new boss, a Navy commander in one of the ships alongside the pier. He was sympathetic but I could see he had limited resources himself.

"You are the senior officer in that nest," he said. He didn't tell me I was responsible for the other seven ships in the nest and I didn't ask because I was afraid he might say "yes."

He then summarized what I had to do in the next few weeks or months.

Figure 295: **Green Cove Springs after construction of piers.**

"Inventory everything on the ship. Make sure that it is accurate and that all the 'title B' equipment is accounted for." (Title B was our internal list of valuable equipment like sextants, radio equipment, and all portable items of value.)

"Be especially careful in preparing your inventory of all classified papers, publications and equipment," he continued, and handed me a memorandum which covered my duties. "Your job now is to get the ship ready for preservation and help supervise the actual preservation itself." We discussed personnel matters and he agreed to help me with the boating needed to get my men back and forth to the ship.

I returned to the ship as upbeat as I could be and explained everything to my skeleton crew of about 50 enlisted men and 4 officers. They were more curious about what would happen next rather than going ashore. And that made it a little easier for me.

It didn't take us long to get into a daily routine as we started our chores to decommission and preserve the ship (decommission means to take the ship out of active service and reassign the

23. Life Span

crew).

One morning we were surprised to see a large water moccasin snake on our main deck forward. We were told that they came aboard via the anchor chain. The sailors promptly rigged large rat guards (sheets of metal about two feet in diameter) around the anchor chains, and we didn't see any more snakes.

There wasn't much to do in Green Cove Springs. It was a sleepy little town about 30 miles inland from the Atlantic Ocean and 25 miles south of Jacksonville, Florida. And for some reason, probably poor transportation, the sailors weren't too interested in going ashore.

It was my first experience with a reserve fleet. And to tell the truth I never did meet anyone there who had any experience with reserve fleets. For a while, it was difficult to find out what was in store for us. However, I soon learned that once alongside a pier, our topside gun mounts would all be "cocooned" (covered with some kind of plastic asbestos to withstand the elements). Because of these cocooned ships, it was also known as the "mothball fleet."

One afternoon we were warned that a hurricane was on the way up the Florida coast, and that it might hit our anchorage and Green Cove Springs. The prospect of a hurricane didn't bother me too much. After all, we were veterans of really rough North Atlantic storms, and didn't think hurricanes could be much worse.

That was my attitude until I read all the literature they sent out to me from our "reserve" headquarters there in Green Cove Springs.

I read that the steel chains and beams anchoring our ships were designed to withstand hurricane force winds... but this would be their first test. Also, I read that the extreme high velocity of the winds could actually make it difficult to breathe, and that some type of rescue breathing mask should be worn if we experienced really high winds.

I got my small group together, distributed the masks, did what we could to secure the lines between the unmanned ships, and told them what I had read about the dangers of a hurricane.

I think I scared them more than I helped them confront the hurricane.

As for myself, yes, now I was worried. This seemed far worse than just being in a heavy storm at sea, where no other ships are tied to you and in a position to inflict heavy damage. I had been in many rough seas, even a roll of 62 degrees, but deep down, I never thought my ship would roll over.

There was a dearth of information about what to do in a hurricane. In those days these monsters were not named and tracked as they are today. Unfortunately, I had read just enough about the December 18, 1944 typhoon that devastated the U.S. Navy's powerful Third Fleet in the Philippine Sea to make me nervous. Three destroyers sank in that storm, and that was the part that had me worried. Yes, this time I was scared.

The hurricane hit, but fortunately the ships all held together. The "I" beams embedded in the river held, as did all our anchor chains. There was considerable thrashing and bouncing together among the ships, but no real damage. When the wind reached a velocity where I thought it wise to put on the masks, I first tried it myself to see if it made any difference ... and it didn't. The mask was much more of a bother than an asset. I don't know if the wind velocity wasn't high enough to warrant its use, or whether it was just a plain dumb idea. I told my men to forget it.

In my subsequent experience and research about hurricanes, the need for the masks has never been mentioned.

We rode out the hurricane nicely. I am rather certain, however, we did not even receive hurricane force winds.

It was very lonesome sitting out there with all those silent dark ships. I'd look out my porthole at the rows and rows of unmanned DEs and get a lump in my throat.

We were now care-takers for our warship in the twilight of its life. Everyone was getting discharged and going home. But for various reasons I was sticking around. Of course, I knew what those reasons were.

23. Life Span

In less than five years I had jumped from college student to being a task unit commander with responsibilities, challenges, excitement, and professional growth opportunities seen by few guys my age.

I also discovered that I adapted well to a sea-going life and naval routines. The quick promotions and rapid ascent to command added a lot of luster to the prospects of a Naval career. I can truthfully say that in my 31 months aboard the Willis I had grown from an immature officer to a hardened professional.

It is easy to forget that warships are also homes. They are homes to men who live together, eat together, laugh together, grow in knowledge together, fight together, and face dangers – even death – together.

These men bond to each other. They become shipmates, many for the remainder of their lives.

The warship hull itself, in the beginning, is nothing more than a mass of metal beams, and a multitude of engineering and other separate parts. Then, when it is commissioned, it somehow takes on a personality of its own. And the men in the crew bond with it too. And, just as the bonds between men are strong, so is the bond between the men and the warship.

I never felt that bond so strongly until it all came to an end at Green Cove Springs. It was sad and almost painful to see the Willis and hundreds of individual lifeless, destroyer escorts nested quietly in the St. Johns River.

A few days after the hurricane scare, and that's what it was, we were moved to one of the newly completed piers. That made life much easier for us.

There was a large barracks-like ship nearby into which the entire crew moved. We kept a watch on the ship but no one, including myself, lived aboard. The preservation work proceeded on schedule and I found myself with less and less to do. It was at that point that my boss told me I would be attached to his staff after the Willis was decommissioned.

That's when I started to think about life without the ship which had been my home for so long. It's hard to describe what it's like to live aboard a ship from its birth to death, or, in Navy terms, from commissioning to decommissioning. For my ship, the USS Willis (DE 395), that was 31 months.

I was the only officer to spend the entire 31 months on the Willis.

It was my home and my life for all that time, as well as my first command. I have racked my brain trying to find something in civilian life comparable to a "first command." I can't.

The Willis was the source of unforgettable adventures, many of which I have described in these chapters. It was also the source of mind numbing boredom, bottomless despair, and sky high elation.

But, more than anything else, we were always just one second away from real excitement. Whether it was an echo at the end of a ping, or a "man overboard" alarm after a quiet dinner, it was like sitting on a powder keg. We never knew if or when it would go off.

I thought the need for staying on my toes would fade somewhat after the war ended, but I was wrong. Yes, a war brings its own built-in threats and excitement, but simply going to sea in a ship does the same. And in the years to come, I went to sea in many different kinds of ships, and each had its own different kind of excitement piled on top of the massive, unpredictable oceans.

About three months after arriving at Green Cove Springs the Willis was officially decommissioned. I was handed the commissioning pennant which had flown at the highest part of the ship all during its active life. About a foot and a half long and a few inches wide, it was weather beaten and ragged, but is a symbol which I still have and revere.

Acknowledgements and Alibis

During World War II I spent so much time at sea, out of touch with events reported in the media, that anyone who read their local newspapers or listened to the radio would probably know more about what I was doing than I did.

Of course, that all changed when the war ended. But there remained for me a large information void for that world-shaking period – a void I never thought about filling until 74 years later when I started writing my memoirs.

That's when I discovered how much I didn't know about many war-time operations in which I was involved.

That discovery put a new zip into my life as my research started filling in holes that I hadn't known even existed.

However, writing *Living with the Torpedo* taught me that there is a tremendous gulf between writing a memoir and getting it published.

But lucky for me, I have family and friends who have those skills and graciously made them available to me.

On these pages I wish to extend to them my heartfelt gratitude for the time and effort spent in my behalf and acknowledge that the book wouldn't be what it is without their contributions. My many thanks to:

- The terrific people who read the entire manuscript and offered invaluable comments: John R. Catsis; Kevin W. Olden,

23. Life Span

    CAPT, MC, USN (Ret.); Kenneth Pollock; George A. Sotos; Tanya A. Roth, Esq.; and Georgette C. Sotos.

- Admiral James Stavridis, USN (Ret.), for writing the forward.

- My family for their unflagging support: George A. Sotos, MD (my younger son) John G. Sotos, MD (my older son), and Georgette C. Sotos – my wife of 60 years, and a strict grammar disciplinarian! I am especially grateful to John, who, after completion of the first draft, took charge and inserted the illustrations, and organized and managed the book through succeeding drafts.

    Many thanks to all!

* * *

    Among the large number of individuals mentioned in this memoir, the following are not real names: Holidan, Ray, Skyzanski, Muldoon, Collins, Ridge, Hoover, Hart, Greenwald, Harris, Morgan, Randolph, Roger, Marty's bar, Bob Norman, Bowman, Tim Maloney, Takis Adams, Mike Turner, Harris, John (xo), Deers, Elise, Greg, and Stewart.

    Of the many ways to present information to readers, I have chosen to use dialog liberally, given that spoken words are the cornerstone of a Navy officer's life aboard ship and on shore – or were, until the advent of email. Although perfect recall of decades-old conversation is, of course, not possible, the tenor and tone of the conversations are accurate, as are any operational or technical matters discussed.

    Similarly, ship courses, speeds, and time details in the text (as on pages 105, 165, 177) are subject to the author's memory lapses. Moreover, in situations such as that on page 183, we moved about so frequently that specific course and speed details were not always maintained or recorded in the deck logs.

Instead, watch standers would use broad entries such as "maneuvering to change screening stations for flight operations" or "to investigate sonar contact" or "to investigate possible enemy submarine" or "to attack possible enemy submarine" or "to pick up survivors." However, those considerable details were recorded by our Combat Information Center (CIC) which maintained a running track of all ship movements.

Nevertheless, the contribution of these elements to the stories they tell are factually correct and I have used specific courses and speeds to provide a clear and accurate picture of the scope of these maneuvers.

Appendix A

The Walter Willis Story

My ship, the USS Willis, was named after Ensign Walter M. Willis, who died at Pearl Harbor. What sort of deeds merit the naming of a ship after a person? This appendix provides an answer.

It also presents an interesting and all but unknown story showing how close the Navy came to detecting the Japanese fleet before the Pearl Harbor attack. In fact, the Navy *did* detect the fleet – Ensign Willis saw it, and reported it, but his report was overruled by a more senior officer, allowing the Japanese to attack with surprise.

Because such a story seems fantastic, we should examine its source. This appendix contains almost the entirety of a letter written in 1997 by retired Navy Captain Norman J. "Dusty" Kleiss, who was a squadron-mate of Ensign Willis' and who personally witnessed Willis endeavoring to make his report.

Willis and a lieutenant (whom Kleiss names) were pilots assigned to Scouting Squadron 6 aboard the USS Enterprise. On December 4, 1941 – three days before the December 7 attack – Willis, flying on the lieutenant's wing, indicated the presence of ships with hand signals, but the lieutenant saw no ships, even after flying ahead some miles. In his letter, Kleiss devotes much space to describing Willis' keen vision, and recalls other exceptionally keen-eyed pilots who were doubted by others having only normal visual acuity.

Capt. Kleiss gained great distinction as a pilot at the Battle of Midway in 1942. He died in 2016 at age 100. His letter is reprinted at length to show that, 56 years after the events he reports, his memories were clear and his confidence strong. Kleiss was writing to the leader of the Willis reunion group, Daniel McHugh. A copy of the letter is reportedly deposited at the Minnesota Historical Society in Minneapolis. (Ensign Willis was from Minnesota.)

The letter follows.

• • •

23 October 1997

Dear Daniel:

It is indeed strange that you should write to me concerning Walter Willis since the circumstances of his final hours (or minutes) remains [sic] the greatest enigma, or unsolved mystery, of my naval career. More about that later.

I remember the incident of Walter's sighting of ships on 4 December 1941 as vividly as though it happened yesterday. Lt. Clarence Dick[inson] and Ens. Willis came into the ready room at about the same time.

"I tell you there were no ships out there," yelled Dickinson.

"But I distinctly saw ships out there!" firmly replied Willis.

"We went ahead miles and miles and there were no ships," responded Dickinson.

"But we didn't go nearly far enough!" Willis insisted; and with uncharacteristic assertiveness he demanded that RADM Halsey be informed.

There was no question which pilot I believed. Walter was quiet and not likely to engage in idle conversation, but when he talked his facts were indeed facts and his message was not garbled. Clarence Dickinson, unfortunately, was quite the opposite.

One other of Walter's characteristics was his remarkable eyesight. Long before the 4 December incident he established his ability to spot things earlier than his fellow pilots. Even today I use his eyesight as a standard of comparison.

For example, when the newspaper reported the last supersonic flight of Gen. Chuck Yeager at age 79 and his still 20/10 eyesight, I immediately thought of Walter.

When fellow astronauts ridiculed the detailed observations of one of their crew, and his observations were later verified, I thought of him.

Likewise in the days following Pearl Harbor day, when Adm. Kimmel insisted that ship crews have inspection in white service uniforms, I was one of the pilots who reported that we could spot the ENTERPRISE from 50 miles away. First we saw a glimmer of reflected light from an aircraft canopy and then a tiny patch of white. Then we trained our gunnery telescope on the spot and saw the superstructure of the ship. I immediately thought, "Walter wouldn't have needed the telescope."

Of course RADM Halsey wasted no time in getting Adm. Kimmel to cancel the order and have khaki uniforms worn at all times and covers put over aircraft canopies.

One other inconsequential thing I always recall about him was his ever-present bunch of keys. Instead of the usual tag, or oddity, his chain included a small pair of red dice.

One of my duties, after Pearl Harbor day, was Assistant Personnel Officer which included finding out what happened to who. Of course we made some mistakes. For example we inventoried Frank "Pat" Patriarca's personal effects and had crossed him off the list of the living because he was last seen heading out to sea with three zero's [sic] after him and many days had passed with no report of his survival.

To our amazement, as the ENTERPRISE pulled into port, there sat Pat on a bollard, with his usual "chessie cat grin," waving to us.

"The devil wouldn't have me. Said I could raise more hell on earth than he could down there!" was his greeting.

One report I got from a pilot, probably not from our squadron, was that Walter was seen to shoot down an enemy plane, and later encounter still another enemy plane. Apparently out of bullets, he was seen to chop off the tail of the enemy plane but both planes then crashed into the side of a cliff. About the same time a report was made that his remains had been identified because his unusual key chain with the red dice had been found in the wreckage.

305

A. THE WALTER WILLIS STORY

His photo ID card was turned over to me (I do not recall who gave it to me or whether the key chain was turned in) and I kept it as a memento hoping to turn it over to a family member some time. I had it when we moved to Berkeley Springs, W.V. in 1965 but somewhere after that time I lost it.

I have been told several times, by several different people, that my recollection of Walter Willis' last flight was erroneous, that they saw him shot down at sea or saw the wreckage of his plane elsewhere, but I still believe the first report given to me was true.

I do not doubt for an instant that Walter would have noticed what was happening as he approached Barber's Point, and that his gunnery with his .50 cal. fixed guns was sufficient to bring down an enemy plane and that his dedication was sufficient that he would try to chop off the tail of an enemy plane when he ran out of ammo. Or that he would fly with his keychain.

The report of Walter's sacrifice was so believable and so much in character that I did not write down the details in my log book or other records.

I find so many errors in books and movies and other reports of Pearl Harbor day that unfolding the truth is most difficult. Walter Lord asked for information from my log book when he re [sic] researched for his book "Incredible Victory." I had pointed out to him some errors in his "Day of Infamy."

I wish I could be present for the December Seventh occasion but I cannot make it. ...

After the Battle of Midway, Scouting Six was disbanded, or merged, with the remaining personnel of VB-6, to form VB-13. This accounts for the confusion in identifying personnel of VS-6 or VB-6. The excerpt on page 3 of *Steady Nerves and Stout Hearts** is in error, as Jack Leaming** has indicated. The fact is that Walter Willis indicated to Clarence Dickinson by hand signals (as he flew wing on him) that he saw ships ahead. Dickinson flew ahead a few miles and then flew back to the ship despite Walter's continued hand signals. (We were under strict radio silence.)

I hope the above will be of some help to you.

... I hope to meet some of Walter's relatives sometime.

Sincerely,
N.J. "Dusty" Kleiss
CAPT USN (Ret.)

---

* See in bibliography: Cressman & Wenger.
** ARM2/c Jack Leaming was another Enterprise crew-member and Dec. 7 aviator.

From the *Dictionary of American Naval Fighting Ships*:

Commissioned an ensign on 10 September, Willis soon joined Bombing Squadron (VB) 6, based in Enterprise (CV-6), and flew Douglas SBD Dauntless dive bombers until early in December 1941. On the morning of 7 December, as Enterprise was returning from Wake Island to Hawaii, the carrier sent up a flight of SBD's to scout the water ahead. Willis took off in one of these bombers for what was intended to be a routine flight to Ford Island, the naval air station at Pearl Harbor. However, instead of enjoying an ordinary scouting mission, these planes ran head-on into a war, for they arrived almost simultaneously with the start of the Japanese attack upon Pearl Harbor. In the ensuing aerial melee, Willis and his gunner were among the Americans shot down.

Appendix B

Photo Credits

Boxes contain the figure numbers, each of which matches the page number where the figure appears. The credit appears after the figure number.

Images for which formal permission is not acknowledged below are either historical artifacts now in the public domain or are used by the author for purposes of comment, criticism, and scholarship pursuant to the Fair Use Doctrine of the U.S. Copyright Act.

<u>Front Cover</u> Author <u>2</u> US Navy photograph <u>16</u> Morison, page 15. <u>19</u> Churchill, page 473. <u>20</u> U.S. Navy photo via Capt. Jerry Mason, USN (Ret.) and uboatarchive.net. <u>27</u> Author. <u>30</u> Author. Photo by Georgette Sotos. <u>36</u> U.S. National Archives and Records Administration, photograph 520819. <u>52</u> Author. <u>58</u> Author. <u>68</u> Author <u>73</u> Library of Congress LC-USW33-017643-ZC. Cover of *Newsweek* magazine, Oct. 26, 1942. Cover of *Bureau of Naval Personnel Information Bulletin*, January 1943. <u>84</u> U.S. Navy photo via navsource.org via former crewmember SM3 Lannie Walker. <u>98</u> Author. <u>108</u> navsourec.org via CMoMM Anthony J. Pellachio. <u>128</u> Author. <u>134</u> navsource.org. <u>139</u> Author's collection. <u>144</u> USN photo #80-G-7251 from National Archives and Records Administration, College Park, Maryland, via Sean Hert and navsource.org – bit.ly/1g66rIs <u>152</u> Author. <u>160</u> Author. <u>170</u> Author. <u>172</u> Author. <u>176</u> Author. <u>184</u> Top: Author. Bottom: Royal Navy, via Wikimedia, via photograph A 31000 from the collections of the Imperial War Museums (collection no. 4700-01). <u>187</u> Naval Historical Center photograph NH 98868 http://1.usa.gov/1aqFDSR <u>198</u> Author. <u>207</u> Captain Jerry Mason, USN (Ret.) <u>210</u> Capt. Jerry Mason, USN (Ret.) and uboatarchive.net. <u>217</u> Author. <u>218</u> Author. <u>226</u> Author. <u>234</u> U.S. Navy photograph (USS Hubbard) via Wikimedia – bit.ly/565OUj <u>238</u> U.S. Navy photograph via Wikimedia.org. <u>240</u> Adapted from Navpers 16116. <u>241</u> Author. <u>243</u> Author. <u>246</u> Author. <u>247</u> Author. <u>250</u>

B. Photo Credits

Author. [252] Author. [260] Author. [272] Author. [286] Author. [292] Author's collection. [294] Clay County Historical Society via navsource.org via RM2/c Ken Adams. [295] Clay County Historical Society via navsource.org via RM2/c Ken Adams. **Back Cover** Christopher Michel via Wikimedia. Cropped and brightened.

Appendix C

Bibliography

PRINT PUBLICATIONS

Anderson, Walter. "AM-FM Mystery." *Radio Age: The Vintage Radio Journal of the Mid-Atlantic Antique Radio Club*. September 2004: 7.

Bercuson, David J.; Herwig, Holger H. *One Christmas in Washington: the Secret Meeting between Roosevelt and Churchill that Changed the World*. Woodstock, NY: Overlook Press, 2005.

Billings, Richard N. *Battleground Atlantic: How the Sinking of a Single Japanese Submarine Assured the Outcome of World War II*. New York: NAL Caliber, 2006.

Churchill, Winston S. *The Second World War. Volume VI. Triumph and Tragedy*. New York: Houghton Mifflin, 1953.

Cremer, Peter; Wilson, Lawrence (transl.). *U-Boat Commander: A Periscope View of the Battle of the Atlantic*. Annapolis: Naval Institute Press, 1984. (First Published in Great Britain as *U-333* by the Bodley Head Ltd, 1984.)

Cressman, Robert J.; Wenger, Michael. *Steady Nerves and Stout Hearts: The Enterprise (CV-6) Air Group and Pearl Harbor, 7 December 1941*. Missoula, MT: Pictorial Histories Publishing Co., 1991.

Davis, James Martin. *"Top Secret," the story of the invasion of Japan*. Ranger Publications, P.O. Box 1385, Omaha, NE 68101.

Hickam, Homer H. *Torpedo Junction*. Annapolis, MD: Naval Institute Press, 1989.

C. BIBLIOGRAPHY

Hornfischer, James D. *The Last Stand of the Tin Can Sailors*. New York: Bantam Books, 2004.

Just, Paul. *Vom Seeflieger zum Uboot-Fahrer: Feindfluge und Feindfarhten, 1939-1945*. Motorbuch Verlag, 1979. [An anonymous translation was supplied to the author in 2012.]

Keith, Don. *Final Patrol: True Stories of World War II Submarines*. New York: New American Library, 2006.

Morison, Samuel E. *History of the United States Naval Operations in World War II. Volume I. The Battle of the Atlantic*. Edison, NJ: Castle Books, Reprint of 1947 Little, Brown edition. [This volume is cited in footnotes as "Morison-I"]

Morison, Samuel E. *History of the United States Naval Operations in World War II. Volume X. The Atlantic Battle Won*. Edison, NJ: Castle Books, Reprint of 1956 Little, Brown edition. [This volume is cited in footnotes as "Morison"]

Navpers 16116. *Naval Ordnance and Gunnery*. Washington, D.C.: U.S.G.P.O., 1944. 564 pages.

Roscoe, Theodore. *United States Destroyer Operations in WWII*. Annapolis: Naval Institute Press, 1953.

Sweeney, Charles W. *War's End: An Eyewitness Account of America's Last Atomic Mission*. New York: Avon Books, 1997.

Wynn, Kenneth. *U-boat Operations of the Second World War, Volume 2: Career Histories, U511-UIT25*. Annapolis: Naval Institute Press, 1998.

Y'Blood, William T. *Hunter Killer*. Annapolis: Naval Institute Press, 1983.

INTERNET RESOURCES

www.pearlharborsurvivorsonline.org/html/invasion%20plans.htm

www.uboatarchive.net/U549blockislandreport.htm

wikipedia.org/wiki/operation_downfall#kamikaze

Index

This index, containing only ship names, is in strict alphabetical order, which is not always numerical order.

Ahrens, 212–214
Arizona, 244
Arkansas, 90
Asphodel, 202
Barr, 213, 215
Basiljka, 130
Blenny, 264
Block Island, 204, 210, 212–215, 221
Bogue, 152, 157, 160, 161, 163, 164, 166, 167, 170–174, 176–178, 181–183, 188, 191, 196, 198, 201–207, 211, 214–217, 219, 226, 227, 229–231, 235, 249, 261, 263
Chatelain, 222
Cockrill, 250
Comfort, 256
Core, 230
DuPont, 72–74
Edmund Lukenbach, 130
Elmore, 213, 214
Enterprise, 304–306
Franklin, 238, 242
Frederick C. Davis, 227, 231–233
Guadalcanal, 222, 223
Gunvor, 130
Haverfield, 157, 158, 202, 203, 214
Hobson, 202
I-52, 206–208

Janssen, 68, 157, 198, 245, 260
Jean Barte, 212
Liverpool, 40
Long Island, 84
Lycoming, 245
Massachusetts, 212
Miantonomah, 130
Mont-Blanc, 28
Nitro, 21, 22, 25–28, 32, 34, 36, 37, 39, 41, 44, 47, 50, 52–54, 63–65, 67, 69–72, 74–76, 78–81, 85, 88–90, 93, 96, 100, 101, 104, 114, 124, 132, 228, 239, 277, 278
Noah, 140
PC 451, 108, 109, 113, 131, 133–139, 145, 147, 149, 150, 153
PC 476, 21, 84, 85, 87, 92, 98, 100, 101, 114, 115, 124, 130–133, 135, 154
Paine, 214
Pillsbury, 20, 222, 223
Pollux, 76, 77
Prince Rupert, 202
Pyro, 36, 39
R-12, 144–147
RO 501, 203, 204
Ranger, 212
Robinson, 203, 204

INDEX

Royal Sovereign, 69, 71
SC 449, 145
Santa Fe, 238
Sarsfield, 187
Sperry, 245, 246, 260–263
Sturtevant, 129, 130, 140
Swenning, 157, 191, 194, 195, 245, 250, 260, 275
Titanic, 72
Truxton, 76, 77
U-1224, 203
U-1229, 227, 229
U-1235, 230, 231
U-156, 221
U-234, 236
U-333, 136–138
U-505, 20, 222–224
U-518, 230
U-530, 205, 206, 236
U-546, 231–234
U-549, 213–215
U-575, 198, 202
U-802, 174
U-880, 230, 231
U-977, 236
Wharton, 245
Wilhoite, 157, 214
Wilkes, 76, 77
Willis, ii, 98, 128, 148, 150, 152–155, 163, 166, 170, 178, 181, 184, 189, 191, 196, 205, 206, 221, 223, 226, 229, 233–235, 238, 240, 241, 245, 247, 248, 250, 257, 260, 264, 272, 276, 277, 280, 284, 292, 298, 299, 304, 313

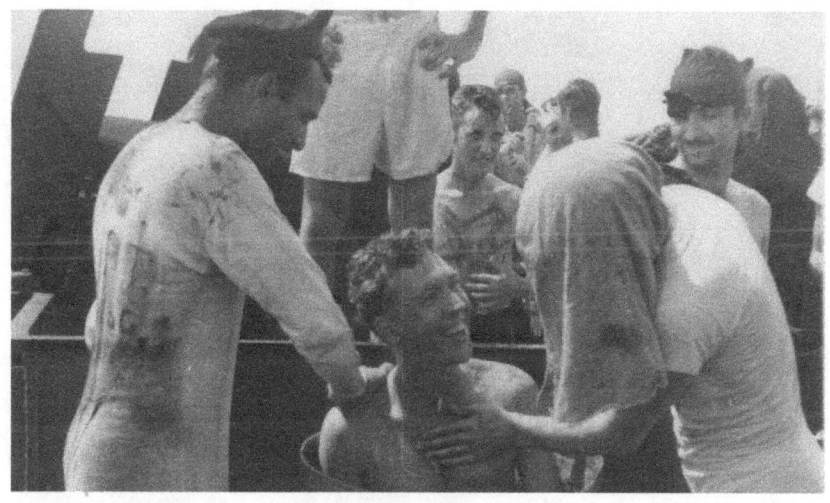

Figure 313: **About the author.** George P. Sotos, a Chicago native, retired as a Captain from the US Navy in 1972 after having six commands at sea over a career of more than 32 years. Above, he is shown on the left, participating in the ancient "crossing the line" ceremony in 1945. Below, he is conning the Willis into its berth alongside another ship in Guam.

www.ingramcontent.com/pod-product-compliance
Lightning Source LLC
Chambersburg PA
CBHW071736150426
43191CB00010B/1590